Good
Housekeeping

Weeknight
Easy

Soy and Whiskey Glazed Pork Chops (recipe page 42)

Good Housekeeping

Weeknight Easy

185 Really Quick, Simply Delicious Recipes

HEARST BOOKS
New York

HEARST BOOKS
New York

An Imprint of Sterling Publishing
387 Park Avenue South
New York, NY 10016

GOOD HOUSEKEEPING

Rosemary Ellis	*Editor in Chief*
Courtney Murphy	*Creative Director*
Susan Westmoreland	*Food Director*
Samantha B. Cassetty, MS, RD	*Nutrition Director*

Designer: Christine Heun
Project Editor: Sarah Scheffel

Photography credits on page 243

Library of Congress Cataloging-in-Publication Data

Good housekeeping weeknight easy : 185 really quick, simply delicious recipes.
    pages cm
  "Rosemary Ellis, editor in chief"--Title page verso.
  Includes index.
  ISBN 978-1-61837-130-0
1. Quick and easy cooking. I. Ellis, Rosemary. II. Good housekeeping.
III. Title: Weeknight easy.
  TX833.5.G673 2014
  641.5'55--dc23
                                    2013031717

ALL RECIPES
· GOOD ·
HOUSEKEEPING
Since ★ 1909
COOKBOOKS
Triple TESTED

The Good Housekeeping Cookbook Seal guarantees that the recipes in this cookbook meet the strict standards of the Good Housekeeping Research Institute. The Institute has been a source of reliable information and a consumer advocate since 1900, and established its seal of approval in 1909. Every recipe has been triple-tested for ease, reliability, and great taste.

Published by Hearst Books
A division of Sterling Publishing Co., Inc.
387 Park Avenue South, New York, NY 10016

Good Housekeeping is a registered trademark of Hearst Communications, Inc.
www.goodhousekeeping.com

For information about custom editions, special sales, premium and corporate purchases, please contact Sterling Special Sales Department at 800-805-5489 or specialsales@sterlingpublishing.com.

Distributed in Canada by Sterling Publishing
C/o Canadian Manda Group, 165 Dufferin Street
Toronto, Ontario, Canada M6K 3H6

Distributed in Australia by Capricorn Link (Australia) Pty. Ltd.
P.O. Box 704, Windsor, NSW 2756 Australia

Manufactured in China

Sterling ISBN 978-1-61837-130-0

Shrimp and Tomato Summer Salad (recipe page 219)

Sizzling Sesame Beef (recipe page 33)

Contents

Foreword

We give public tours of the GH test kitchens every month (if you're coming to NYC, go to our website and sign up for one!) and the two questions we're asked without fail are "With your jobs, how do you all stay so thin?" and "After a day of cooking, do you cook at home, too?" Yes, we do cook at home most nights, and it's one of the reasons we're (mostly) able to control our weight. We're by no means cooking diet food. Instead, we're cooking our version of fast food with fresh ingredients, and eating hearty home portions, not oversized restaurant ones. Working all day, we know firsthand that it's a challenge to get dinner on the table. Open a page in *Weeknight Easy*—loaded with 185 family-friendly recipes—and it'll help you put a delicious dinner on the table in half an hour or less. Plus, these simple recipes will help you enjoy the process as much as the food.

The great-tasting meals include stir-fries like Sizzling Sesame Beef and Caramelized Chili Shrimp and healthy-in-a-hurry meals such as Five-Spice Pork with Gingered Vegetables and Grilled Chicken and Greens. Serve them over healthy whole-grains like instant brown rice (cooks in just 10 minutes!), bulgur, quinoa, or whole-wheat couscous. Dinners like Barbecued Shrimp and Peach Kabobs and Chicken with Tex-Mex Salsa boast the incomparable flavor that only comes from a grill. Many of these dishes can be made indoors in a grill pan for the same great grilled flavor. And, of course we haven't forgotten the noodles: Lasagna Toss Bolognese is a simpler twist on an old favorite, while Spicy Szechuan Noodles and Peanut Noodles with Chicken make Chinese takeout a thing of the past.

When weeknights get busy, why not wrap up the day with one of our tasty wraps, tacos, or sandwiches? Quick Mu Shu Pork incorporates ready-to-use coleslaw mix, while Chicken Tostadas with Avocado Sauce employs supermarket rotisserie chicken to create a fast and yummy meal. Main-dish salads are another great way to get dinner on the table fast: Our Grilled Steak Salad and Tex-Mex Turkey Cobb Salad will satisfy even the biggest appetites. And a perennial hit: Breakfast for dinner. Check out easy dishes like Bacon and Eggs Over Asparagus and Shrimp and Fresh Corn Grits. They're hearty enough for the dinner table, too.

If you prefer to prep early then let dinner cook itself, choose a cozy oven dish like Turkey Enchiladas (made with boneless turkey breast from the deli) or our comforting Upside-Down Shepherd's Pie. Slow-cooker dishes like Red Wine–Braised Short Ribs and Chicken Fricassee are the ultimate fix-it-and-forget it meals, allowing you to prep in the A.M. and enjoy a delicious dinner in the P.M. with ease. (To take full advantage of this convenient device, check out our tips for slow-cooker success.)

But the dinner-in-a-flash recipes are just one facet of weeknight-easy cooking. Planning, shopping, and organizing your kitchen efficiently are the others. Be sure to read the introduction for lots of great *Good Housekeeping* advice on ways to save time even before you cook. You'll also find recommendations for hard-working tools, quick and easy techniques, and other meal preparation short-cuts that'll cut down your cooking time once you're in the kitchen. Tip boxes throughout suggest timesaving techniques and express-lane ingredients; items like instant brown rice, quick-cooking grits, preshredded carrots, rotisserie chicken, and more will help you get dinner on the table without a fuss. Recipe icons indicating low-calorie ☺, heart-healthy ♥, and make-ahead 🍱 options help you select meals that are as good for your family as they are easy on the cook.

With *Weeknight Easy* as your guide, cook fast, cook simple, cook delicious—and enjoy!

—Susan Westmoreland
Food Director, *Good Housekeeping*

Introduction

It's the end of a busy day, you're running late, and there's still more to do before you head home to start dinner. Wondering how you are ever going to put supper on the table? Preparing a meal for your family that is quick, healthy, and delicious *is* an attainable goal. *Good Housekeeping Weeknight Easy* serves up 185 mouthwatering recipes for homemade dinners that can be prepped and cooked in thirty minutes or less with ease — without sacrificing valued time with your family.

We open with a chapter on quick stir-fries and sautés featuring poultry, meat, vegetables, and tofu too. Many can be made in a nonstick skillet. Then it's on to Healthy in a Hurry: Fast recipes that each feature a protein, whole grain, and vegetables so you can be sure your family is getting all the nutrients they need. Pasta is always a weeknight favorite, so we've included a whole chapter of inspiring recipes — including Asian noodle dishes that'll make the expense of Chinese takeout unnecessary.

Firing up the grill is a great way to get a tasty dinner on the table quickly: Choose from our succulent recipes for steaks, burgers, kabobs, tacos, and more. And a slow cooker is another tool that makes weeknight meals easy on the chef. We share lots of tempting recipes for roasts, stews, casseroles, and even a risotto that are a cinch to slow cook. The oven is another fix-it-and-forget-it tool; choose from our selection of comforting oven-baked dishes, from enchiladas to shepherd's pie to everyone's favorite — mac and cheese.

Sometimes, hearty sandwiches or a main-dish salad is just the thing on a busy weeknight. Whether you choose to make Chicken Gyros, Zucchini and Mixed-Bean Burritos, or a Grilled Steak Salad, just wrap it up or toss it together, and dinner is served! And for those of you who love your omelets and frittatas, we've included an entire chapter of breakfast-for-dinner options. Hearty meals like Lox Scrambled Eggs, Shrimp and Fresh Corn Grits, and Tostada Stacks are as sure to satisfy in the P.M. as they are in the A.M.

Plan Ahead

Making quick meals requires some organization. Follow these tips, then it's ready, set, cook!

KEEP IT SIMPLE. Choose recipes with a limited number of ingredients that use simple cooking techniques. The aim is to spend dinnertime with your family, not to be bustling in the kitchen.

MAKE A LIST. Put aside some time once a week to plan menu ideas. Read the recipes you want to cook, taking note of all ingredients called for. Check your pantry, your freezer, and your refrigerator to see what you already have. Then plan your shopping list. Consider downloading an app for your smartphone to help you keep an ongoing list at your fingertips.

BUY IN BULK. With your shopping list in hand, navigate the supermarket for staples, sale items, and all the components you'll need for the week's menus. Doing a "big" shopping trip once a week and limiting or eliminating midweek trips to the market is a simple yet effective time and money saver. Once you get home, be sure to wrap, pack, and store perishables properly to avoid waste.

COOK AHEAD. Weekends are great times for making large batches of soups, stews, or casseroles. Serve some right away and freeze the rest for another day. If you can, prepare a few basics that can be incorporated into meals during the week ahead: cook up a pot of rice or other grain, make pasta sauce, roast potatoes or a mix of seasonal vegetables.

Shop Smart, Shop Quickly!

Most supermarkets are arranged in a similar manner. Produce is often in the front of the store; meats, dairy, deli, baked goods, and frozen items are usually around the perimeter, while the aisles are stocked with bottled, canned, and packaged goods. Arrange your shopping list by grocery departments and use it as a map to your local market. You'll know exactly where to find everything you need and won't waste time browsing. Start with the staples, move on to the perishables, then the refrigerated items. Save frozen foods for last so they'll stay cold; they'll also help cool your perishable and refrigerated groceries.

Strategic shopping helps makes weeknight cooking fast and easy. Keep these tips in mind as you push your cart through the aisles.

+ **Take advantage of sales** on meats, poultry, seafood, or frozen foods you use. For meats, poultry, and seafood, separate what you plan to cook within two days, then wrap the rest in meal-size portions and freeze them immediately. For more tips, see "Stock Up" on page 12.

+ **Choose items that cook up fast.** Use chicken tenders instead of whole chicken pieces and thinly sliced medallions of pork instead of thick loin chops; select vegetables cut into matchstick-size pieces, which cook evenly and more quickly than whole veggies or large chunks.

- **Choose convenience products** that are nutritious and have the fewest preservatives and artificial ingredients. Some options include whole-wheat tortilla wraps and pre- or partially baked pizza shells, quick-cooking rice or whole-grain pilafs, rotisserie chicken, preshredded cabbage or broccoli slaw, pre-washed salad greens, and peeled, chopped fruit and veggies (fresh or frozen).
- **Think outside the box**—or bottle or package. Spice blends in any of a variety of flavors can be mixed into ground beef to give meatballs, burgers, or meat loaf an exotic twist. Bottled creamy salad dressings can top mashed or baked potatoes instead of butter or sour cream; you can sauté fresh vegetables with a tablespoon of vinaigrette dressing instead of oil. Garlic-flavored spreadable cheese thinned with a little milk makes a delectable sauce for pasta or vegetables.

Stock Up

Keeping your kitchen stocked with foods you use on a regular basis will not only cut down on your shopping and prepping time, it will ensure that no matter how busy you are, you'll always have the makings of a healthy meal.

FOR YOUR PANTRY (nonperishables and non-refrigerated long-lasting items): Every week or so, check your larder and add any items that are running low to your big shopping list.

- Quick-cooking white and brown rice, cous-cous, and other quick-cooking grains
- A variety of pasta shapes (include some healthy whole-grain noodles!)
- Canned broths and soups, packaged soup mixes
- Canned tomato products: whole, crushed, diced, and sauce

- Canned tuna and salmon
- Canned and dried fruit
- Nuts
- Peanut/nut butters (check the label to see if refrigeration is required once opened)
- Oils: extra-virgin and light olive oils, vegetable oil, Asian sesame oil, and a nut oil (check the label to see if the oil should be refrigerated)
- Dried herbs and spices (alone and in blends)
- Condiments: vinegars, relishes, pickles, chutneys, mustards, ketchup, olives, sun-dried tomatoes, pesto, salsas (most condiments require refrigeration once opened)
- Salad dressings and bottled sauces such as steak, soy, teriyaki, peanut, and curry (check the label to see if refrigeration is required once opened)
- Sweeteners: sugar or sugar substitute, honey, jams (refrigerate jams once opened)
- Onions, garlic, shallots
- Potatoes

FOR YOUR REFRIGERATOR: Place items that are used most often in the front of the fridge and lesser-used items behind them. Take note of the rear items you have in stock about every other week, so you remember to use them.
- Fresh meats, fish, and poultry
- Fresh vegetables and salad greens
- Fresh pasta (cooks faster than dried)
- Sliced deli meats and whole sausages
- Cheeses: sliced deli cheeses, feta, blue, Cheddar, and Parmesan
- Milk, yogurt, and sour cream
- Butter and cream cheese
- Mayonnaise
- Citrus fruits
- Juices and other beverages

Chicken and Orzo Pilaf (recipe page 165)

FOR YOUR FREEZER: Wrap meat and poultry in freezer wrap or heavy-duty foil, pressing out all the air. Label each package with the name of the cut, the number of servings, and the date. Freeze seafood only if it's very fresh, and wrap it in both plastic wrap and heavy-duty foil. Always freeze foods in meal-sized or recipe-sized portions unless it will be a simple matter to remove the amount you need from the frozen package. Take inventory at least once a month.

+ Fresh meat, fish, and poultry to be used at a later date
+ Raw vegetables chopped and prepared for cooking: onions, carrots, bell peppers, celery, leeks, broccoli, and cauliflower florets
+ Packaged frozen vegetables and vegetable combos
+ Flash-frozen fruits and berries
+ Breads, tortillas, pita pockets
+ Cooked rice and pasta
+ Leftovers—casseroles, soups, stews, grilled meats, and steamed vegetables
+ Sliced pound cake (to top with fruit or berries, ice cream, or puddings for a quick dessert)

Cut Down on Kitchen Time

Spend a minute or two organizing your work area. Start by clearing an adequate workspace with plenty of elbow room. Assemble all your ingredients, cookware, and tools so that everything is within easy reach. Get the kids to help out by setting the table, pouring drinks, and doing any other simple tasks that will save you time. And be sure to quickly read your chosen recipe before you begin, so you don't have to stop to read each step while you work.

Taking the time to gather together the following hard-working utensils will help speed your preparations along.

+ **Knives:** a paring knife for trimming veggies and fruits, a chef's knife for fast slicing and chopping, and a serrated knife to cut through delicate foods like bread, tomatoes, and cake
+ **A heavy 12-inch nonstick skillet,** for browning, sautéing, stir-frying, and making sauces; choose one with a lid
+ **Heatproof silicone spatulas** in a few sizes
+ **Spring-action tongs** are the best for turning meats without piercing them. They'll also keep you at a safe distance from the heat when you're grilling or frying foods.
+ **Kitchen scissors** for snipping fresh herbs
+ **A Microplane grater** for grating hard cheeses, citrus peels, and ginger

Investing in the following time-saving appliances is sure to pay off in the long run. If you don't already own these handy devices, keep an eye out for them at tag sales or pick them up at a kitchenware retailer when they're on sale. You'll never look back!

+ **Mini food processor** with changeable cutting disks for chopping, slicing, and shredding
+ **Immersion blender** for pureeing soups and making gravies, dips, and sauces
+ **Microwave oven** for defrosting frozen meats, fish, and poultry; precooking ingredients that take a long time to cook, such as potatoes and winter squash; reheating leftovers; steaming vegetables; melting butter and cheese
+ **Grill pan** (uses very little oil, preheats fast, and leaves the familiar grill marks on burgers, chicken breasts, and more)
+ **Slow cooker** (lets you prep, set, and forget—then enjoy a hot homemade dinner at the end of a long day)

PREPPED AND PREMADE FOODS

You deserve a little convenience come mealtime! Supermarkets carry a vast selection of foods that are available already prepared and that make feeding a hungry family on the go a breeze. For more ideas, look for "Express-Lane Ingredient" boxes throughout the book.

+ Premade items such as rotisserie chicken, as well as choices from the salad bar, can form the basis of a hearty no-cook dinner.

+ Cleaned and ready to use, sliced, diced, and shredded fresh vegetables can be found in the produce section along with packaged peeled and sliced fresh fruits.

+ Packaged salad greens come cut, washed, and mixed with other veggies to go straight from the bag to the salad bowl. Just be sure to check the packaging to make sure it says *washed* and *ready-to-eat*, as some bagged salad greens must be rinsed before eating.

+ Frozen vegetables—available in a variety of styles and combinations, including ethnic mixes like Asian and Mediterranean—aren't just for side dishes. They can be tossed into stir-fries and pasta dishes.

+ Meats, fish, and poultry are sold pre-seasoned and marinated, even prepared as kabobs or stuffed rolls. All you provide is the grilling, roasting, steaming, stir-frying, or sautéing.

+ Precooked and packaged chicken pieces, meatballs, and flavored sausages can help you get meals on the table in a flash.

Quick and Easy Cooking Techniques

When it comes to fast weeknight meals, not all cooking methods are created equal. In the recipes that follow, we take full advantage of the following speedy techniques, and so should you!

STIR-FRYING: The fastest of cooking methods, stir-frying yields quick, tasty results and requires only a small amount of oil. Small pieces of food are cooked over high heat in a skillet, stirred constantly to keep the food from sticking or burning. Vegetables should be sliced or chopped to roughly the same size to ensure even cooking; the fastest-cooking ingredients should be the last items you add to the pan. Lean cuts of meat should be sliced very thinly across the grain or cubed. Shrimp can be stir-fried with their shells on or off. Tip: A nonstick skillet is a convenient tool for this method. It heats up

quickly and makes cleanup a breeze. For safety's sake, don't preheat an empty nonstick pan or cook at temperatures above medium heat.

GRILLING: Whether you grill outdoors on a gas or charcoal grill or indoors in a ridged grill pan, the intense heat caramelizes the crust and lends delicious smoky flavor to whatever meat, poultry, seafood, or vegetable you're grilling. Much of the fat drips away during the process, making this quick and easy method an excellent choice for those looking to lighten up. Tip: To intensify flavor, use a dry rub or marinade. The longer an ingredient marinates, the more intense the flavor; use the leftover marinade to baste the food as it cooks.

STEAMING: Cooking vegetables in a steamer basket over simmering water is a great way to add a quick side dish. Steaming preserves the veggies' natural color, flavor, and nutritional value, and it doesn't require any added fat. Tip: You can also steam vegetables in the microwave.

In a covered, microwave-safe dish, cook one pound chopped vegetable of choice with ¼ cup water on High until tender, stirring once halfway through cooking time. (Green beans, asparagus, broccoli, cauliflower, carrots, peas, spinach, and zucchini are all good options.) Take care not to overcook; the finished veggies should be crisp and brightly colored, never mushy. Season with salt and pepper to serve.

SLOW COOKING: It may sound like an oxymoron, but a slow cooker is an amazing way to get dinner on the table fast—with a minimum of effort. It's magic when it comes to making stews, poultry, and meat dishes, and you can even slow-cook delicate items like seafood and risotto in one. Just add your ingredients to the bowl of the cooker in the morning, and you'll have a home-cooked meal come dinnertime. Tip: See "Slow- Cooker Success" on page 137 for how to get the most out of this handy appliance.

MORE SHORTCUTS TO MEAL PREPARATION

We're always looking for ways to make dinnertime easier for you. Here are some of our favorite time-saving tips.

+ Choose lean cuts of meat, such as sirloin, which will cook faster than fattier cuts like chuck. Save tougher cuts for the slow cooker.

+ Put water on to boil for pasta or rice, or preheat the oven, as soon as you get home. While the heating begins, you can gather your ingredients, brown meat, or sauté onions, according to the recipe's requirements.

+ If you are using ground beef in a recipe, brown it the previous evening, then let it cool, bag it, and refrigerate.

+ Cook enough for two meals and turn the leftovers into different dishes later in the week. For example, the leftovers from a pot of chili can be used to make tacos and nachos—or as a great baked potato topping.

+ Freeze leftovers in individual servings, and you'll have a stockpile of quick and healthy meals to serve whenever you want.

+ Incorporate restaurant leftovers into fast and easy meals: Extra white rice becomes quick fried rice when you add some vegetables and scrambled eggs; leftover pasta with marinara sauce can be tossed with sautéed sausage or chicken pieces.

Linguine with Frisée, Bacon, and Egg (recipe page 102)

1

Stir-Fries & Sautés

These fast and easy skillet dishes are just right for weeknight cooking. All of them can be made, from start to finish, in a half hour or less. Just heat some oil in a pan, add your ingredients, and toss them in the pan to create a wholesome and delicious meal. This is your go-to chapter when you're shuttling between one child's track meet and another's dance lesson.

Start by picking your protein: We include recipes featuring everything from quick-cooking flank steak or chicken tenders to shrimp, salmon, and tofu, too. If you choose tofu, just be sure to pat it dry before adding it to the pan so that it browns nicely. And don't stir it too vigorously, or it'll start to come apart.

Stir-fries are a tasty way to cook up all sorts of vitamin- and antioxidant-rich vegetables. Feel free to substitute veggies you happen to have on hand or add your favorites; snow peas, asparagus, cauliflower, broccoli, carrots, bell peppers—they're all wonderful thrown into a hot pan and cooked just until tender-crisp.

Whatever the combination, you can serve these stir-fries and sautés over white rice or experiment with whole-grains: brown rice is available in quick-cooking bags that take just ten minutes to prepare. Pasta, including Asian noodles and whole-wheat couscous, makes an equally good—and speedy—base.

Caramelized Chile Shrimp (recipe page 43)

Tangerine Chicken Stir-Fry

Toss stir-fried chicken and vegetables with a citrus-infused sauce for a quick and delicious meal.

ACTIVE TIME: 20 minutes
TOTAL TIME: 30 minutes
MAKES: 4 main-dish servings

3	tangerines
¼	cup dry sherry
1	tablespoon grated, peeled fresh ginger
1	teaspoon Asian sesame oil (see page 33)
1	tablespoon plus 1 teaspoon cornstarch
2	tablespoons reduced-sodium soy sauce (see Tip)
1½	pounds skinless, boneless chicken-breast halves, cut into ½-inch-wide strips
1	cup quick-cooking (10-minute) brown rice (see page 57)
4	teaspoons vegetable oil
1	bag (12 ounces) broccoli flowerets
2	medium carrots, thinly sliced diagonally
3	green onions, cut into 1-inch pieces
⅓	cup water

1. From 1 tangerine, with vegetable peeler, remove peel in strips. Using small knife, remove and discard any white pith from peel; set peel aside. Into 1-cup liquid measuring cup, squeeze ½ cup juice from tangerines. Stir in sherry, ginger, sesame oil, and 1 teaspoon cornstarch; set juice mixture aside.

2. In medium bowl, combine soy sauce and remaining 1 tablespoon cornstarch. Add chicken and toss to coat; set aside.

3. Cook rice as label directs. Meanwhile, in 12-inch skillet, heat 2 teaspoons vegetable oil over medium-high heat. Add peel and cook 1 minute or until lightly browned. With tongs or slotted spoon, transfer peel to large bowl.

4. To same skillet, add broccoli, carrots, and green onions; stir to coat with oil. Add water; cover and cook 4 minutes, stirring once. Uncover and cook, stirring frequently, 1 minute longer or until vegetables are tender-crisp. Transfer vegetables to bowl with peel.

5. To same skillet, add remaining 2 teaspoons vegetable oil; reduce heat to medium. Add chicken mixture and cook, stirring frequently, 6 to 7 minutes or until chicken is golden and cooked through (165°F). Transfer chicken to bowl with cooked vegetables.

6. Add juice mixture to skillet and heat to boiling over medium-high heat; boil 1 minute, stirring until browned bits are loosened. Return chicken and vegetables to skillet and cook, stirring, 1 minute to heat through. To serve, spoon brown rice into shallow dinner bowls; top with chicken and vegetables.

EACH SERVING: About 390 calories, 45g protein, 32g carbohydrate, 9g total fat (1g saturated), 5g fiber, 99mg cholesterol, 420mg sodium ☺ ♥

TIP: *Reduced-sodium soy sauce is available at most grocery stores. If you can't locate it, dilute regular soy sauce by half with water.*

Chicken with Olives and Peppers

With just a few rustic-rich-tasting add-ins—sherry, slivers of green olive, comforting cubes of bread—chicken thighs gain savory Spanish flavor.

ACTIVE TIME: 25 minutes
TOTAL TIME: 30 minutes
MAKES: 4 main-dish servings

2	tablespoons olive oil
4	garlic cloves, thinly sliced
4	cups cubed (1-inch) Italian bread
1	pound skinless, boneless chicken thighs, trimmed and cut into 1-inch chunks
3/8	teaspoon salt
1/4	teaspoon freshly ground black pepper
3	medium peppers (6 to 8 ounces each), preferably red, yellow, and orange, very thinly sliced
1	medium shallot, chopped
3	tablespoons dry sherry
2	tablespoons water
1	tablespoon fresh lemon juice
1/4	cup pitted green olives, slivered
2	tablespoons fresh parsley leaves, finely chopped

1. In 12-inch skillet, heat 1 tablespoon oil and half of garlic over medium heat until garlic begins to sizzle. Add bread and stir until well coated. Cook 5 to 6 minutes or until golden brown and crisp, stirring occasionally. Transfer to large platter.

2. Wipe out same skillet and add remaining tablespoon oil; heat on medium-high. Add chicken and sprinkle with 1/4 teaspoon each salt and pepper. Cook 3 minutes or until browned, stirring occasionally. Transfer to medium bowl.

3. Reduce heat to medium and add peppers. Cook 2 to 3 minutes or until peppers are just beginning to soften. Add shallots and remaining garlic; cook 2 minutes, stirring constantly. Stir in sherry and water, scraping up any browned bits. Cook 3 to 4 minutes longer or until peppers are very soft. Return chicken to skillet along with any juices. Cook 4 minutes or until chicken is no longer pink inside, stirring occasionally.

4. Remove skillet from heat and stir in lemon juice, olives, parsley, and remaining 1/8 teaspoon salt. Pour chicken mixture over croutons. Serve immediately.

EACH SERVING: About 385 calories, 28g protein, 36g carbohydrate, 14g total fat (3g saturated), 3g fiber, 94mg cholesterol, 730mg sodium F ☺

Chicken Sauté with Artichokes, Lemon, and Mint

Frozen, ready-to-serve artichoke hearts are the secret to this streamlined, Greek-style favorite, with its light and zesty add-ins.

ACTIVE TIME: 15 minutes
TOTAL TIME: 30 minutes
MAKES: 6 main-dish servings

4	medium skinless, boneless chicken-breast halves (1½ pounds total)
¼	teaspoon salt
⅛	teaspoon freshly ground black pepper
4	teaspoons olive oil
1	package (8 to 10 ounces) frozen artichoke hearts, thawed (see page 235)
¾	cup chicken broth
¼	cup loosely packed fresh mint leaves, chopped, plus additional for garnish
1	tablespoon fresh lemon juice
¼	cup crumbled feta cheese

1. Place chicken between two sheets plastic wrap. With meat mallet or bottom of skillet, pound chicken to even ½-inch thickness; sprinkle with salt and pepper on both sides.

2. In 12-inch skillet, heat 2 teaspoons oil over medium heat. Add chicken and cook, turning once, 12 to 14 minutes or until chicken is browned on both sides and loses pink color throughout. (Instant-read thermometer inserted horizontally into center of chicken should reach 165°F.) Transfer chicken to shallow serving bowl; cover with foil to keep warm.

3. To same skillet, add remaining 2 teaspoons oil and heat over medium heat. Add artichokes and cook, stirring occasionally, 3 minutes or until browned. Stir in broth and heat to boiling over medium-high heat; boil 2 to 3 minutes or until liquid is reduced by half. Remove skillet from heat; stir in mint leaves and lemon juice.

4. To serve, spoon artichoke sauce over chicken; top with feta. Garnish with additional chopped mint leaves.

EACH SERVING: About 285 calories, 43g protein, 7g carbohydrate, 9g total fat (3g saturated), 3g fiber, 107mg cholesterol, 515mg sodium ☺

Basil Chile Chicken Stir-Fry

Whip up this simple, make-it-fast supper in a single skillet. To make this Thai-inspired dish a bit more spicy, leave the seeds in the chile pepper.

ACTIVE TIME: 25 minutes
TOTAL TIME: 30 minutes
MAKES: 4 main-dish servings

1	cup quick-cooking (10-minute) short-grain brown rice (see page 57)
4	garlic cloves
1	tablespoon plus 1 teaspoon vegetable oil
1	pound green beans, trimmed and cut into 1-inch pieces
¼	cup plus 2 tablespoons water
¼	teaspoon salt
¼	teaspoon freshly ground black pepper
1	fresh Thai or serrano chile, stem and seeds discarded, finely chopped
1¼	pounds chicken-breast tenders, very thinly sliced crosswise
2	tablespoons plus 1 teaspoon reduced-sodium Asian fish sauce
1	teaspoon reduced-sodium soy sauce
2	teaspoons sugar
1	cup packed fresh basil leaves, plus additional for garnish

1. Prepare rice as label directs, but do not add any salt.

2. Very thinly slice 2 garlic cloves; finely chop remaining 2 cloves.

3. In 12-inch skillet, heat 1 teaspoon oil over medium-high heat. Add thinly sliced garlic and cook 10 seconds or until garlic is golden. Add green beans, ¼ cup water, salt, and pepper. Cook, stirring frequently, 4 to 5 minutes or until beans are tender-crisp and water has evaporated. Transfer bean mixture to large plate or bowl.

4. In same skillet, heat remaining 1 tablespoon oil over medium-high heat. Add chile and chopped garlic and cook, stirring, 10 seconds or until garlic is golden. Add chicken tenders in single layer and cook, stirring mixture occasionally, 2 to 3 minutes or until chicken just loses pink color throughout.

5. Add fish sauce, soy sauce, sugar, and remaining 2 tablespoons water. Cook, stirring, 1 minute or until chicken is just cooked through (165°F). Stir in basil leaves and cook 15 to 20 seconds or until just wilted.

6. To serve, divide cooked rice, green beans, and chicken with sauce among serving plates. Garnish with 2 or 3 basil leaves.

EACH SERVING: About 325 calories, 35g protein, 28g carbohydrate, 9g total fat (1g saturated), 4g fiber, 91mg cholesterol, 815mg sodium ☺

EXPRESS-LANE INGREDIENT: ASIAN FISH SAUCE

An integral flavoring in Southeast Asian cooking, this pungent sauce made from fermented fish adds an amazing depth of flavor to stir-fries and noodle dishes. It's available in reduced-sodium versions in Asian markets and most grocery stores.

Chicken Tikka Masala

Put this enticing Indian chicken dish on the table in just twenty minutes.

Total time: 20 minutes
Makes: 4 main-dish servings

1	cup basmati rice
1	tablespoon vegetable oil
1	medium onion (6 to 8 ounces), chopped
2	teaspoons grated, peeled fresh ginger
1	garlic clove, crushed with garlic press
2	tablespoons Indian curry paste
1¼	pounds skinless, boneless chicken-breast halves, cut into 1-inch chunks
¼	teaspoon salt
¼	teaspoon freshly ground black pepper
1	cup canned crushed tomato (from 15-ounce can)
½	cup half-and-half or light cream
¼	cup loosely packed cilantro leaves, chopped, plus additional for garnish

1. Prepare rice as label directs.

2. Meanwhile, in nonstick 12-inch skillet, heat oil over medium heat 1 minute. Add onion and cook 6 minutes, stirring frequently. Add ginger, garlic, and curry paste; cook 3 minutes longer.

3. Add chicken, salt, and pepper and cook, stirring occasionally, 2 minutes or until chicken is no longer pink on the outside. Add tomato; cover and cook 3 to 4 minutes longer or until chicken just loses pink color throughout (165°F).

4. Uncover and stir in half-and-half and cilantro. Spoon rice into shallow bowls; top with chicken mixture and garnish with cilantro.

Each serving: About 430 calories, 39g protein, 42g carbohydrate, 13g total fat (4g saturated), 6g fiber, 93mg cholesterol, 685mg sodium ☺

Chicken and Zucchini Mole

This quick version of mole incorporates the traditional flavors of the original: cocoa, dried chiles, oregano, and cinnamon.

ACTIVE TIME: 20 minutes
TOTAL TIME: 30 minutes
MAKES: 4 main-dish servings

1   small onion (4 to 6 ounces), cut into quarters

3   garlic cloves, peeled

1   ounce dried guajillo or pasilla chiles, stems and seeds discarded

3   tablespoons roasted almonds

1   can (14½ ounces) fire-roasted tomatoes

½   teaspoon dried oregano

½   teaspoon ground cinnamon

13   (6-inch) corn tortillas

1   cup reduced-sodium chicken broth

1   tablespoon vegetable oil

1   pound zucchini, cut into half-moons

1   pound skinless, boneless chicken breasts, cut into ½-inch chunks

1   ounce semisweet chocolate, chopped

½   teaspoon salt

3   green onions, thinly sliced

1. In blender, puree onion, garlic, chiles, almonds, tomatoes, oregano, cinnamon, 1 tortilla, and ½ cup broth 2 minutes or until completely smooth. (Can be made ahead and stored, covered, in refrigerator up to 24 hours.)

2. In 12-inch skillet, heat oil over medium-high heat. Add chile mixture and cook 4 minutes, stirring constantly. Reduce heat to medium and cook, stirring frequently, 8 minutes longer or until mixture is brick red and the consistency of tomato paste. Stir in remaining ½ cup broth and heat to simmering.

3. Add zucchini and chicken; simmer, stirring occasionally, 5 minutes or until vegetables are tender and meat just loses pink color throughout (165°F). Add chocolate and salt and stir until chocolate melts.

4. Wrap remaining 12 corn tortillas in damp paper towels; microwave on High 45 seconds or until warm and pliable.

5. Transfer mole to serving bowl; garnish with green onions. Serve with tortillas.

EACH SERVING: About 490 calories, 34g protein, 57g carbohydrate, 14g total fat (3g saturated), 9g fiber, 73mg cholesterol, 810mg sodium

Pan-Seared Chicken Thighs with Pear and Celery Slaw

This heart-healthy meal pairs skinless, boneless thighs with a warm pear-and-celery slaw and can be prepared on the fly!

TOTAL TIME: 20 minutes
MAKES: 4 main-dish servings

1	teaspoon olive oil
1	pound skinless, boneless chicken thighs, cut into 1-inch-wide strips
½	teaspoon salt
¼	teaspoon freshly ground black pepper
2	medium Bartlett pears, not peeled
2	stalks celery
2	tablespoon fresh lemon juice
1	shallot, finely chopped
¾	cup apple cider
1	tablespoon Dijon mustard
1	tablespoon chopped fresh parsley leaves

1. In nonstick 12-inch skillet, heat oil over medium heat. Add chicken thighs to skillet and sprinkle with salt and pepper. Cook chicken, turning once, 8 to 10 minutes or until cooked through (165°F). Transfer to warm plate.

2. Meanwhile, cut each pear lengthwise in half; discard core. Cut halves lengthwise into matchstick-thin strips (see Tip). Thinly slice celery on diagonal. In large bowl, toss pear and celery with lemon juice; set slaw aside.

3. To same skillet, add shallot and cook, stirring constantly, 30 seconds to 1 minute or until it begins to brown. Add cider and heat to boiling; whisk in mustard. Pour cider dressing over pear mixture and toss to coat. Serve slaw with thighs. Sprinkle with parsley.

EACH SERVING: About 230 calories, 23g protein, 21g carbohydrate, 6g total fat (1g saturated), 94mg cholesterol, 430mg sodium ☺ ♥

TIP: *To turn pears into even, matchstick-thin strips quickly and effortlessly, use a mandoline or V-slicer.*

QUICK TECHNIQUE: SEEDLESS LEMON JUICE

Place a lemon half, cut side down, on a square of cheesecloth. Bring the cheesecloth up over the top and fasten with a twist-tie, then squeeze out the juice, seed free. The same technique works for any citrus fruit, from limes to grapefruit.

Crispy Duck Breasts with Tart Cherry Sauce

This streamlined classic recipe is also great made with pork. You can substitute four 6-ounce, ³⁄₄-inch-thick boneless pork-loin chops for the duck breasts. In step 2, season the chops and cook them in 1 teaspoon vegetable oil over medium heat for about 8 minutes, turning them once. Then proceed as directed.

ACTIVE TIME: 25 minutes
TOTAL TIME: 30 minutes
MAKES: 4 main-dish servings

1	package (8¹⁄₂ ounces) precooked whole-grain pilaf (optional)
4	small duck-breast halves (6 ounces each; see Tip)
¹⁄₂	teaspoon salt
¹⁄₂	teaspoon ground black pepper
²⁄₃	cup port wine
2	cans (14¹⁄₂ ounces each) tart cherries in water, well drained
¹⁄₄	cup sugar

Steamed green beans (optional)

1. Prepare pilaf, if desired, as package label directs. Keep warm.

2. Meanwhile, pat duck breasts dry with paper towels. Make several ¹⁄₄-inch-deep diagonal slashes in duck skin. Place breasts, skin side down, in nonstick 10-inch skillet; sprinkle with salt and pepper. Cook over medium heat until skin is deep brown, about 12 minutes; turn breasts and cook 3 minutes longer for medium. (Instant-read thermometer inserted horizontally into center of duck should reach 165°F.) Transfer breasts, skin side down, to cutting board; let stand 5 minutes for easier slicing. Discard fat from skillet but do not wash.

3. While duck is standing, add port to skillet; heat to boiling over medium heat. Boil until reduced by half, about 5 minutes. Add cherries and sugar; simmer, stirring occasionally, until most of liquid has evaporated, 3 to 4 minutes.

4. To serve, slice breasts crosswise. Transfer slices, skin side up, to dinner plates. Spoon cherry sauce over duck. Serve with pilaf and green beans, if you like.

EACH SERVING: About 320 calories, 23g protein, 36g carbohydrate, 10g total fat (3g saturated), 1g fiber, 120mg cholesterol, 380mg sodium ☺ ♥

TIP: If you can only find the larger duck breasts, which weigh in at 12 to 13 ounces each, buy two and cook them, skin side down, over medium-low heat 20 minutes; turn breasts and continue cooking 4 minutes longer. Slice to serve, as in step 4, and divide slices among dinner plates.

Turkey Cutlets with Pears and Tarragon

This good-for-you recipe contains lean proteins (turkey) and green veggies (spinach). The best pears for this recipe are Anjou and Bosc, which are juicy and keep their shape when cooked.

TOTAL TIME: 25 minutes
MAKES: 4 main-dish servings

1	tablespoon olive oil
4	turkey-breast cutlets (1 pound total)
¼	teaspoon salt
⅛	teaspoon ground black pepper
2	large firm, ripe pears, peeled, cored, and cut into ½-inch-thick wedges (see Tip)
1	cup chicken broth
¼	cup dried tart cherries or cranberries
2	tablespoons Dijon mustard with seeds
½	teaspoon dried tarragon
1	bag (9 ounces) microwave-in-bag spinach

1. In 12-inch skillet, heat oil over high heat. Sprinkle cutlets with salt and pepper. Add cutlets to skillet and cook, turning once, until turkey is golden brown on both sides and has just lost pink color throughout, 3 to 4 minutes. (Instant-read thermometer inserted horizontally into center of cutlets should reach 165°F.) Transfer cutlets to plate; keep warm.

2. To same skillet, add pears. Reduce heat to medium-high and cook pears, turning occasionally, until browned, about 3 minutes. Add broth, cherries or cranberries, mustard, and tarragon to skillet. Increase heat to high and cook, stirring occasionally, until sauce thickens slightly and pears are tender, 4 to 5 minutes.

3. Meanwhile, in microwave oven, cook spinach in bag as label directs.

4. Return cutlets to skillet; heat through, spooning pear sauce over them.

5. To serve, spoon spinach onto dinner plates. Top with cutlets, pears, and sauce.

EACH SERVING: About 255 calories, 31g protein, 20g carbohydrate, 6g total fat (1g saturated), 8g fiber, 71mg cholesterol, 565mg sodium ☺

TIP: Peel and cut the pears just before you are ready to use them; like cut apples, they discolor. If you want to prep them in advance, place them in a bowl of cold water to which you've added 1 teaspoon lemon juice. Drain and pat dry before using.

Savory Steak and Pepper Stir-Fry

Steak and peppers are a classic combo, and for good reason. Colorful bell peppers add sweetness to this savory and satisfying beef dish.

ACTIVE TIME: 20 minutes
TOTAL TIME: 25 minutes
MAKES: 4 main-dish servings

2   teaspoons canola oil
1½   pounds beef flank steak, thinly sliced
⅛   teaspoon Chinese five-spice powder
     (see page 160)
½   teaspoon plus pinch salt
1   medium red pepper, thinly sliced
1   medium green pepper, thinly sliced
1   small onion (4 to 6 ounces), thinly sliced
5   tablespoons water
2   tablespoons brown sugar
1   tablespoon reduced-sodium soy sauce
     (see Tip)
1   tablespoon cornstarch
¼   teaspoon freshly ground black pepper
Cooked rice for serving

1. In 12-inch skillet, heat oil over medium-high heat. Sprinkle steak with five-spice powder and ½ teaspoon salt; add to skillet. Cook, stirring occasionally, 3 minutes or until just browned. With slotted spoon, transfer to medium bowl.

2. To skillet, add red and green peppers, onion, 2 tablespoons water, and pinch salt. Cover and cook, stirring occasionally, 5 minutes or until slightly softened.

3. In small bowl, whisk together brown sugar, soy sauce, cornstarch, 3 tablespoons water, and black pepper until smooth. Add to skillet; heat to simmering. Simmer 1 minute or until thickened. Add beef and any accumulated juices to skillet. Cook 1 minute or until beef is heated through (145°F). Serve with rice.

EACH SERVING: About 345 calories, 37g protein, 15g carbohydrate, 15g total fat (5g saturated), 2g fiber, 110mg cholesterol, 500mg sodium ☺

TIP: Want a slightly sweeter flavor? Use teriyaki sauce instead of soy.

Sizzling Sesame Beef

Try our streamlined version of the popular Chinese dish — it's almost as quick as ordering takeout. For photo, see page 6.

TOTAL TIME: 30 minutes
MAKES: 4 main-dish servings

1	pound beef sirloin or rib-eye steak, cut 1 inch thick
1	cup short-grain or jasmine rice
2	green onions, white portions cut into 2-inch chunks, green portions thinly sliced
4	garlic cloves, crushed with garlic press
4	teaspoons Asian sesame oil
¼	teaspoon salt plus additional to taste
2	teaspoons sugar
2	tablespoons reduced-sodium soy sauce

Freshly ground black pepper to taste

1	pound broccoli flowerets

1. Place steak in freezer. Prepare rice as label directs. Meanwhile, in large bowl, combine 1 tablespoon sliced green onions, 1 teaspoon garlic, 2 teaspoons sesame oil, and ¼ teaspoon salt; set aside.

2. Cut cold steak across grain into very thin slices; in shallow bowl, toss with sugar, 1 tablespoon soy sauce, green-onion chunks, and remaining garlic.

3. In 12-inch skillet, heat *1 inch water* to boiling over high heat. Add broccoli; cook 3 minutes or until just tender. Drain well; place in same bowl as onion-garlic mixture. Toss well. In same skillet, heat remaining 2 teaspoons sesame oil over high heat. Add beef in single layer; cook 1 minute. Stir in remaining sliced green onions and salt and pepper to taste; cook 1 minute longer. Stir in remaining 1 tablespoon soy sauce. Serve with rice and broccoli.

EACH SERVING: About 510 calories, 30g protein, 50g carbohydrate, 21g total fat (7g saturated), 5g fiber, 75mg cholesterol, 585mg sodium

EXPRESS-LANE INGREDIENT: ASIAN SESAME OIL

Pressed from roasted sesame seeds, this dark brown-orange oil adds a rich, toasty flavor to stir-fries and other Chinese, Japanese, and Korean dishes. It can be found in the international section of most supermarkets, or along with the other oils. Because of its strong flavor and fragrance, it is often used in combination with other lighter cooking oils. Don't confuse it with regular sesame oil, which is light in flavor and color and an excellent choice for frying because of its high smoke point (420°F).

Chili-Crusted Flank Steak

Heed the heat. Chili powder—a blend of garlic, oregano, cumin, coriander, cloves, and ground dried chiles—ranges in flavor and hotness depending on the brand, so adjust the amount to suit your taste.

TOTAL TIME: 30 minutes
MAKES: 6 main-dish servings

2	tablespoons chili powder
1	tablespoon brown sugar
¼	teaspoon salt
2	tablespoons fresh lime juice
1	large garlic clove, crushed with garlic press
1	beef flank steak (1½ pounds)
3	large red onions (8 ounces each), each cut into 6 wedges
1	tablespoon olive oil

1. Preheat outdoor grill for direct grilling over medium heat.

2. Meanwhile, in cup, with fork, stir chili powder, brown sugar, salt, lime juice, and garlic until blended. Rub mixture on both sides of steak. In medium bowl, toss red onions with oil.

3. Place steak and onions on grill. Grill steak 10 to 15 minutes for medium-rare or until desired doneness, turning once. (Instant-read thermometer inserted into center of steak should reach 145°F.) Grill onions, turning occasionally, until browned and just tender, about 15 minutes.

4. Transfer steak and onions to cutting board. Let steak stand 10 minutes to set juices. Thinly slice steak and serve with onions.

EACH SERVING: About 270 calories, 24g protein, 15g carbohydrate, 13g total fat (5g saturated), 57mg cholesterol, 200mg sodium ☺ ♥

Veal Scaloppine Marsala

Simple, elegant, and scrumptious, this quintessential Italian dish is quick and easy to prepare. The purpose of pounding the cutlets is twofold: to tenderize the meat and to ensure even cooking.

TOTAL TIME: 25 minutes
MAKES: 6 main-dish servings

1	pound veal cutlets
¼	cup all-purpose flour
¼	teaspoon salt
⅛	teaspoon coarsely ground black pepper
3	tablespoons butter or margarine
½	cup dry Marsala wine
½	cup chicken broth
1	tablespoon chopped fresh parsley

1. With meat mallet, pound cutlets to even ⅛-inch thickness. Cut veal into roughly 3-inch squares. On waxed paper, combine flour, salt, and pepper; use to coat both sides of veal pieces, shaking off excess.

2. In nonstick 10-inch skillet, melt butter over medium heat. Cook veal in batches until lightly browned, 45 to 60 seconds per side (145°F), using slotted spatula to transfer pieces to warm platter as they are browned; cover with foil to keep warm.

3. Stir Marsala and broth into veal drippings in pan; cook until syrupy, 4 to 5 minutes, stirring until browned bits are loosened from bottom of skillet. To serve: pour sauce over veal and sprinkle with parsley.

EACH SERVING: About 180 calories, 17g protein, 5g carbohydrate, 7g total fat (4g saturated), 0g fiber, 75mg cholesterol, 288mg sodium ☺ ♥

QUICK TECHNIQUE: POUNDING CUTLETS

For even cooking, it's a good idea to pound veal, turkey, or chicken cutlets to a uniform thickness. Here's how: Place one piece of veal or other cutlet between two sheets of plastic wrap. With a meat mallet, rolling pin, or heavy skillet, pound three or four times until cutlet is ¼ inch thick, or whatever thickness is specified in the recipe.

Steak with Apple-Horseradish Relish

Blasted with blazing-high heat and basted in butter, this aged, succulent strip steak brings chophouse authenticity to the table fast.

ACTIVE TIME: 20 minutes
TOTAL TIME: 30 minutes
MAKES: 4 main-dish servings

2	tablespoons prepared horseradish, drained
1	tablespoon plus 2 teaspoons apple cider vinegar
1	tablespoon fresh lemon juice
1	tablespoon maple syrup
3/4	teaspoon salt
3/4	teaspoon freshly ground black pepper
1	Golden Delicious apple
1	Granny Smith apple
2	strip loin steaks (each 1½ inches thick and 12 ounces), preferably dry-aged
1	tablespoon vegetable oil
1	tablespoon butter or margarine
2	sprigs fresh thyme

1. Arrange oven rack in lowest position. Preheat oven to 450°F.

2. In medium bowl, combine horseradish, vinegar, lemon juice, syrup, and ¼ teaspoon each salt and pepper. Using large holes of box grater, grate apples; discard cores. Immediately stir apples into horseradish mixture. Set apple relish aside.

3. Heat ovenproof 12-inch skillet over high heat. Pat steaks dry with paper towels. Sprinkle with remaining ½ teaspoon each salt and pepper to season both sides. Add oil to pan and swirl to coat bottom evenly. When oil shimmers and is almost smoking, add steaks.

4. Cook 2 minutes. With tongs, lift each steak from pan and put back down on same side. Cook 1 minute longer, then turn steaks over. Transfer to lowest rack of oven. Roast 4 minutes.

5. Carefully add butter and thyme to skillet. Baste steaks with melted butter. Roast 2 to 3 minutes longer for medium-rare, or until desired doneness. (Instant-read thermometer inserted horizontally into center of steak should reach 145°F.)

6. Remove pan from oven and baste again. Transfer steaks to cutting board and let rest 5 minutes.

7. Slice steaks against grain at angle. Spoon pan juices on top and serve with apple relish.

EACH SERVING: About 505 calories, 35g protein, 17g carbohydrate, 32g total fat (13g saturated), 3g fiber, 102mg cholesterol, 585mg sodium

Red Wine Steaks with Green Beans

Low in carbs and added fat, and accompanied by healthful veggies, this steak dinner is sauced with a rich red-wine reduction.

ACTIVE TIME: 15 minutes
TOTAL TIME: 25 minutes
MAKES: 4 main-dish servings

1½	pounds beef strip steaks (each 1 inch thick)
⅜	teaspoon salt
⅜	teaspoon freshly ground black pepper
1	tablespoon butter or margarine
1	package (12 ounces) microwave-in-bag green beans
1	teaspoon red wine vinegar
2	shallots, finely chopped
1	cup dry red wine
¼	cup packed fresh tarragon leaves, finely chopped

1. Sprinkle steaks with ¼ teaspoon each salt and pepper to season both sides. In 12-inch skillet, melt ½ tablespoon butter over medium-high heat. Add steaks and cook, turning once, 7 minutes for medium-rare or until desired doneness. (Instant-read thermometer inserted horizontally into center of steak should reach 145°F.)

2. Meanwhile, in microwave oven, cook green beans as label directs. Transfer beans to large bowl and toss with vinegar, remaining ⅛ teaspoon each salt and pepper, and 1 tablespoon shallots.

3. Transfer steaks to plate. Reduce heat to medium-low and add remaining shallots to skillet. Cook, stirring occasionally, 5 minutes or until tender.

4. Add wine, increase heat to medium-high, and simmer 2 minutes, stirring and scraping up browned bits from pan. Remove skillet from heat and stir in tarragon, accumulated steak juices, and remaining ½ tablespoon butter until butter melts.

5. To serve, slice steak across grain. Divide steak and green beans among serving plates. Spoon sauce over steak.

EACH SERVING: About 455 calories, 37g protein, 9g carbohydrate, 29g total fat (11g saturated), 2g fiber, 97mg cholesterol, 340mg sodium

Gingered Pork and Vegetable Stir-Fry

Fast and fresh, this Asian-inspired dish delivers lean pork loin in a flavorful, gingery sauce without the fat and sodium of greasy takeout.

TOTAL TIME: 30 minutes
MAKES: 4 main-dish servings

1	pork tenderloin (12 ounces), trimmed
1	tablespoon rice vinegar
3	tablespoons soy sauce
¾	cup reduced-sodium chicken broth
1	tablespoon grated, peeled fresh ginger
1	tablespoon honey
2	teaspoons cornstarch
1	garlic clove, crushed with garlic press
3	teaspoons canola oil
8	ounces snap peas, strings removed from both sides
1	large red pepper, cut into ¼-inch-thick strips
3	green onions, cut into 1-inch pieces

Quick-cooking (10-minute) brown rice (optional; see page 57)

1. Cut pork tenderloin crosswise into three pieces. Cut each piece lengthwise in half, then cut lengthwise into thin slices.

2. In medium bowl, toss pork with vinegar and 1 tablespoon soy sauce. In small bowl, mix 2 tablespoons soy sauce with broth, ginger, honey, cornstarch, and garlic until blended. Set aside.

3. In nonstick 12-inch skillet, heat 1 teaspoon oil over medium heat until hot. Add peas, pepper, and green onions and cook 7 to 8 minutes or until lightly browned and tender-crisp, stirring frequently. Transfer vegetables to bowl.

4. In same skillet, heat remaining 2 teaspoons oil until hot. Add pork mixture and cook 2 to 3 minutes or until pork just loses pink color throughout (145°F), stirring constantly. With slotted spoon, transfer pork to bowl with vegetables.

5. Stir broth mixture, then add to skillet; heat to boiling. Boil 1 minute or until slightly thickened. Return pork and vegetables to skillet; stir until heated through. Serve with rice, if you like.

EACH SERVING: About 260 calories, 28g protein, 17g carbohydrate, 8g total fat (2g saturated), 3g fiber, 71mg cholesterol, 960mg sodium ☺

Orange Pork and Asparagus Stir-Fry

The secrets to a perfect orange pan sauce are simple: Wash and pat dry the orange first, and avoid the bitter white pith just below the peel when grating.

TOTAL TIME: 25 minutes
MAKES: 4 main-dish servings

2	navel oranges
1	teaspoon olive oil
1	pork tenderloin (12 ounces), trimmed and thinly sliced on diagonal
¾	teaspoon salt
¼	teaspoon ground black pepper
1½	pounds thin asparagus, trimmed and cut in half
1	garlic clove, crushed with garlic press
¼	cup water

1. From 1 orange, grate 1 teaspoon peel and squeeze ¼ cup juice. Cut peel from remaining orange and set aside, then remove and discard white pith. Cut orange crosswise into ¼-inch-thick slices; cut each slice into quarters.

2. In nonstick 12-inch skillet, heat ½ teaspoon oil over medium heat until hot but not smoking. Add half of pork slices and sprinkle with ¼ teaspoon salt and ⅛ teaspoon pepper. Cook, stirring frequently, until pork just loses pink color thoughout, about 2 minutes (145°F). With slotted spoon, transfer pork to plate. Repeat with remaining ½ teaspoon oil, pork, ¼ teaspoon salt, and remaining ⅛ teaspoon pepper.

3. To same skillet, add asparagus, garlic, orange peel, remaining ¼ teaspoon salt, and water; cover and cook, stirring occasionally, until asparagus is tender-crisp, about 2 minutes. Return pork to skillet. Add orange juice and orange pieces; heat through, stirring often.

EACH SERVING: About 165 calories, 24g protein, 8g carbohydrate, 4g total fat (1g saturated), 2g fiber, 50mg cholesterol, 495mg sodium ☺

Soy and Whiskey Glazed Pork Chops

Add a kick to juicy pork chops with a "shot" of garlic-and-ginger-infused whiskey glaze. For photo, see page 2.

ACTIVE TIME: 20 minutes
TOTAL TIME: 30 minutes
MAKES: 4 main-dish servings

1	piece (2 inches long) fresh ginger, peeled
2	tablespoons vegetable oil
1	pound broccoli florets
8	ounces fresh shiitake mushrooms, stems discarded, cut into 1-inch pieces
½	cup plus 3 tablespoons water
¼	cup plus 1 tablespoon reduced-sodium soy sauce
¼	teaspoon freshly ground black pepper
4	center-cut boneless pork chops (each ¾ inch thick)
2	garlic cloves, lightly smashed
2	tablespoons whiskey
2	tablespooons sugar

Thinly sliced green onions for garnish

1. Cut half of ginger into 4 chunks and finely chop remaining half.

2. In 12-inch skillet, heat 1 tablespoon oil over medium-high heat. Add finely chopped ginger; cook 10 seconds, stirring. Add broccoli and mushrooms. Cook 1 minute; stir in ½ cup water and 1 tablespoon soy sauce. Cover and cook 3 minutes or until vegetables are tender and liquid has evaporated. Transfer to serving plates; keep warm.

3. Wipe out skillet and heat remaining 1 tablespoon oil over medium heat. Sprinkle pepper on pork to season both sides. Add pork to skillet and cook, turning once, 7 to 8 minutes or until browned on the outside and barely pink in center. (Instant-read thermometer inserted horizontally into center of pork should reach 145°F.) Transfer pork chops to plate.

4. To skillet, add garlic, whiskey, sugar, ginger chunks, remaining ¼ cup soy sauce, and remaining 3 tablespoons water; simmer, stirring occasionally, 4 to 6 minutes or until consistency of thin syrup. Stir in any accumulated pork juices from plate. Remove and discard garlic and ginger.

5. To serve, divide pork chops among plates with broccoli mixture. Spoon sauce over pork.

EACH SERVING: About 505 calories, 40g protein, 17g carbohydrate, 31g total fat (9g saturated), 5g fiber, 102mg cholesterol, 865mg sodium

Caramelized Chile Shrimp

Thanks to a trio of insta-ingredients—preshelled shrimp, thin vermicelli, and bagged broccoli—this streamlined seafood stir-fry is ideal on time-is-tight nights. Red pepper flakes add a bit of heat. For photo, see page 18.

ACTIVE TIME: 15 minutes
TOTAL TIME: 25 minutes
MAKES: 4 main-dish servings

6   ounces rice stick noodles (rice vermicelli)
1   pound broccoli florets
1   green onion, finely chopped
¼   teaspoon salt
3   tablespoons sugar
1   tablespoon water
1   tablespoon vegetable oil
3   garlic cloves, very thinly sliced
¼   teaspoon crushed red pepper
1   tablespoon reduced-sodium Asian fish sauce (see page 24)
1   pound jumbo shrimp, shelled and deveined
¼   cup packed fresh cilantro leaves
¼   teaspoon ground black pepper

1. In heavy 12-inch skillet, heat *1 inch water* to boiling on high heat. Add noodles and cook 1 to 2 minutes or until just tender. With tongs, transfer noodles to colander. Rinse noodles under cold water and drain.

2. When water in skillet returns to boiling, add broccoli. Cook 3 minutes or until tender-crisp; drain and transfer to large bowl. Toss with green onion and salt. Wipe skillet dry.

3. In same skillet, cook sugar and water on medium-high heat (stirring just until sugar dissolves), 3 to 4 minutes or until mixture turns dark amber. Stir in oil, garlic, and red pepper. Cook 10 seconds, then stir in fish sauce and shrimp.

4. Cook 2 to 3 minutes or until shrimp just turn opaque throughout, stirring frequently. Remove from heat, and stir in cilantro and black pepper.

5. Divide noodles and broccoli among serving plates. Spoon shrimp with sauce on noodles.

EACH SERVING: About 340 calories, 22g protein, 53g carbohydrate, 5g total fat (1g saturated), 4g fiber, 168mg cholesterol, 600mg sodium ☺

Halibut in Thai Curry Sauce

This speedy fish dish boasts authentic Indian flavors. Nutty basmati rice is perfect for soaking up the boldly spiced, creamy sauce.

ACTIVE TIME: 10 minutes
TOTAL TIME: 25 minutes
MAKES: 4 main-dish servings

1   can (13½ to 14 ounces) light coconut milk
1   teaspoon grated, peeled fresh ginger
1   teaspoon brown sugar
½   teaspoon Thai red or green curry paste or curry powder
1   garlic clove, finely chopped
4   pieces skinless halibut fillet (6 ounces each)
2   green onions, chopped
¼   cup firmly packed fresh cilantro leaves, chopped
1   lime, cut into wedges
Cooked basmati or jasmine rice (optional)

1. In nonstick 12-inch skillet, whisk together coconut milk, ginger, brown sugar, curry paste or powder, and garlic until blended; heat to boiling over high heat, stirring. Reduce heat to medium-low and cook 5 minutes, stirring occasionally.

2. Add halibut fillets to skillet and cook 4 to 5 minutes on each side or just until fish turns opaque in the center. (Instant-read thermometer inserted horizontally into center of fillet should reach 145°F.) Transfer halibut to warm deep platter. Remove skillet from heat. Stir green onions and cilantro into sauce in skillet; pour sauce over halibut. Serve halibut with lime wedges and rice, if you like.

EACH SERVING: About 290 calories, 37g protein, 4g carbohydrate, 13g total fat (6g saturated), 1g fiber, 54mg cholesterol, 120mg sodium ☺

Crunchy Salmon with Lemony Squash Salad

Sourdough bread is the key to the crunch of this quick and easy salmon dinner. For photo, see page 8.

ACTIVE TIME: 15 minutes
TOTAL TIME: 25 minutes
MAKES: 4 main-dish servings

1	loaf (round) country or sourdough bread
4	center-cut skinless salmon fillets (6 ounces each)
½	teaspoon salt
½	teaspoon freshly ground black pepper
1	large zucchini, trimmed
2	tablespoons water
1	large yellow squash, cut into very thin half-moons
½	teaspoon pure honey
1	tablespoon plus 1 teaspoon olive oil
1	lemon
1	tablespoon chopped fresh dill, plus additional for garnish

1. With serrated knife, cut top off bread. Cut two horizontal ½-inch-thick slices from loaf, then cut off crusts. With rolling pin, roll slices to ¼-inch thickness. Cut each slice in half and trim to match dimensions of skin sides of salmon fillets. Reserve leftover bread for another use. Sprinkle ¼ teaspoon each salt and pepper on salmon. Press 1 bread slice onto skin side of each salmon fillet.

2. With vegetable peeler, peel zucchini into wide ribbons. In nonstick 12-inch skillet, heat water to boiling over high heat. Add yellow squash and zucchini and cook, gently stirring, 2 minutes or until just tender. Transfer to large bowl and toss with honey. Wipe skillet dry.

3. In skillet, heat 1 tablespoon oil over medium heat 1 minute. Add salmon, bread sides down, in single layer. Cook 7 minutes or until bread is golden brown. With spatula, carefully turn salmon over and cook 4 minutes longer or until salmon just turns opaque in center. (Instant-read thermometer inserted horizontally into center of salmon should reach 145°F.)

4. Meanwhile, from lemon, grate ½ teaspoon peel and squeeze 1 tablespoon juice. Gently stir into squash mixture along with dill, remaining ¼ teaspoon each salt and pepper, and remaining 1 teaspoon oil.

5. To serve, divide salmon and squash mixture among dinner plates. Garnish with additional dill.

EACH SERVING: About 335 calories, 38g protein, 18g carbohydrate, 12g total fat (2g saturated), 2g fiber, 80mg cholesterol, 515mg sodium ☺

Seared Salmon with Sweet Potatoes

Simple salmon and sweet potatoes become a gourmet meal in minutes when topped with an easy, tangy lemon-caper sauce and spiked with a hit of spicy cayenne.

ACTIVE TIME: 15 minutes
TOTAL TIME: 30 minutes
MAKES: 4 main-dish servings

1	pound sweet potatoes, peeled and cut into ½-inch cubes
¼	cup water
⅜	teaspoon salt
¼	teaspoon freshly ground black pepper
1	bag (6 ounces) baby spinach
⅛	teaspoon cayenne (ground red) pepper
4	pieces skinless center-cut salmon fillet (5 ounces each)
1	lemon
1	cup dry white wine
2	teaspoons capers, rinsed
¼	cup chopped fresh flat-leaf parsley

1. In large microwave-safe bowl, combine potatoes, water, and ¼ teaspoon each salt and pepper. Cover with vented plastic wrap; microwave on High 9 minutes or until tender, stirring halfway through. Add spinach; re-cover and microwave 2 minutes longer.

2. Meanwhile, sprinkle cayenne and remaining ⅛ teaspoon salt on salmon to season both sides. In nonstick 12-inch skillet over medium heat, cook salmon 10 minutes or until knife pierces center easily, turning once halfway through. (Instant-read thermometer inserted horizontally into center of fillet should reach 145°F.) Transfer to plate. From lemon, finely grate ½ teaspoon peel onto fish; into cup, squeeze 1 tablespoon juice.

3. To skillet, add wine and capers. Boil over high heat 2 minutes or until liquid is reduced by half, scraping browned bits from pan. Remove from heat; stir in lemon juice and parsley.

4. Divide potato mixture among plates; top with fish. Spoon sauce over fish.

EACH SERVING: About 300 calories, 31g protein, 22g carbohydrate, 9g total fat (1g saturated), 4g fiber, 78mg cholesterol, 430mg sodium ☺ ♥

2

Healthy in a Hurry

If you're like us, you're always on the lookout for wholesome family dinner recipes that are speedy to prepare. Look no further: In this chapter, we've collected fast and healthy recipes that everyone will love. All are 450 calories or less per serving and contain no more than 5 grams of saturated fat. Many include a side of whole grains—like quick-cooking brown rice, quinoa, or barley—so they deliver a healthy dose of fiber, too.

Lean chicken breasts are a natural choice for quick and healthy meals. Maple-Walnut Chicken includes a whole-grain pilaf and a side of spinach. Grilled Chicken and Greens offers both watercress and asparagus and can be made in a grill pan or on an outdoor grill.

Skip the Chinese takeout and make our Beef and Pepper Stir-Fry. It's served on quick-cooking brown rice and uses only a little oil, which makes it a healthy alternative. Pork Medallions with Pears is made from lean pork tenderloin and served on quinoa, which has the highest protein content of any whole grain.

Fish and seafood are low in fat and a rich source of protein, vitamins, and minerals, which makes them a great choice for healthy-in-a-hurry meals. Our Almond-Crusted Tilapia and Shrimp and Asparagus Stir-Fry are so tasty, they'll win over even reluctant fish eaters.

A pasta dinner can be a healthy choice, too, especially when it's loaded with vegetables and whole-grain noodles. Try our Vegetable Lasagna Toss, which includes white beans and an assortment of veggies, or Whole-Grain Rotini with Asparagus and Snap Peas.

Spiced Chicken Skewers (recipe page 51)

Sweet and Savory Chicken

Prunes provide the sweet while olives provide the savory in this easy chicken-and-whole-grain dinner recipe.

TOTAL TIME: 30 minutes
MAKES: 4 main-dish servings

1¾ cups reduced-sodium chicken broth
1   cup water
1   cup bulgur
1½ pounds chicken-breast tenders
¼   teaspoon salt
¼   teaspoon ground black pepper
1   tablespoon olive oil
1   small onion (4 to 6 ounces), chopped
¼   cup chopped pimiento-stuffed olives
¼   cup chopped prunes
1   teaspoon capers, drained and chopped

1. In 2-quart saucepan, heat 1 cup broth and water to boiling. Stir in bulgur. Cover and simmer over low heat 15 minutes or until liquid is absorbed.

2. Meanwhile, place chicken tenders between two sheets of plastic wrap. With meat mallet, pound to ¼-inch thickness. Sprinkle chicken with salt and pepper to season both sides.

3. In 12-inch skillet, heat oil over medium-high heat. Add chicken and cook, turning once, 4 minutes or until no longer pink throughout (165°F). Transfer to plate; cover and keep warm.

4. Add onion to skillet; cook over medium heat, stirring occasionally, 5 minutes or until beginning to soften. Add olives, prunes, capers, remaining ¾ cup broth, and juices from chicken on plate; heat to boiling, stirring. Boil 1 minute. Serve chicken and sauce over bulgur.

EACH SERVING: About 385 calories, 45g protein, 35g carbohydrate, 7g total fat (1g saturated), 8g fiber, 99mg cholesterol, 670mg sodium ☺

Spiced Chicken Skewers

Spice up your usual chicken routine with this quick and healthy recipe seasoned with chili powder and fresh lemon. For photo, see page 48.

TOTAL TIME: 30 minutes
MAKES: 4 main-dish servings

1	cup bulgur
1¾	cups water
1	pound skinless, boneless chicken breasts, cut into 1-inch chunks
2	teaspoons chili powder
2	teaspoons extra-virgin olive oil
½	teaspoon salt
½	teaspoon freshly ground black pepper
2	pints cherry tomatoes
4	(10-inch) metal skewers
2	lemons
1	garlic clove, crushed with garlic press
1	cup chopped fresh flat-leaf parsley leaves

EXPRESS-LANE INGREDIENT: BULGUR

Bulgur is cracked wheat that has been parboiled and dried so it cooks faster. Better still, it's a nutritional powerhouse that contains thirteen B vitamins, vitamin E, protein, and essential fatty acids. So enjoy it as the base for our Spiced Chicken Skewers, above, and in other fast weeknight meals.

1. Prepare outdoor grill for direct grilling or preheat large grill pan over medium-high heat.

2. In large microwave-safe bowl, combine bulgur and water. Microwave on High, stirring once, 10 minutes or until bulgur is tender and water is absorbed.

3. In medium bowl, toss chicken with chili powder, 1 teaspoon oil, and ¼ teaspoon each salt and pepper until well coated. Thread chicken and tomatoes alternately onto skewers, spacing ¼ inch apart.

4. Place skewers on hot grill grate and grill, turning occasionally, 7 to 8 minutes or until chicken is cooked through (165°F).

5. Meanwhile, into bowl with bulgur, from 1 lemon, finely grate 1 teaspoon peel and squeeze 3 tablespoons juice. Add garlic, parsley, remaining ¼ teaspoon each salt and pepper, and remaining 1 teaspoon oil. Stir well.

6. Divide bulgur mixture and chicken skewers among serving plates. Serve with remaining lemon, cut into wedges.

EACH SERVING: About 305 calories, 29g protein, 37g carbohydrate, 6g total fat (1g saturated), 10g fiber, 63mg cholesterol, 390mg sodium ☺ ♥

Grilled Chicken and Greens

Lighten up with watercress and asparagus, served with easy flash-grilled chicken breasts. The greens deliver disease-fighting antioxidants and fiber — and almost no calories.

TOTAL TIME: 30 minutes
MAKES: 4 main-dish servings

1	cup packed fresh mint leaves
1 to 2 lemons	
2	garlic cloves, crushed with garlic press
1	tablespoon plus 2 teaspoons extra-virgin olive oil
¼	teaspoon plus pinch salt
¼	teaspoon plus pinch freshly ground black pepper
1	pound skinless, boneless chicken-breast halves, pounded to even ⅓-inch thickness
1	pound asparagus, ends trimmed
1	pound radishes, trimmed and very thinly sliced
2	packages (4 ounces each) watercress

1. Preheat large ridged grill pan or outdoor grill for direct grilling over medium-high heat.

2. Finely chop half of mint. From lemons, finely grate 1 teaspoon peel and squeeze ¼ cup juice. In 9-inch pie plate, combine chopped mint, lemon peel, 1 tablespoon lemon juice, half of garlic, 1 teaspoon oil, and ⅛ teaspoon each salt and pepper. Add chicken and rub with mint mixture to coat evenly.

3. On jelly-roll pan, toss asparagus with 1 teaspoon oil, 1 pinch each salt and pepper, and remaining garlic. Grill, turning occasionally, 4 to 6 minutes or until charred in spots.

4. Meanwhile, in large bowl, toss radishes and watercress with remaining 3 tablespoons lemon juice, 1 tablespoon oil, and ⅛ teaspoon each salt and pepper, and mint. Divide among plates.

5. Place hot asparagus on top of greens. Place chicken on grill. Cook 2 to 3 minutes per side or until meat just loses pink color throughout (165°F). Divide hot chicken among plates with greens (see Tip).

EACH SERVING: About 225 calories, 27g protein, 10g carbohydrate, 9g total fat (2g saturated), 5g fiber, 63mg cholesterol, 315mg sodium ☺ ❤

TIP: *Enjoy ASAP! Watercress, like other delicate greens, starts to wilt and lose its tangy bite as soon as you add dressing.*

Balsamic Chicken and Pears

Star ingredient: skinless, boneless chicken breasts, which deliver plenty of protein with almost no artery-clogging saturated fat. Whole-wheat couscous and pears add beneficial fiber, and Roma beans (long, flat-podded Italian-style green beans available frozen in supermarkets) serve up multiple plant nutrients.

TOTAL TIME: 25 minutes
MAKES: 4 main-dish servings

1	package (9 ounces) frozen Roma beans
1⅓	cups whole-wheat couscous
1	tablespoon plus 1 teaspoon olive oil
4	small skinless, boneless chicken-breast halves (1 pound total)
2	Bosc pears, not peeled, each cored and cut into 8 wedges
1	cup chicken broth
3	tablespoons balsamic vinegar
2	teaspoons cornstarch

1. Prepare beans and couscous as labels direct.

2. Meanwhile, in 12-inch skillet, heat 1 tablespoon oil over medium heat. Add chicken and cook, turning once, 10 to 12 minutes or until instant-read thermometer inserted horizontally into breast reaches 165°F. Transfer to plate.

3. In same skillet, in remaining 1 teaspoon oil, cook pear wedges 3 to 4 minutes or until lightly browned and tender.

4. In cup, mix broth, vinegar, and cornstarch; add to skillet with pears. Heat to boiling over medium-high heat. Boil 1 minute. Return chicken and any juice on plate to skillet; lower heat to medium and heat through heat through.

EACH SERVING: About 450 calories, 36g protein, 61g carbohydrate, 7g total fat (1g saturated), 10g fiber, 66mg cholesterol, 235mg sodium ☺ ♥

Maple-Walnut Chicken

Maple syrup adds a sugary glaze to lean chicken breasts, while spinach, walnuts, and whole-grain pilaf deliver heart-boosting antioxidants and loads of fiber.

TOTAL TIME: 30 minutes
MAKES: 4 main-dish servings

4	skinless chicken-breast halves (6 to 7 ounces each)
1	tablespoon olive oil
1	tablespoon packed fresh thyme leaves
¼	teaspoon salt
¼	teaspoon freshly ground black pepper
½	cup walnuts
5	tablespoons cider vinegar
3	tablespoons maple syrup
½	cup water
1	package (8½ ounces) precooked whole-grain pilaf
1	package (9 ounces) microwave-in-bag spinach

1. Rub chicken with oil, then rub with thyme, salt, and pepper. Let stand.

2. Meanwhile, in nonstick 12-inch skillet, toast walnuts over medium heat, stirring occasionally, 4 to 6 minutes or until golden and fragrant. Transfer walnuts to dish; do not remove skillet from heat.

3. Add chicken to same skillet; cook, turning frequently, 12 minutes or until chicken is golden brown and cooked through. (Instant-read thermometer inserted horizontally into breast should reach 165°F.) Transfer chicken to clean plate; do not remove skillet from heat.

4. To same skillet, add vinegar and cook, stirring, 1 minute. Add syrup and water; simmer, stirring occasionally, 6 to 7 minutes or until mixture has thickened.

5. Meanwhile, in microwave, cook pilaf, then spinach, as labels direct.

6. Stir walnuts and any chicken juices into sauce. Divide pilaf and spinach among dinner plates. Top with chicken; spoon maple-walnut sauce all around.

EACH SERVING: About 435 calories, 40g protein, 33g carbohydrate, 17g total fat (2g saturated), 10g fiber, 82mg cholesterol, 310mg sodium ☺ ♥

Herb-Grilled Turkey Cutlets

Super-lean turkey cutlets, seasoned with fresh herbs and served with fiber-rich bulgur and tomato salsa, deliver a meal that's light on fat, calories, and effort.

TOTAL TIME: 30 minutes
MAKES: 4 main-dish servings

1	lemon
1	large tomato, chopped
2	cups water
1	cup bulgur
¼	cup loosely packed fresh parsley leaves, chopped
⅜	teaspoon salt
⅜	teaspoon freshly ground black pepper
1	tablespoon chopped fresh oregano leaves
1	tablespoon chopped fresh mint leaves
2	teaspoons olive oil
1	pound turkey breast cutlets

1. Prepare outdoor grill for direct grilling over medium heat. From lemon, grate ¼ teaspoon peel and squeeze 2 tablespoons juice. In small bowl, stir together 1 tablespoon juice and tomato; set aside.

2. Prepare bulgur: In 3-quart saucepan, heat water to boiling over high heat. Stir in bulgur and reduce heat to low; cover and simmer about 15 minutes or until all liquid has been absorbed. Stir in parsley, ⅛ teaspoon each salt and pepper, lemon peel, and remaining 1 tablespoon juice.

3. Meanwhile, in small bowl, combine oregano, mint, and oil. Pat cutlets dry; rub with herb mixture on both sides. Sprinkle with remaining ¼ teaspoon each salt and pepper to season both sides. Grill turkey, turning once, 3 to 4 minutes, or until instant-read thermometer inserted horizontally into cutlet reaches 165°F. Top turkey with tomato; serve with bulgur.

EACH SERVING: About 285 calories, 32g protein, 30g carbohydrate, 5g total fat (1g saturated), 7g fiber, 66mg cholesterol, 280mg sodium ☺ ♥

Spicy Turkey Sausage Jambalaya

This hearty Creole classic gets slimmed down with chicken tenders and turkey sausage (in place of high-fat pork). Brown rice boosts the fiber, while peppers and tomatoes deliver half the recommended daily amount of vitamin C——and it's all cooked in one skillet!

ACTIVE TIME: 10 minutes
TOTAL TIME: 25 minutes
MAKES: 4 main-dish servings

8   ounces turkey andouille sausage, sliced ¼ inch thick

1   green or yellow pepper, chopped

1   can (14½ ounces) stewed tomatoes

1   cup quick-cooking (10-minute) brown rice

8   ounces chicken tenders, each cut crosswise in half

½   cup water

¼   teaspoon salt

1   bunch green onions, sliced

1. Heat 12-inch skillet over medium heat. Add sausage and pepper and cook 5 minutes, stirring occasionally.

2. Stir in tomatoes with their juice, rice, chicken, water, and salt; heat to boiling over high heat. Reduce heat to low; cover and simmer 10 minutes or until rice is just tender. Remove skillet from heat; stir in green onions.

EACH SERVING: About 265 calories, 26g protein, 30g carbohydrate, 6g total fat (2g saturated), 4g fiber, 73mg cholesterol, 830mg sodium ☺ 🍱

EXPRESS-LANE INGREDIENT: INSTANT BROWN RICE

We all know how healthy brown rice is, but it takes a lot longer to cook than white rice. The solution? Instant brown rice: It cooks in just ten minutes and there's no appreciable difference in the nutrition profile from regular brown rice. Both are considered whole grains, and both are good sources of fiber, manganese (a mineral that helps produce energy), magnesium (which helps build bones), and selenium (key to a healthy immune system). So, enjoy instant brown rice as the base for the jambalaya above and in other healthy-in-a-hurry meals.

Beef and Pepper Stir-Fry

A Chinese restaurant favorite gets a makeover: Lean top round stays tender when flash-fried in a hot skillet, while tomatoes add a flavor twist (and extra antioxidants) to the usual veggie combo. Instant (cooks in 10 minutes!) brown rice delivers the fiber missing from white rice.

TOTAL TIME: 30 minutes
MAKES: 4 main-dish servings

1	cup quick-cooking (10-minute) short-grain brown rice (see page 57)
12	ounces beef top round, thinly sliced across the grain
1	tablespoon plus 1 teaspoon reduced-sodium soy sauce
1	teaspoon sugar
½	teaspoon freshly ground black pepper
2	teaspoons vegetable oil
3	peppers (preferably red, yellow, and orange), thinly sliced
2	garlic cloves, crushed with garlic press
2	ripe tomatoes, cored, cut into ½-inch wedges

1. Prepare brown rice as label directs.

2. In bowl, combine beef, 1 teaspoon soy sauce, ½ teaspoon sugar, and ¼ teaspoon black pepper.

3. In 12-inch skillet, heat 1 teaspoon oil over medium-high heat. Add beef in single layer. Cook, without stirring, 1 minute. Transfer to plate; return skillet to medium-high heat without cleaning.

4. Add remaining 1 teaspoon oil to skillet. Add peppers and garlic; stir-fry 4 to 5 minutes or until tender-crisp. Add tomatoes and remaining ½ teaspoon sugar. Cook, stirring, 3 to 4 minutes or until saucy. Return beef to skillet; add remaining ¼ teaspoon black pepper and 1 tablespoon soy sauce. Cook 1 minute, stirring. Serve stir-fry over rice.

EACH SERVING: About 285 calories, 26g protein, 28g carbohydrate, 16g total fat (5g saturated), 3g fiber, 59mg cholesterol, 305mg sodium ☺ ♥

Pork Medallions with Pears

Tenderloins finished with a sweet and tangy pear sauce are hearty and healthful.

TOTAL TIME: 30 minutes
MAKES: 4 main-dish servings

1	cup quinoa, rinsed
1	pork tenderloin (1 pound), cut into 1-inch-thick medallions
¼	teaspoon freshly ground black pepper
⅜	teaspoon salt
1	tablespoon extra-virgin olive oil
2	teaspoons fennel seeds
4	green onions, sliced
⅓	cup water
2	garlic cloves, chopped
1½	pounds ripe Anjou or Bartlett pears, peeled, cored, and sliced
1	tablespoon fresh lemon juice

EXPRESS-LANE INGREDIENT: QUINOA

Not only is quinoa quick to cook, it's a complete protein that contains all of the essential amino acids the body can't produce for itself. It's also high in iron, manganese, and magnesium. Quinoa has a mildly nutty flavor that makes it a delicious base for salads or sautés, like the Pork Medallions with Pears above. Be sure to wash it well (rub the grains under cold running water, then rinse until the water is clear) to remove any traces of bitterness, the result of a natural substance in quinoa called saponin.

1. Prepare quinoa as label directs. Press pork with palm of hand to flatten. Sprinkle with pepper and ⅛ teaspoon salt.

2. In 12-inch skillet, heat oil over medium-high heat. Add pork; cook, turning once, 5 to 6 minutes or until browned on both sides. Transfer to plate; set aside.

3. Reduce heat to medium. To same skillet, add fennel seeds; cook 30 seconds, stirring. Add green onions, water, and garlic; cook 1 minute, stirring. Add pears, lemon juice, and remaining ¼ teaspoon salt; cook, stirring occasionally, 2 minutes or until pears begin to soften. Return pork to pan, along with any juices. Cook 3 to 6 minutes or until pork is slightly pink in center. (Instant-read thermometer inserted horizontally into center of pork should reach 145°F.)

4. Serve pork with quinoa alongside; top with pear mixture.

EACH SERVING: About 415 calories, 31g protein, 54g carbohydrate, 9g total fat (2g saturated), 9g fiber, 74mg cholesterol, 285mg sodium ☺ ♥

Five-Spice Pork with Gingered Vegetables

In this simple meal, gingery veggies and bulgur pair perfectly with pork medallions seasoned with Chinese five-spice powder.

ACTIVE TIME: 15 minutes
TOTAL TIME: 25 minutes
MAKES: 4 main-dish servings

1½	cups bulgur
1	tablespoon plus 1 teaspoon canola oil
¾	teaspoon Chinese five-spice powder (see page 160)
⅜	teaspoon salt
1	pork tenderloin (1 pound), cut into 1-inch-thick medallions
5	medium carrots, very thinly sliced on diagonal
8	ounces stringless snap peas
4 to 5	tablespoons grated, peeled fresh ginger
¼	cup water, plus additional if necessary

1. Prepare bulgur as label directs.

2. Meanwhile, in 12-inch skillet, heat oil over medium-high heat. Sprinkle ½ teaspoon five-spice powder and ¼ teaspoon salt on pork to season all sides. Add to hot oil in single layer. Cook, turning once, 6 to 7 minutes or until instant-read thermometer inserted horizontally into pork reaches 145°F. Transfer to plate.

3. To same skillet, add carrots, snap peas, ginger, ¼ cup water, and remaining ¼ teaspoon five-spice powder and ⅛ teaspoon salt. Cook, stirring, 2 minutes or until carrots are just tender, adding 1 tablespoon water if pan seems too dry. Serve vegetables over bulgur with pork.

EACH SERVING: About 405 calories, 32g protein, 53g carbohydrate, 8g total fat (1g saturated), 13g fiber, 74mg cholesterol, 345mg sodium ☺ ♥

Almond-Crusted Tilapia

Appealingly lean tilapia is coated with crunchy, antioxidant-boosting almonds and served with a side of mushrooms and green beans.

TOTAL TIME: 25 minutes
MAKES: 4 main-dish servings

2	lemons
2	tablespoons olive oil
½	teaspoon salt
¼	teaspoon coarsely ground black pepper
4	tilapia fillets (6 ounces each)
¼	cup sliced natural almonds
1	small onion (4 to 6 ounces), chopped
1	bag (12 ounces) trimmed fresh green beans
1	package (10 ounces) sliced white mushrooms
2	tablespoons water

1. Preheat oven to 425°F. From 1 lemon, grate 1 teaspoon peel and squeeze 3 tablespoons juice; cut second lemon into wedges. In cup, mix lemon peel and 1 tablespoon juice, 1 tablespoon oil, ¼ teaspoon salt, and ⅛ teaspoon pepper.

2. Spray 13" by 9" glass baking dish with nonstick spray; place tilapia, dark side down, in dish. Drizzle tilapia with lemon mixture; press almonds on top. Bake 15 minutes or until tilapia turns opaque and instant-read thermometer inserted horizontally into center of fillet reaches 145°F.

3. Meanwhile, in 12-inch skillet, heat remaining 1 tablespoon oil over medium-high heat 1 minute. Add onion and cook, stirring occasionally, 5 to 6 minutes or until golden. Stir in green beans, mushrooms, water, and remaining ¼ teaspoon salt and ⅛ teaspoon pepper. Cook until most of liquid evaporates and green beans are tender-crisp, about 6 minutes. Toss with remaining 2 tablespoons lemon juice. Serve bean mixture and lemon wedges alongside tilapia.

EACH SERVING: About 315 calories, 33g protein, 15g carbohydrate, 15g total fat (1g saturated), 5g fiber, 0mg cholesterol, 380mg sodium ☺ ♥

Steamed Scrod Fillets

Fish is steamed on a bed of bok choy and carrots and drizzled with soy sauce and ginger.

ACTIVE TIME: 15 minutes
TOTAL TIME: 25 minutes
MAKES: 4 main-dish servings

3	tablespoons reduced-sodium soy sauce
2	tablespoons seasoned rice vinegar
1	tablespoon finely chopped, peeled fresh ginger
1	garlic clove, crushed with garlic press
1	pound bok choy, coarsely chopped
1¾	cups shredded carrots
4	scrod fillets (6 ounces each)
3	green onions, sliced

1. In small bowl, with fork, mix soy sauce, vinegar, ginger, and garlic.

2. In 12-inch skillet, toss bok choy and carrots; place scrod on top. Pour soy-sauce mixture over scrod and sprinkle with green onions; cover and heat to boiling. Reduce heat to medium; cook until scrod is opaque throughout (145°F), about 10 minutes.

EACH SERVING: About 200 calories, 34g protein, 12g carbohydrate, 2g total fat (0g saturated), 3g fiber, 73mg cholesterol, 820mg sodium ☺

Steamed Scrod Fillets

Salmon with Ginger and Green Onions

Why it's good for you: Salmon is rich in protein, low in saturated fat—and loaded with heart-protecting omega-3 fatty acids. A gingery sauce and a bed of rice noodles give it Asian flair fast.

ACTIVE TIME: 5 minutes
TOTAL TIME: 12 minutes
MAKES: 4 main-dish servings

1   package (7 to 8 ounces) thin rice noodles (vermicelli style)
4   green onions
1   teaspoon Asian sesame oil (see page 33)
2   tablespoons reduced-sodium soy sauce
2   tablespoons water
2   teaspoon grated, peeled fresh ginger
4   pieces salmon fillet (6 ounces each)

1. Prepare noodles as label directs.

2. Thinly slice dark-green tops from green onions and reserve for garnish; cut remaining white and light-green parts into ½-inch pieces.

3. In 9-inch glass pie plate, toss green-onion pieces with sesame oil. Cover and cook in microwave oven on High 2 to 3 minutes or until green onions are tender.

4. Stir soy sauce, water, and ginger into green onions in pie plate; top with salmon, skin side up, with thinner ends toward center. Cook, covered, on High 5 minutes (see Tip) or until salmon turns opaque throughout. (Instant-read thermometer inserted horizontally into center of fillet should reach 145°F.) Let stand, covered, 2 minutes.

5. To serve, divide noodles among shallow bowls; top with salmon, liquid from pie plate, and reserved green-onion tops.

EACH SERVING: About 465 calories, 36g protein, 50g carbohydrate, 13g total fat (2g saturated), 1g fiber, 94mg cholesterol, 440mg sodium ♥

TIP: *Microwaving note: This recipe was tested in a 1,000-watt microwave oven. If your microwave has more or less power, you may need to adjust the cooking time.*

Salmon Provençal with Zucchini

Salmon, like other cold-water fish, is brimming with omega-3 fatty acids, which improve the ratio of good (HDL) to bad (LDL) cholesterol and also lower heart-damaging triglycerides.

TOTAL TIME: 25 minutes
MAKES: 4 main-dish servings

1	tablespoon olive oil
4	pieces skinless salmon fillet (6 ounces each)
¼	teaspoon salt
⅛	teaspoon ground black pepper
1	can (28 ounces) whole tomatoes in juice
1	small onion (4 to 6 ounces), chopped
¼	cup Kalamata olives, chopped
1	tablespoon capers, drained and chopped
3	medium zucchini (8 ounces each)
1	tablespoon fresh lemon juice

1. In 12-inch skillet, heat oil over medium-high heat. Evenly season salmon on both sides with salt and pepper. Add salmon to skillet and cook 3 minutes. Reduce heat to medium; turn salmon over and cook 3 to 5 minutes longer or until opaque throughout. (Instant-read thermometer inserted horizontally into center of fillet should reach 145°F.)

2. Meanwhile, drain tomatoes, reserving ¼ cup juice. Chop tomatoes.

3. Transfer salmon to plate; cover with foil to keep warm. To same skillet, add onion and cook 5 minutes or until tender. Stir in tomatoes with reserved juice; heat to boiling. Cook, stirring, 2 minutes or until sauce thickens. Remove skillet from heat; stir in olives and capers.

4. While tomato sauce is cooking, cut each zucchini lengthwise in half, then cut crosswise into ¼-inch-thick slices.

5. In microwave-safe medium bowl, place zucchini and *2 tablespoons water*. Cover with vented plastic wrap and cook in microwave on High 5 minutes or until just fork-tender. Drain zucchini; add lemon juice and toss to coat.

6. Place salmon on dinner plates; top with tomato-olive-caper mixture and serve with zucchini.

EACH SERVING: About 240 calories, 29g protein, 24g carbohydrate, 5g total fat (1g saturated), 8g fiber, 172mg cholesterol, 740mg sodium ☺

Easy Seafood Stew

Low in fat and rich in protein, this speedy version of a classic fisherman's stew also delivers an abundant serving of stewed red tomatoes, which contain lycopene, an antioxidant that lowers your risk of heart disease and certain cancers.

Active time: 10 minutes
Total time: 30 minutes
Makes: 4 main-dish servings

2	teaspoons olive oil
1	large yellow pepper, coarsely chopped
1	medium onion, chopped
2	garlic cloves, crushed with garlic press
1	can (14½ ounces) stewed tomatoes
1	cup spicy tomato-vegetable juice
½	cup water
¼	teaspoon salt
1	pound skinless cod fillet, cut into 1-inch chunks
8	ounces shelled and deveined medium shrimp

1. In 4-quart saucepan, heat oil over medium heat. Add yellow pepper and onion, and cook, stirring frequently, 5 to 6 minutes or until softened and lightly browned. Stir in garlic and cook 1 minute, stirring constantly.

2. Stir in stewed tomatoes, vegetable juice, water, and salt; cover and heat to boiling over high heat. Reduce heat to low and simmer, covered, 10 minutes.

3. Stir in cod and shrimp; cover and simmer, gently stirring once, 3 to 4 minutes or until cod and shrimp just turn opaque throughout. Ladle stew into large soup bowls.

EACH SERVING: About 245 calories, 34g protein, 17g carbohydrate, 4g total fat (1g saturated), 3g fiber, 135mg cholesterol, 715mg sodium ☺

Shrimp and Asparagus Stir-Fry

Enjoy this Asian-influenced entrée, flavored with ginger, soy, and sesame and rich in vitamins and minerals (thanks to brown rice and asparagus). It's low in calories and fat, too.

TOTAL TIME: 30 minutes
MAKES: 4 main-dish servings

1	cup quick-cooking (10-minute) brown rice (see page 57)
3	teaspoons Asian sesame oil (see page 33)
1½	pounds asparagus, trimmed and cut into 1-inch pieces
1	pound peeled and deveined shrimp
1	tablespoon grated, peeled fresh ginger
2	tablespoons reduced-sodium soy sauce
2	tablespoons fresh lime juice
¼	cup loosely packed fresh basil leaves, thinly sliced

1. Cook rice as label directs.

2. Meanwhile, in nonstick 12-inch skillet, heat 2 teaspoons oil over medium heat 1 minute. Add asparagus and cook, stirring occasionally, 7 to 8 minutes or until tender-crisp. Add shrimp and ginger; cook, stirring occasionally, 5 to 6 minutes or until shrimp are opaque throughout.

3. Stir in soy sauce, lime juice, basil, and remaining 1 teaspoon oil; remove from heat. Serve stir-fry over rice.

EACH SERVING: About 265 calories, 29g protein, 22g carbohydrate, 7g total fat (1g saturated), 2g fiber, 172mg cholesterol, 455mg sodium ☺ ♥

Sautéed Shrimp on Warm Black Bean Salad

Sure, shrimp has more cholesterol than other seafood, but it's still heart smart because it's so low in fat and calories. And fiber-packed black beans outscore all other beans in antioxidants.

TOTAL TIME: 25 minutes
MAKES: 4 main-dish servings

1¼ pounds large shrimp, shelled and deveined (see Tip)

½ teaspoon salt

⅜ teaspoon coarsely ground black pepper

2 teaspoons olive oil

1 lime

1 small onion (4 to 6 ounces), chopped

1 medium red pepper, chopped

1 teaspoon ground cumin

1 can (15 to 19 ounces) black beans, rinsed and drained

2 tablespoons chopped fresh cilantro leaves

1. Sprinkle shrimp with ¼ teaspoon salt and ⅛ black pepper. In nonstick 12-inch skillet, heat 1 teaspoon oil over medium heat 1 minute. Add shrimp and cook, stirring occasionally, about 6 minutes or until opaque throughout.

2. Meanwhile, from lime, grate 1 teaspoon peel and squeeze 2 tablespoons juice; set aside.

3. Transfer shrimp to small bowl; cover with foil to keep warm. In same skillet, heat remaining 1 teaspoon oil over medium heat 1 minute. Add onion and red pepper and cook 8 minutes or until tender. Stir in cumin; cook 1 minute. Add black beans, lime peel and juice, and remaining ¼ teaspoon each salt and black pepper. Cook 3 minutes or until heated through.

4. Spoon black-bean mixture onto dinner plates. Top with shrimp and any liquid in bowl; sprinkle with chopped cilantro.

EACH SERVING: About 240 calories, 29g protein, 24g carbohydrate, 5g total fat (1g saturated), 8g fiber, 172mg cholesterol, 740mg sodium ☺

TIP: *You can save yourself a few minutes by purchasing already shelled and deveined shrimp. You'll need 1 pound to make this recipe.*

Scallops and Parsnip Puree

Proof that you can never be too rich (creamy parsnip puree) or too thin (low-fat, low-cal scallops).

TOTAL TIME: 30 minutes
MAKES: 4 main-dish servings

1¾	pounds parsnips
1	head Savoy cabbage (1½ pounds), cored and cut into ½-inch slices
2	garlic cloves, crushed with garlic press
¼	cup water
½	teaspoon salt
⅜	teaspoon freshly ground black pepper
1	tablespoon extra-virgin olive oil
1	pound sea scallops (8 to 12 large)
¼	cup reduced-fat sour cream
1	tablespoon finely chopped fresh chives
1	lemon, cut into wedges

EXPRESS-LANE INGREDIENT: SEA SCALLOPS

If you haven't prepared scallops at home, we encourage you to try this recipe or the Scallops, Scampi-Style, opposite. Not only are they quick cooking, they have a firm texture and sweet flavor. Choose those that are creamy pink in color; avoid scallops that are very white and plump—they have been soaked in a preservative solution. Soaked scallops tend to expel a lot of liquid while cooking, which means they don't brown nicely. Before cooking, pull the tough, crescent-shaped muscle from the side of each scallop and discard. Rinse to remove sand from crevices.

1. Fill 4-quart covered saucepan with *water;* heat to boiling over high heat. Meanwhile, peel parsnips and remove center core if woody; cut into ½-inch pieces. Add parsnips to boiling water; return water to boiling. Reduce heat to medium; cover and simmer parsnips 15 minutes or until tender. Remove and reserve ¼ *cup cooking water* from pot; drain parsnips.

2. Meanwhile, in microwave-safe large bowl, combine cabbage, garlic, and water. Cover with vented plastic wrap and microwave on High 7 to 8 minutes or until tender. Drain; sprinkle with ⅛ teaspoon each salt and pepper.

3. While cabbage is cooking, in 12-inch skillet, heat oil over medium-high heat until very hot. Sprinkle ⅛ teaspoon salt on scallops. Add to pan in single layer. Cook, turning once, 4 to 6 minutes or until browned on both sides.

4. In food processor with knife blade attached, puree parsnips, sour cream, remaining ¼ teaspoon each salt and pepper, and reserved cooking water. Divide among serving plates; top with scallops. Serve with cabbage. Garnish with chives and lemon wedges.

EACH SERVING: About 340 calories, 24g protein, 45g carbohydrate, 10g total fat (2g saturated), 14g fiber, 42mg cholesterol, 840mg sodium ☺

Scallops, Scampi-Style

Scallops are low in fat, calories, and cholesterol, and high in vitamin B$_{12}$. Zucchini and squash deliver some fiber, but to boost it even more, we've added a side of whole-wheat couscous.

ACTIVE TIME: 15 minutes
TOTAL TIME: 25 minutes
MAKES: 4 main-dish servings

1   cup whole-wheat couscous

1¼   pounds sea scallops (12 to 16 large)

1   lemon

1   garlic clove, crushed with garlic press

¼   teaspoon salt

¼   teaspoon coarsely grated black pepper

4   zucchini or yellow summer squash (8 ounces each) or 2 of each

1   tablespoon butter or margarine

2   tablespoons chopped fresh chives

1. Prepare couscous as label directs.

2. Meanwhile, pull off and discard crescent-shaped muscle, if any, from edge of each scallop; rinse well and pat dry.

3. From lemon, grate 1 teaspoon peel and squeeze 2 tablespoons juice. Set juice aside. In bowl, toss scallops with garlic, ½ teaspoon lemon peel, salt, and pepper.

4. With vegetable peeler, shave each squash lengthwise into thin, long ribbons until you reach core with seeds; discard core. Set aside squash ribbons.

5. In nonstick 12-inch skillet, heat butter over medium heat until melted. Add scallops and cook, turning once, 5 to 6 minutes or until browned and just opaque throughout; transfer scallops to plate. Add squash to same skillet; cover and cook 2 minutes, stirring once. Uncover and cook 1 minute or until tender-crisp. Remove squash from heat; stir in lemon juice and remaining ½ teaspoon peel.

6. Spoon vegetable mixture onto plates; top with scallops and sprinkle with chives. Serve with couscous.

EACH SERVING: About 355 calories, 33g protein, 48g carbohydrate, 4g total fat (1g saturated), 9g fiber, 47mg cholesterol, 416mg sodium ☺ ♥

Stuffed Portobellos

This healthy meal is low in calories, yet hearty enough to serve as a main course. Meaty portobello mushrooms combine with protein-rich quinoa, creamy feta, and vitamin-dense Brussels sprouts to create a flavorful dish that's packed with nutrients.

TOTAL TIME: 30 minutes
MAKES: 4 main-dish servings

½   cup quinoa, rinsed
¾   cup water
1¼   pounds Brussels sprouts (see Tip)
4   teaspoons extra-virgin olive oil
⅜   teaspoon salt
¼   teaspoon freshly ground black pepper
4   large portobello mushroom caps
1   teaspoon fresh thyme leaves
⅔   cup frozen corn
3   ounces feta cheese, crumbled (¾ cup)
½   teaspoon ground cumin

1. Preheat oven to 450°F. In 2-quart saucepan, combine quinoa and water. Heat to boiling over high heat; reduce heat to medium-low. Cover and cook 15 minutes or until liquid is absorbed.

2. Meanwhile, trim and halve sprouts. In 18″ by 12″ jelly-roll pan, toss sprouts, 2 teaspoons oil, and ¼ teaspoon each salt and pepper to coat evenly. Roast 10 minutes.

3. While sprouts cook, brush mushrooms with remaining 2 teaspoons oil and sprinkle with remaining ⅛ teaspoon salt. Finely chop thyme and add to medium bowl along with corn, feta, cumin, and cooked quinoa.

4. Push sprouts to one side of pan and arrange mushrooms, gilled sides up, on other side. Divide quinoa mixture among mushroom tops; roast 10 minutes or until mushrooms are tender.

EACH SERVING: About 290 calories, 14g protein, 38g carbohydrate, 11g total fat (4g saturated), 9g fiber, 19mg cholesterol, 500mg sodium ☺

TIP: *Brussels sprouts not a favorite? Roasted broccoli would deliver just as much crunch.*

3

Oodles of Noodles

Pasta is the very definition of weeknight easy. Just get a big pot of water boiling on the stovetop for your noodles—don't forget to salt the water generously! Then prepare one of our quick sauces: We offer oodles of options to please every pasta fan.

Pasta is a great playground for vegetables and fresh herbs. Summer Herb Pasta mingles the bright, fresh flavors of parsley, mint, and basil with ricotta and feta cheeses. Enjoy a bounty of spring vegetables in Pasta Primavera, a colorful mix of everything from asparagus and zucchini to grape tomatoes and garbanzos.

For meat lovers, we've included plenty of hearty dishes, from Penne with Sausage and Broccoli Rabe to Lasagna Toss Bolognese, which allows you to enjoy all the irresistible ingredients that compose a classic meat lasagna in a fraction of the time. Or dig into Chicken Carbonara, our luscious twist on this classic pasta, which adds chicken breast to the creamy bacon-studded sauce.

Italians aren't the only ones who know how to cook noodles. Whip up our Spicy Szechuan Noodles or Thai Noodles with Beef and Basil for delicious Asian dinners at a fraction of the cost of takeout. We include tips on choosing and preparing tofu—it's a quick and healthy protein alternative to poultry or seafood.

Pasta Primavera (recipe page 79)

Summer Herb Pasta

This light summer pasta recipe is flavored with ricotta, feta, and fresh herbs.

TOTAL TIME: 30 minutes
MAKES: 4 main-dish servings

1   pound campanelle or corkscrew pasta
1   cup part-skim ricotta cheese
1   ounce feta cheese, crumbled (¼ cup)
½   teaspoon freshly grated lemon peel
¼   teaspoon salt
¼   teaspoon freshly ground black pepper
½   cup loosely packed fresh parsley leaves, chopped
½   cup loosely packed fresh mint leaves, chopped
½   cup loosely packed fresh basil leaves, chopped
4   plum tomatoes, chopped

1. Cook pasta in *boiling salted water* as package label directs.

2. Meanwhile, in bowl, combine ricotta, feta, lemon peel, salt, and pepper.

3. Reserve *⅓ cup pasta cooking water*. Drain pasta and return to saucepot. Stir reserved cooking water into ricotta mixture; toss with pasta to coat. Stir in herbs and chopped tomatoes.

EACH SERVING: About 560 calories, 24g protein, 94g carbohydrate, 9g total fat (5g saturated), 5g fiber, 28mg cholesterol, 500mg sodium

QUICK TECHNIQUE: PERFECT PASTA

Perfectly cooked pasta is firm yet tender to the bite, or *al dente* as Italians say, with sauce coating each delicious mouthful. Some of the most common mistakes—mushy (or sticky) spaghetti, watery lasagna, sauce that pools in the bottom of the bowl instead of clinging to the noodles as it should—can easily be avoided by following these simple guidelines.

+ **Use plenty of boiling water.** A good rule of thumb is 4 quarts for each pound of pasta. Bring it to a rolling boil, then add about 2 teaspoons of salt per pound of pasta. Salted water takes longer to boil, so add the salt just before adding the pasta.

+ **Stir frequently to prevent sticking.** Once you've salted the water and it's at a full boil, stir in the pasta. Cook, stirring often, until the noodles separate. There's no need to add oil to pasta cooking water. Stirring is all you need to prevent sticking.

+ **Cook according to package directions.** There's no set rule for how long each pasta shape should cook. Spaghetti from one manufacturer may take longer than the spaghetti from another. So always read the directions on the box—they will give you the correct cooking time.

+ **Check for doneness often,** before the suggested cooking time has elapsed. The goal is pasta that's tender yet still slightly firm. The only way to test it is by tasting. Remove a piece from the pot and rinse it briefly under warm water, then bite into it. There should be no hard white center. Remember that pasta will continue cooking from the residual heat even after you drain it. If the cooked pasta will be baked later, be sure to undercook it slightly.

+ **Drain well in a colander,** shaking to make sure all excess water has been removed. Don't rinse pasta unless the recipe specifies to do so. Rinsing can remove starch that helps the sauce cling to the noodles and provides important nutrients, too.

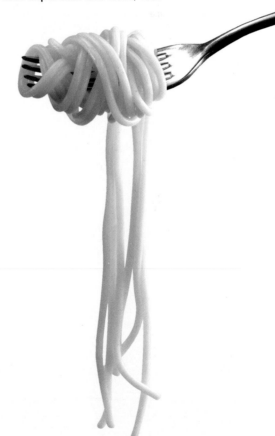

Tortellini Toss with Herbed Goat Cheese

Requiring only five ingredients and just twenty-five minutes of prep time, this delicious pasta recipe will win over any busy family cook.

ACTIVE TIME: 10 minutes
TOTAL TIME: 25 minutes
MAKES: 4 main-dish servings

2	packages (9 ounces each) refrigerated cheese tortellini
1	bag (5 to 6 ounces) baby spinach
¼	cup oil-packed sun-dried tomatoes
½	teaspoon grated lemon peel
2	ounces herbed goat cheese, crumbled (½ cup)

1. Cook tortellini in *boiling salted water* as package label directs.

2. Reserve *¼ cup pasta cooking water;* drain tortellini and return to saucepot with reserved cooking water. Stir in spinach.

3. Drain tomatoes, reserving 1 tablespoon oil, then chop tomatoes. Into saucepot with cooked tortellini, stir lemon peel and chopped sun-dried tomatoes and their oil; toss to coat. Transfer to serving bowls and sprinkle with goat cheese.

EACH SERVING: About 485 calories, 23g protein, 60g carbohydrate, 16g total fat (7g saturated), 9g fiber, 77mg cholesterol, 880mg sodium

EXPRESS-LANE INGREDIENT: SUN-DRIED TOMATOES

Although rarely dried in the sun anymore (they're processed by more commercial methods), these intensely flavored dehydrated tomatoes are a quick way to perk up a business-as-usual pasta dish. Sun-dried tomatoes can be purchased loose in a package or in a jar, packed with oil. (Save a little of the oil to add flavor to the pasta sauce, if you like.) Loose-packed dried tomatoes should be soaked in boiling water to cover until softened, then drained before using.

Pasta Primavera

Celebrate spring with a bright pasta dish chock-full of vegetables. For photo, see page 74.

ACTIVE TIME: 20 minutes
TOTAL TIME: 30 minutes
MAKES: 4 main-dish servings

12 ounces whole-wheat spaghetti
1 tablespoon olive oil
1 medium onion (6 to 8 ounces), finely chopped
3 garlic cloves, finely chopped
1 pint grape tomatoes
12 ounces asparagus, trimmed and cut into 2-inch pieces
1 medium zucchini, cut into half-moons
¼ cup water
½ teaspoon salt
1 can (15 to 19 ounces) no-salt-added garbanzo beans (chickpeas), rinsed and drained
1 medium carrot, grated
2 tablespoons freshly grated Parmesan cheese
2 tablespoons fresh lemon juice
Fresh basil leaves for garnish

1. Cook spaghetti in *boiling salted water* as package label directs.

2. Meanwhile, in 12-inch skillet, heat oil over medium heat. Add onion and garlic; cook, stirring occasionally, 2 to 3 minutes or until golden. Add grape tomatoes; cook 5 minutes or until beginning to soften. Add asparagus, zucchini, water, and ¼ teaspoon salt. Cover and cook 5 to 7 minutes or until tomatoes begin to burst. Stir in beans and carrot; cook 2 to 3 minutes or until beans are heated through.

3. Reserve ½ *cup pasta cooking water*. Drain pasta; return to saucepot and add vegetable mixture, Parmesan, lemon juice, reserved cooking water, and remaining ¼ teaspoon salt; toss until combined. Divide among serving bowls; garnish with basil.

EACH SERVING: About 495 calories, 22g protein, 95g carbohydrate, 6g total fat (1g saturated), 18g fiber, 2mg cholesterol, 375mg sodium ♥

Grown-Up Mac and Cheese

This macaroni and cheese may be reminiscent in spirit of the scrumptious dish you had as a kid, but the rich, complex flavors will surely please your mature taste buds. Pair with a simple salad of greens and wild mushrooms for a delightful, easy-to-make dinner for two.

TOTAL TIME: 30 minutes
MAKES: 2 main-dish servings

6 ounces mini penne or small shell pasta

1 ounce pancetta, cut into ¼-inch pieces

Olive oil

2 tablespoons all-purpose flour

1 cup reduced-fat (2%) milk

4 ounces Fontina cheese (see Tip), shredded (1 cup)

¼ cup plus 2 tablespoons freshly grated Pecorino-Romano cheese

¼ teaspoon freshly ground black pepper

2 tablespoons panko (Japanese-style bread crumbs)

1. Cook pasta in *boiling salted water* as package label directs.

2. Meanwhile, place rack in bottom third of oven and preheat broiler. In 3-quart saucepan, cook pancetta over medium heat 5 minutes or until browned; with slotted spoon, transfer to paper towels to drain.

3. Add enough oil to drippings in pan to equal 1 tablespoon; whisk in flour and cook 30 seconds, whisking constantly. Gradually whisk in milk and heat to boiling over medium-high heat, stirring frequently. Boil 1 minute, stirring. Remove saucepan from heat; add Fontina, ¼ cup Romano, and pepper and stir until cheese melts. In cup, combine remaining 2 tablespoons Romano with panko.

4. Drain pasta well. Stir pasta and pancetta into cheese mixture until evenly coated. Spoon mixture into 4-cup shallow gratin dish or 9-inch pie plate. Sprinkle with panko mixture.

5. Broil 3 to 6 minutes or until browned.

EACH SERVING: About 750 calories, 35g protein, 79g carbohydrate, 31g total fat (17g saturated), 2g fiber, 92mg cholesterol, 840mg sodium

TIP: *For robust flavor, opt for an Italian Fontina cheese rather than domestic.*

Vegetable Lasagna Toss

This free-form lasagna is loaded with fresh vegetables and beans—a perfect choice for a casual family dinner.

ACTIVE TIME: 10 minutes
TOTAL TIME: 20 minutes
MAKES: 4 main-dish servings

8	ounces lasagna noodles
1	tablespoon extra-virgin olive oil
2	garlic cloves, crushed with garlic press
1	bag (12 ounces) broccoli florets
1	cup reduced-sodium chicken broth
1	can (15 to 19 ounces) white kidney beans (cannellini), drained and rinsed
3	large tomatoes, coarsely chopped
⅓	cup freshly grated Romano cheese, plus additional for serving

1. In large saucepot, cook noodles in *boiling salted water* as label directs, but increase cooking time by about 2 minutes so that noodles are al dente.

2. Meanwhile, in nonstick 12-inch skillet, heat oil over medium heat; add garlic and broccoli and cook 1 minute, stirring frequently. Add broth; cover and cook 8 minutes. Stir in beans; cover and cook 2 to 3 minutes longer or until broccoli is very tender. Stir in tomatoes; remove from heat.

3. Drain lasagna noodles; add to broccoli mixture in skillet and sprinkle with cheese. Toss to coat noodles. Serve with additional cheese on the side.

EACH SERVING: 425 calories, 19g protein, 71g carbohydrate, 8g total fat (2g saturated), 11g fiber, 8mg cholesterol, 380mg sodium ☺ ♥

Rotini with Asparagus and Snap Peas

Fresh snap peas and asparagus lighten up a pasta dinner (and add plenty of vitamins). Choosing whole-grain pasta over regular triples the cholesterol-lowering fiber.

TOTAL TIME: 30 minutes
MAKES: 4 main-dish servings

1	package (13¼ ounces) whole-grain rotini or fusilli pasta
8	ounces asparagus, ends trimmed, cut into 1-inch pieces
1	bag (8 ounces) stringless snap peas
1	tablespoon olive oil
1	small onion (4 to 6 ounces), chopped
1	lemon
½	cup freshly grated Pecorino-Romano cheese
¼	cup loosely packed fresh basil leaves, thinly sliced
½	teaspoon salt
¼	teaspoon coarsely ground black pepper

1. Heat large covered saucepot of *salted water* to boiling over high heat. Add pasta and cook as label directs, adding asparagus and snap peas when 3 minutes of cooking time remain.

2. Meanwhile, in nonstick 10-inch skillet, heat oil over medium heat. Add onion and cook 10 to 12 minutes or until tender and browned. From lemon, grate 1 teaspoon peel and squeeze 2 tablespoons juice.

3. Reserve *½ cup pasta cooking water;* drain pasta and vegetables. In large serving bowl, toss pasta and vegetables with reserved cooking water, onion, lemon peel and juice, cheese, basil, salt, and pepper.

EACH SERVING: About 405 calories, 18g protein, 72g carbohydrate, 8g total fat (2g saturated), 9g fiber, 10mg cholesterol, 545mg sodium ☺

Pasta with Chicken and Brussels Sprouts

Combining two quick and easy favorites, this pasta with chicken will make any night of the week delicious.

ACTIVE TIME: 25 minutes
TOTAL TIME: 30 minutes
MAKES: 4 main-dish servings

12   ounces cavatappi pasta
1   pound skinless, boneless chicken thighs, cut into 1/2-inch chunks
3/8   teaspoon salt
1/4   teaspoon ground black pepper
2   teaspoons olive oil
10   ounces Brussels sprouts, sliced
1/4   cup water
1   tablespoon butter or margarine
1/4   teaspoon crushed red pepper
1/4   cup dried plain bread crumbs
3   garlic cloves, crushed with garlic press
1/4   cup freshly grated Parmesan cheese
2   tablespoons finely chopped fresh parsley

1. Cook cavatappi in *boiling salted water* as package label directs.

2. Meanwhile, season chicken with 1/4 teaspoon each salt and black pepper. In 12-inch skillet, heat oil over medium-high heat. Add chicken; cook, stirring, 6 minutes or until cooked through (165°F). Transfer chicken to bowl.

3. To skillet, add sprouts, water, butter, crushed red pepper, and remaining 1/8 teaspoon salt; cook 3 minutes, stirring. Add bread crumbs and garlic. Cook, stirring, 2 minutes to toast bread crumbs.

4. Reserve *1/2 cup pasta cooking water*. Drain pasta; return to pot. Stir in chicken, sprouts, and cooking water. Serve with Parmesan and parsley.

EACH SERVING: About 570 calories, 39g protein, 75g carbohydrate, 13g total fat (3g saturated), 6g fiber, 99mg cholesterol, 545mg sodium

Chicken Carbonara

A decadent dinner doesn't mean hours in the kitchen with this pasta, tossed with a creamy, bacon-studded cheese-and-egg sauce.

ACTIVE TIME: 20 minutes
TOTAL TIME: 30 minutes
MAKES: 4 main-dish servings

12	ounces linguine
4	slices bacon
12	ounces skinless, boneless chicken breasts, cut into ½-inch chunks
¼	teaspoon salt
1	medium shallot, finely chopped
2	garlic cloves, crushed with garlic press
4	large eggs
⅓	cup freshly grated Pecorino-Romano cheese
¼	teaspoon freshly ground black pepper
2	tablespoons finely chopped fresh parsley (optional)

1. Cook linguine in *boiling salted water* as package label directs.

2. Meanwhile, in 12-inch skillet, cook bacon over medium heat 6 to 9 minutes or until browned and crisp. Sprinkle chicken with salt.

3. Transfer cooked bacon to paper towel. Add chicken to same skillet with drippings. Increase heat to medium-high. Cook chicken, stirring occasionally, 2 minutes or until just starting to turn opaque. Add shallot. Cook 2 minutes, stirring. Add garlic. Cook, stirring, 1 minute or until chicken is cooked through (165°F). Remove from heat; cool slightly. Crumble bacon.

4. In large bowl, whisk together eggs, cheese, and pepper until well combined. Add bacon and cooled chicken mixture to egg mixture.

5. When pasta is cooked, drain well. Add to sauce in large bowl, tossing to coat. Divide among serving plates. Garnish with parsley, if desired.

EACH SERVING: About 635 calories, 43g protein, 65g carbohydrate, 22g total fat (8g saturated), 3g fiber, 269mg cholesterol, 795mg sodium

Minted Chicken and Artichoke Rotini

Fresh mint adds bright spring flavor to this ultra-quick chicken-and-artichoke pasta.

ACTIVE TIME: 15 minutes
TOTAL TIME: 25 minutes
MAKES: 6 main-dish servings

2	tablespoons olive oil
1	pound ground chicken
4	garlic cloves, chopped
2	packages (9 ounces each) frozen artichokes
½	cup packed fresh mint leaves, finely chopped
1	box (13½ to 14½ ounces) multi-grain rotini
1	ounce Parmesan cheese, grated
½	teaspoon salt
¼	teaspoon freshly ground black pepper

1. Heat large covered saucepot of *salted water* to boiling over high heat.

2. Meanwhile, in 12-inch skillet, heat 1 tablespoon oil over medium-high heat. Add chicken, half of garlic, and ¼ teaspoon each salt and pepper. Cook 4 to 5 minutes or until chicken is browned, stirring and breaking up chicken with spoon. With slotted spoon, transfer to plate.

3. In same skillet, heat remaining 1 tablespoon oil over medium heat. Add artichokes, one-fourth of mint, and remaining garlic. Cover and cook 5 minutes or until artichokes are tender, stirring occasionally and breaking artichokes into pieces with side of spoon.

4. Meanwhile, add pasta to boiling water. Cook, stirring occasionally, 1 minute less than minimum time that label directs. Reserve *1 cup pasta cooking water*. Drain pasta and return to pot.

5. Add Parmesan, reserved chicken, artichokes, remaining ¼ teaspoon salt, and remaining mint to pot. Cook, tossing, over medium heat 2 minutes or until pasta is al dente and coated. If mixture seems dry, toss with some reserved cooking water.

EACH SERVING: About 460 calories, 29g protein, 52g carbohydrate, 17g total fat (4g saturated), 14g fiber, 69mg cholesterol, 565mg sodium

Cauliflower and Anchovy Spaghetti

Heart-healthy anchovies contribute lots of low-cal protein and omega-3s to this quick-cooking pasta dish.

Active time: 15 minutes
Total time: 25 minutes
Makes: 4 main-dish servings

3   tablespoons olive oil
1   small head cauliflower (1½ pounds), cored and finely chopped
¼   teaspoon salt
¼   cup water
16   anchovy fillets (1 ounce total), rinsed and patted dry
3   cloves garlic, finely chopped
1   box (14½ ounces) multigrain thin spaghetti
¼   cup packed fresh flat-leaf parsley leaves, finely chopped
½   teaspoon freshly ground black pepper

1. Heat large covered pot of *salted water* to boiling on high heat.

2. In 12-inch skillet, heat 2 tablespoons oil over medium-high heat. Add cauliflower and ¼ teaspoon salt. Cook 2 minutes or until browned, stirring occasionally. Add water and cook 3 minutes or until tender, stirring occasionally. Reduce heat to medium and add anchovies, garlic, and remaining 1 tablespoon oil. Cook 1 to 2 minutes or until fragrant, stirring to break up anchovies into small pieces.

3. Meanwhile, add pasta to boiling water in pot. Cook 1 minute less than minimum time label directs, stirring occasionally. Reserve *1 cup pasta cooking water*. Drain pasta and return to pot.

4. Add parsley, cauliflower mixture, *½ cup pasta cooking water*, and pepper to pot. Cook on medium 1 minute or until pasta is al dente and well coated, tossing and stirring. If mixture seems dry, toss with additional cooking water.

Each serving: About 500 calories, 18g protein, 81g carbohydrate, 13g total fat (2g saturated), 5g fiber, 6mg cholesterol, 490mg sodium

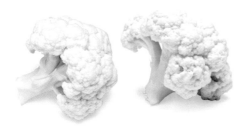

Rustic Pasta Toss with Tuna and Tomatoes

This pasta salad is loaded with farm-stand squash and zucchini — and two pounds of tomatoes. Just combine the raw veggies with canned tuna and campanelle pasta for a beat-the-heat — and beat-the-clock — meal.

ACTIVE TIME: 15 minutes
TOTAL TIME: 30 minutes
MAKES: 6 main-dish servings

1	pound campanelle or fusilli pasta
2	medium zucchini
1	medium yellow squash
1	pint cherry or grape tomatoes (see Tip)
¼	cup pitted Kalamata olives
¼	cup fresh flat-leaf parsley leaves
3	tablespoons red wine vinegar
¼	cup extra-virgin olive oil
1	garlic clove, crushed with garlic press
¼	teaspoon salt
⅛	teaspoon freshly ground black pepper
2	cans (5 ounces each) tuna in water, drained

1. Cook pasta in *boiling salted water* to minimum time that label directs.

2. Meanwhile, trim zucchini and squash, cut into quarters lengthwise, then cut into thin slices crosswise. Slice tomatoes in half. Slice olives and finely chop parsley.

3. In large bowl, whisk together vinegar, oil, garlic, salt, and pepper; stir in tomatoes.

4. Drain pasta well. Add to tomato mixture along with tuna, zucchini, squash, olives, and parsley. Toss until well mixed.

EACH SERVING: About 470 calories, 21g protein, 66g carbohydrate, 14g total fat (2g saturated), 5g fiber, 16mg cholesterol, 435mg sodium ♥

TIP: *If you're lucky enough to find some nice, ripe regular tomatoes, substitute 2 pounds of them for the cherry tomatoes called for here. Chop them in step 2 and add along with the other vegetables in step 3. Their extra juices will add more moisture to the sauce.*

Fettuccine with Lemony Shrimp

Light and aromatic with the scent of fresh lemon, this pasta dish looks and tastes as good as any restaurant meal.

ACTIVE TIME: 20 minutes
TOTAL TIME: 30 minutes
MAKES: 6 main-dish servings

2   large leeks
1   tablespoon plus 2 teaspoons olive oil
1½ pounds shrimp (16 to 20 count), shelled and deveined, with tail part of shell left on if you like
½   teaspoon salt
¼   teaspoon freshly ground black pepper, plus additional for serving
2   garlic cloves, very thinly sliced
¼   teaspoon crushed red pepper
1   cup dry white wine
1   pound fettuccine
1   tablespoon butter or margarine
2   tablespoons finely chopped fresh basil leaves
2   tablespoons finely chopped fresh flat-leaf parsley leaves
1   lemon

1. Heat large covered saucepot of *salted water* to boiling over high heat.

2. Trim and discard roots and dark-green tops from leeks. Discard any tough outer leaves. Cut leeks lengthwise in half, then crosswise into ¼-inch-wide slices. Place leeks in large bowl of cold water; with hand, swish to remove any sand. Remove leeks to colander. Repeat process with fresh water, changing water several times until sand is removed. Drain leeks well.

3. In 12-inch skillet, heat 1 teaspoon oil over medium-high heat. Sprinkle shrimp with ¼ teaspoon each salt and black pepper. Add half of shrimp to pan; cook, turning once, 1 to 2 minutes or until shrimp are just pink and curled. Transfer to plate. Repeat with 1 teaspoon oil and remaining shrimp.

4. In same skillet, heat remaining 1 tablespoon oil over medium-low heat. Add leeks, garlic, and crushed red pepper; stir well. Cover and cook, stirring occasionally, 10 minutes or until very tender. Uncover and add wine. Heat to boiling, then reduce heat to medium and simmer 4 to 5 minutes or until wine is reduced by half.

5. Meanwhile, add fettuccine to boiling water. Cook, stirring occasionally, 2 minutes less than minimum time that label directs. Reserve *1 cup cooking water*. Drain pasta; return to pot. Add butter, shrimp, and leek mixture. Cook, tossing frequently, over medium heat 2 minutes or until noodles are al dente and glazed with sauce. Add basil, parsley, and remaining ¼ teaspoon salt. Cook 2 minutes longer, tossing and adding some reserved cooking liquid if mixture seems dry.

6. Divide among serving plates. With zester, grate a little lemon peel directly over pasta. Grind black pepper to taste over pasta.

EACH SERVING: About 445 calories, 28g protein, 60g carbohydrate, 9g total fat (1g saturated), 2g fiber, 137mg cholesterol, 455mg sodium ☺ ♥

Spring Salmon Fettuccine

Meaty salmon holds its own superbly in this creamy fettuccine with asparagus.

ACTIVE TIME: 20 minutes
TOTAL TIME: 30 minutes
MAKES: 6 main-dish servings

2	lemons
1	cup light cream
1	pound thin asparagus, trimmed and cut at an angle into 1½-inch pieces
18	ounces fresh fettuccine or 1 pound dried fettuccine
20	ounces skinless salmon fillet, cut into 1½-inch chunks
½	teaspoon salt
½	teaspoon freshly ground black pepper
1	ounce Parmesan cheese, finely grated

1. Heat large covered saucepot of *salted water* to boiling over high heat.

2. Into small bowl, from lemons, finely grate 1 tablespoon peel. Stir in cream. Into a separate small bowl, squeeze 1 teaspoon lemon juice. Cut remaining lemon into wedges.

3. If using fresh pasta, add asparagus to boiling water in pot. Cook 1 minute, then add fettuccine. Cook, stirring occasionally, 1 minute less than minimum time that label directs. (If using dried pasta, add pasta to boiling water in saucepot. Cook, stirring occasionally, 3 minutes less than minimum time that label directs. Add asparagus and cook 2 minutes longer.) Reserve *1 cup pasta cooking water*. With tongs or slotted spoon, transfer pasta and asparagus to colander; do not discard cooking water in pot.

4. Add salmon to water in pot. Cook 4 to 5 minutes or just until fish turns opaque throughout. Drain carefully; set aside.

5. To same pot, add pasta mixture, cream mixture, lemon juice, salt, and pepper. Cook, tossing and stirring, over medium heat 1 minute or until pasta is al dente and well coated. If mixture seems dry, toss with reserved cooking water. Top pasta with Parmesan and salmon, and serve with lemon wedges.

EACH SERVING: About 530 calories, 39g protein, 51g carbohydrate, 18g total fat (7g saturated), 5g fiber, 147mg cholesterol, 455mg sodium

Penne with Sausage and Broccoli Rabe

Sweet Italian sausage and spicy broccoli rabe make a tasty combination. Serve the finished dish with additional grated Parmesan.

ACTIVE TIME: 10 minutes
TOTAL TIME: 25 minutes
MAKES: 4 main-dish servings

1	bunch broccoli rabe (1 pound)
12	ounces penne pasta
1	link sweet Italian sausage (4 ounces), cut into ½-inch-thick slices
2	shallots, finely chopped
2	garlic cloves, crushed with garlic press
¼	cup freshly grated Parmesan cheese, plus additional for serving
¼	teaspoon salt
¼	teaspoon freshly ground black pepper

1. Heat large covered saucepot of *salted water* to boiling over high heat. Meanwhile, from broccoli rabe, trim any tough stem ends and discard. Cut broccoli rabe into 1-inch pieces and add to boiling water. Cook 4 to 5 minutes or until bright green and just tender. With slotted spoon, transfer to large colander. Return water to boiling. Drain broccoli rabe, rinse with cold water, and drain again. In same saucepot of boiling water, cook penne as label directs.

2. Meanwhile, heat deep 12-inch skillet over medium-high heat. Add sausage in single layer and cook, turning to brown evenly, 4 to 5 minutes or until sausage loses its pink color. (Reduce heat to medium if browning too quickly.) Add shallots and garlic; cook, stirring, 2 minutes or until tender. Remove *1½ cups water* from saucepot with pasta; add to skillet. Heat to boiling, stirring occasionally.

3. Drain pasta and add to skillet with sausage. Stir in Parmesan, broccoli rabe, salt, and pepper until well mixed. Divide among shallow bowls; sprinkle with additional Parmesan and serve.

EACH SERVING: About 470 calories, 20g protein, 70g carbohydrate, 12g total fat (4g saturated), 4g fiber, 26mg cholesterol, 765mg sodium

Lasagna Toss Bolognese

Lasagna is a perennial family favorite, but it takes two and a half hours to prep and bake. Our streamlined version clocks in at just thirty minutes from saucepot to pasta bowl, without losing any of the robust flavors of the original.

ACTIVE TIME: 15 minutes
TOTAL TIME: 30 minutes
MAKES: 6 main-dish servings

1	package (16 ounces) lasagna noodles (see Tip)
2	teaspoons olive oil
1	pound 90% lean ground beef or ground meat for meat loaf (beef, pork, and/or veal)
½	cup dry red wine
1	jar (24 ounces) prepared marinara sauce
⅓	cup whole milk
¾	cup part-skim ricotta cheese
½	cup fresh basil, chopped
¼	cup freshly grated Pecorino-Romano cheese
¼	teaspoon coarsely ground black pepper
⅓	cup shredded part-skim mozzarella cheese

TIP: *Tempted to cook up no-boil lasagna noodles to save time? Don't—they'll break apart when tossed.*

1. Cook lasagna in *boiling salted water* as label directs, but increase cooking time by 2 to 3 minutes so that noodles are al dente.

2. Meanwhile, in 12-inch skillet, heat oil over medium-high heat. Add meat and cook until no longer pink, breaking it up with spoon, about 3 minutes. If using meat-loaf mix, drain off fat. Add wine; cook 2 to 3 minutes or until almost evaporated. Stir in marinara; heat to boiling. Simmer over low heat 5 minutes, stirring occasionally. Stir in milk; simmer 5 minutes.

3. In bowl, stir ricotta with basil, Romano, and pepper; set aside.

4. Drain noodles; return to saucepot. Add meat sauce and mozzarella; toss well. Spoon onto warm plates; top with dollops of ricotta mixture.

EACH SERVING: About 655 calories, 32g protein, 71g carbohydrate, 26g total fat (10g saturated), 5g fiber, 71mg cholesterol, 800mg sodium

Thai Noodles with Beef and Basil

Top off this tasty ground-beef-and-noodle stir-fry with a refreshing garnish of cucumber, cilantro, bean sprouts, and crunchy peanuts.

Total time: 30 minutes
Makes: 4 main-dish servings

8	ounces linguine or flat rice stick noodles (see Tip, opposite)
1	tablespoon vegetable oil
1	medium onion, thinly sliced
4	garlic cloves, thinly sliced
1	piece (3 inches) peeled fresh ginger, cut into thin slivers
½	pound ground beef
½	cup chicken broth
3	tablespoons Asian fish sauce (see page 24)
1	teaspoon sugar
¾	teaspoon crushed red pepper
½	cup chopped fresh cilantro or basil leaves (optional)
1	small cucumber, cut lengthwise in half and thinly sliced crosswise
½	cup bean sprouts
¼	cup unsalted peanuts, chopped
4	Lime wedges for serving (optional)

1. Cook linguine in *boiling salted water* as label directs. If using rice noodles, put them in large bowl and pour *boiling water* over noodles to cover; let soak 15 minutes. Do not soak longer or noodles may become too soft.

2. Meanwhile, in 12-inch skillet, heat oil over medium heat. Add onion, garlic, and ginger; cook, stirring occasionally, until golden, 8 to 10 minutes. Add beef; cook until meat is no longer pink, about 5 minutes, stirring and breaking up beef with wooden spoon. Stir in broth, fish sauce, sugar, and crushed red pepper. Simmer, uncovered, 5 minutes to thicken slightly.

3. Drain noodles. Add noodles and cilantro, if using, to beef mixture, stirring to heat through. Spoon into bowls; top with cucumber, bean sprouts, and peanuts. Serve with lime wedges, if you like.

Each serving: About 455 calories, 25g protein, 60g carbohydrate, 14g total fat (3g saturated), 4g fiber, 40mg cholesterol, 720mg sodium

Pad Thai

Go to a Thai restaurant, and you're certain to find pad Thai — a tasty mix of noodles, shrimp, peanuts, and eggs. It's surprisingly easy to make at home: Just have everything in place before you start because it cooks quickly.

TOTAL TIME: 25 minutes
MAKES: 4 main-dish servings

1	package (7 or 8 ounces) flat rice stick noodles (see Tip), or 8 ounces angel hair pasta (capellini)
½	pound medium shrimp, shelled and deveined
¼	cup fresh lime juice
¼	cup Asian fish sauce (see Tip, page 24)
2	tablespoons sugar
1	tablespoon vegetable oil
2	garlic cloves, crushed with garlic press
¼	teaspoon crushed red pepper
2	large eggs, lightly beaten
6	ounces fresh bean sprouts, rinsed (2 cups)
2	tablespoons unsalted roasted peanuts, coarsely chopped
3	green onions, thinly sliced
½	cup loosely packed fresh cilantro leaves

Lime wedges for serving

1. Break pasta strands in half. In large bowl, soak rice stick noodles in *hot tap water* to cover 20 minutes. (If using angel hair pasta, cook as label directs and rinse with cold running water.)

2. Meanwhile, cut each shrimp horizontally in half. In small bowl, combine lime juice, fish sauce, and sugar; stir to dissolve sugar. Measure all remaining ingredients before beginning to cook and set out within reach.

3. Drain noodles. In a nonstick wok or 12-inch skillet, heat oil over high heat until hot but not smoking. Add shrimp, garlic, and crushed red pepper; cook 1 minute, stirring. Add eggs and cook 20 seconds, stirring. Add drained noodles and cook 2 minutes, stirring. Add fish-sauce mixture, half of bean sprouts, half of peanuts, and half of green onions; cook 1 minute, stirring.

4. Transfer noodle mixture to platter; top with remaining bean sprouts, peanuts, and green onions. Sprinkle with cilantro leaves. Serve with lime wedges.

EACH SERVING: About 495 calories, 25g protein, 65g carbohydrate, 17g total fat (3g saturated), 3g fiber, 235mg cholesterol, 827mg sodium

---

TIP: *Unlike Italian dried pasta, rice stick noodles are soaked before they're cooked, then added to the shrimp mixture near the end of the cook time.*

Peanut Noodles with Shredded Chicken

Pull together a peanut sauce in a flash to top shredded chicken and pasta in this Thai-inspired dish.

ACTIVE TIME: 20 minutes
TOTAL TIME: 30 minutes
MAKES: 6 main-dish servings

12 ounces thick spaghetti or linguine
1   garlic clove, thinly sliced
4   medium skinless, boneless chicken-breast halves (1½ pounds total)
¼   cup rice vinegar
¼   cup reduced-sodium soy sauce
⅓   cup smooth peanut butter
3   tablespoons water
2   tablespoons grated, peeled fresh ginger
1   small (4 to 6 ounces) Kirby cucumber, thinly sliced
1   bag (8 to 10 ounces) shredded carrots
1   medium red pepper (4 to 6 ounces), thinly sliced
Cilantro sprigs for garnish

1. Cook pasta in *boiling salted water* as label directs. Drain pasta. Rinse under cold running water; drain again.

2. Meanwhile, in covered 12-inch skillet, heat garlic and *1 inch water* to boiling over high heat. Add chicken; cover, reduce heat to medium-low, and cook 13 to 14 minutes or until chicken loses its pink color throughout. (Instant-read thermometer inserted horizontally into center of chicken should reach 165°F.) With slotted spoon or tongs, remove chicken from skillet and place in large bowl of ice water; chill 5 minutes. Discard poaching liquid. Drain chicken; with hands, shred chicken.

3. While pasta and chicken cook, in large bowl, whisk together vinegar, soy sauce, peanut butter, water, and ginger until smooth.

4. To bowl with peanut sauce, add drained pasta, shredded chicken, cucumber, carrots, and pepper; toss to coat. To serve, garnish with cilantro sprigs.

EACH SERVING: About 510 calories, 46g protein, 54g carbohydrate, 12g total fat (3g saturated), 4g fiber, 87mg cholesterol, 570mg sodium

Spicy Szechuan Noodles

Try this tasty homemade adaptation of a popular Chinese dish. Replacing the usual pork with ground turkey keeps the fat in check.

TOTAL TIME: 20 minutes
MAKES: 4 main-dish servings

10	ounces Chinese egg noodles or thin spaghetti
¾	cup chicken broth
3	tablespoons reduced-sodium soy sauce
3	tablespoons lime juice
1	tablespoon sugar
1	tablespoon Sriracha hot sauce
1	tablespoon chopped, peeled fresh ginger
2	tablespoons canola oil
8	ounces ground turkey
5	ounces baby spinach

Chopped peanuts for garnish

EXPRESS-LANE INGREDIENT: CHINESE EGG NOODLES

These quick-cooking wheat-based noodles can be found in the produce section of grocery stores or in Asian markets. Because of the egg in the dough, they have a soft texture and rich flavor that creates a delicious base for any sauce you choose to top them with. Consider sprinkling some chopped peanuts on top, as in the recipe above.

1. Cook egg noodles or spaghetti in *boiling salted water* as label directs. Drain and rinse under cold water.

2. In food processor, puree broth, soy sauce, lime juice, sugar, hot sauce, and ginger.

3. In 12-inch skillet, heat oil over high heat.

4. Add ground turkey; cook 5 minutes, breaking up with spoon. Add broth mixture; simmer 5 minutes or until turkey is cooked through.

5. Stir in baby spinach; cook 1 minute.

6. Divide noodles among plates; top with sauce and chopped peanuts.

EACH SERVING: About 420 calories, 20g protein, 53g carbohydrate, 15g total fat (2g saturated), 4g fiber, 89mg cholesterol, 1,145mg sodium ☺

Lo Mein Primavera

Use fresh linguine for this protein-packed vegetarian lo mein — and be sure to pat the tofu dry before cooking.

ACTIVE TIME: 18 minutes
TOTAL TIME: 30 minutes
MAKES: 4 main-dish servings

1   package (14 ounces) extra-firm tofu, drained
1   package (9 ounces) fresh linguine
2   tablespoons vegetable oil
2   stalks celery, thinly sliced
1   medium red pepper (4 to 6 ounces), thinly sliced
3   garlic cloves, crushed with garlic press
1   large zucchini, cut into ¼-inch-thick half-moons
2   large carrots, shredded
¼   cup reduced-sodium soy sauce
½   teaspoon Asian sesame oil (see page 33)
Fresh cilantro leaves for garnish

EXPRESS-LANE INGREDIENT: TOFU

Tofu is a protein-rich alternative to meat or chicken that's quick to prepare. It's made from soybean curd that is drained and pressed in a process similar to cheese-making. It comes in a range of textures: silken (the right choice for dressings and dips), regular and firm (good for stir-fries), and finally extra-firm (which is excellent grilled). To store tofu after opening, cover with cool water and refrigerate up to one week; change water daily.

1. Cut tofu block in half lengthwise. Cut each piece into ½-inch-thick slices. Place slices in single layer between paper towels to remove excess moisture.

2. In nonstick 12-inch skillet, heat *1 inch water* to boiling over high heat. Add linguine and cook as label directs. Drain and rinse under cold running water to prevent pasta from sticking.

3. In same skillet, heat 1 tablespoon oil over medium heat 1 minute. Add tofu in single layer and cook, turning once, 10 minutes or until golden brown. Transfer to plate.

4. In same skillet, heat remaining 1 tablespoon oil over medium heat 1 minute. Add celery, pepper, and garlic; cook, stirring, 2 minutes or until tender-crisp. Add zucchini; cook, stirring, 1 to 2 minutes or until tender-crisp.

5. Add carrots, soy sauce, tofu, and noodles. Cook, stirring to coat with sauce, 2 minutes or until heated through.

6. Remove from heat, stir in sesame oil, and transfer to serving plates. Garnish with cilantro.

EACH SERVING: About 395 calories, 20g protein, 47g carbohydrate, 15g total fat (2g saturated), 6g fiber, 38mg cholesterol, 685mg sodium ☺

Linguine with Frisée, Bacon, and Egg

Bacon-and-egg pasta is a fun and quick dish that will please your whole family. For a healthy upgrade, this recipe includes green peas and frisée. The bitter frisée makes a natural pairing with the salty bacon and fried eggs. For photo, see page 17.

ACTIVE TIME: 20 minutes
TOTAL TIME: 30 minutes
MAKES: 4 main-dish servings

4	slices bacon, chopped
3	garlic cloves, very finely chopped
1/4	teaspoon crushed red pepper
1/2	cup frozen peas
3/8	teaspoon salt
12	ounces linguine or spaghetti
4	large eggs
1/8	teaspoon freshly ground black pepper
1	medium bunch frisée, cut into 1-inch pieces
2	green onions, light- and dark-green parts only, thinly sliced

1. Heat large covered saucepot of *salted water* to boiling over high heat. In nonstick 12-inch skillet, cook bacon over medium heat, stirring occasionally, 8 to 9 minutes or until browned and crisp. With slotted spoon, transfer bacon to plate lined with paper towel to drain; set bacon aside.

2. Discard all but 2 tablespoons bacon fat from skillet. To same skillet over medium heat, add garlic and crushed red pepper. Cook, stirring occasionally, 30 seconds or until garlic is golden. Remove from heat and add peas, stirring to coat and warm through. Transfer mixture to large bowl. Season with 1/4 teaspoon salt and stir well to blend. Set aside.

3. Cook pasta in boiling water as label directs. Meanwhile, wipe out same skillet with paper towel and heat over medium-low heat. Without breaking yolks, carefully add eggs to hot skillet and cook 5 to 6 minutes or until whites are set but yolks are still runny. Sprinkle eggs with 1/8 teaspoon each salt and black pepper.

4. Reserve *1/4 cup pasta cooking water*. Drain pasta and add to bowl with pea mixture, along with frisée, reserved bacon, and pasta cooking water. Toss to combine. Divide among shallow serving bowls. Top each with 1 egg and garnish with green onions.

EACH SERVING: About 545 calories, 23g protein, 76g carbohydrate, 16g total fat (6g saturated), 10g fiber, 224mg cholesterol, 630mg sodium

Borscht and Beef Pasta

Based on the traditional Russian soup, this satisfying pasta supper gets its boldness and bright color from two pounds of beets. Complementing the root vegetable's rusticity and heft: hearty whole-wheat linguine and quick-browning ground beef.

ACTIVE TIME: 15 minutes
TOTAL TIME: 35 minutes
MAKES: 6 main-dish servings

1	pound ground beef chuck
¼	teaspoon ground cloves
¾	teaspoon salt
½	teaspoon freshly ground black pepper
2	pounds beets, well scrubbed (peeled if large) and shredded (see Tip)
¼	cup water
2	tablespoons apple cider vinegar
1	pound whole-wheat linguine
2	tablespoons chopped fresh dill, plus additional for garnish

1. Heat covered 6-quart pot of *salted water* to boiling over high heat.

2. Heat 12-inch skillet over medium-high heat. Add beef, ⅛ teaspoon cloves, ¼ teaspoon salt, and ¼ teaspoon pepper. Cook 3 minutes or until browned, stirring and breaking beef into very small pieces.

3. Add beets, water, and ¼ teaspoon salt. Cook, stirring occasionally, 10 to 12 minutes or until beets are tender. Stir in vinegar.

4. Meanwhile, add pasta to boiling water in pot. Cook, stirring occasionally, 1 minute less than minimum time that label directs. Reserve *1 cup pasta cooking water*. Drain pasta and return to pot.

5. Add beet mixture, dill, remaining ¼ teaspoon each salt and pepper, and ⅛ teaspoon cloves to pot. Cook over medium heat, tossing and stirring, 2 minutes or until pasta is al dente and well coated. If mixture seems dry, toss with some reserved cooking water. To serve, garnish with dill.

EACH SERVING: About 495 calories, 27g protein, 67g carbohydrate, 15g total fat (6g saturated), 12g fiber, 50mg cholesterol, 520mg sodium

TIP: Use the shredding blade on your food processor to shred the beets; it's fast and virtually mess-free.

Quickie Cincinnati Chili Pasta

We take the guilt out of this comfort food by using lean ground beef and multi-grain pasta so you can enjoy every spicy bite.

ACTIVE TIME: 15 minutes
TOTAL TIME: 25 minutes
MAKES: 4 main-dish servings

12	ounces multi-grain spaghetti
2	teaspoons vegetable oil
12	ounces 93% lean ground beef sirloin
1	small onion (4 to 6 ounces), chopped
2	garlic cloves, chopped
2	tablespoons chili powder
1	tablespoon unsweetened cocoa
1	tablespoon brown sugar
1	teaspoon ground cinnamon
1/2	teaspoon ground cumin
1/4	teaspoon salt
1/4	teaspoon freshly ground black pepper
1	can (28 ounces) no-salt-added crushed tomatoes
1	can (15 ounces) no-salt-added kidney beans, rinsed, and drained
2	ounces Cheddar cheese, finely shredded (1 cup)
3	green onions, thinly sliced

1. Cook spaghetti in *boiling salted water* as package label directs.

2. Meanwhile, in 3-quart saucepan, heat oil over medium-high heat. Add beef, onion, and garlic. Cook 2 minutes, stirring and breaking up beef with wooden spoon. Add chili powder, cocoa, sugar, cinnamon, cumin, salt, and pepper. Cook 1 minute, stirring. Add tomatoes.

3. Heat beef mixture to simmering. Simmer 8 minutes or until slightly thickened. Stir in beans. Simmer 2 minutes or until beans are heated through.

4. Drain spaghetti. Divide among serving plates. Top with chili, cheese, and green onions.

EACH SERVING: About 625 calories, 44g protein, 93g carbohydrate, 13g total fat (5g saturated), 25g fiber, 58mg cholesterol, 510mg sodium

4

Grill It
For incomparable flavor and aroma, you can't beat favorites like steak, hamburgers, or kabobs grilled to perfection outdoors—or indoors in a grill pan. They are not only delicious, they're weeknight easy, too. So fire up your grill and prepare one of our go-to recipes.

Classic Barbecue Chicken is always a crowd-pleaser, or kick it up a notch with our Chicken with Tex-Mex Salsa. For a grilled twist on an Italian favorite, prepare our Chicken Parm Stacks, which include grilled yellow squash in the layers. If company's coming Prosciutto-Wrapped Turkey Cutlets with Basil-Melon Salsa is ready in twenty-five minutes—and sure to impress.

Everyone loves meals on a stick; Anise Beef Kabobs and Sweet and Smoky Salmon Kabobs are both easy to make if you follow our "Skewer Know-How" tips. Or if you like tacos, wrap some chargrilled fish—or pork and pineapples—in tortillas. Fish can also be grilled with ease in foil packages. See our recipe for spice-rubbed Nantucket Seafood Packets.

If you're in the mood for burgers or hot dogs, try our creative takes on for size. There's Burgers with French Onions or Bacon-Wrapped Cheeseburgers for the carnivores, and for vegetarians, we have Black Bean Burgers with a zippy chipotle-chili mayonnaise. Or prepare our Grilled Sausages with Mix-and-Match Toppings. Just grill up your favorite sausages or hot dogs and slather on a topping—Red Pepper Relish, Quick Sauerkraut, or Grilled Peppers and Onions—they're all delicious.

Grilled Pork Chops 'n' Peaches (recipe page 120)

Basil-Orange Chicken

Marinating chicken in orange and basil gives it a bright, fresh flavor. Served over whole-wheat couscous with steamed sugar snap peas, this light dish is perfect for warmer weather.

ACTIVE TIME: 20 minutes
TOTAL TIME: 30 minutes
MAKES: 4 main-dish servings

2	large navel oranges
3	lemons
½	cup packed fresh basil leaves, chopped
2	tablespoons olive oil
⅜	teaspoon salt
⅜	teaspoon freshly ground black pepper
4	skinless, boneless chicken-breast halves (1½ pounds total)
½	teaspoon sugar
1	cup whole-wheat couscous
1	package (8 ounces) stringless sugar snap peas

1. From 1 orange, grate 1½ teaspoons peel and squeeze 4 tablespoons juice. From 2 lemons, grate 1½ teaspoons peel and squeeze ⅓ cup juice. Cut remaining orange and lemon into slices; set aside for garnish.

2. In medium bowl, combine 1 teaspoon each of orange and lemon peel and 1 tablespoon orange juice with half of basil, 1 tablespoon olive oil, and ¼ teaspoon each salt and pepper.

3. Place chicken breasts between two sheets of plastic wrap. With flat side of meat mallet, pound chicken breasts to even ½-inch thickness. Add chicken to citrus mixture, turning to coat; set aside.

4. In small pitcher or bowl, combine sugar, ⅛ teaspoon each salt and pepper, and remaining citrus peels, citrus juices, basil, and oil; set aside. (Recipe can be made to this point up to 8 hours ahead. Cover chicken and citrus sauce and refrigerate.)

5. Preheat large ridged grill pan or prepare outdoor grill for direct grilling over medium-high heat.

6. Meanwhile, prepare couscous as label directs. Place vegetable steamer in 4-quart saucepan filled with ½ inch water. Heat to boiling over high heat.

7. Add chicken to hot grill pan or place on hot grill grate; cook 4 minutes. Turn chicken over and cook 3 to 4 minutes longer or until instant-read thermometer inserted horizontally into center of breast reaches 165°F. Briefly grill reserved citrus slices.

8. While chicken is cooking on second side, add snap peas to steamer; cook 2 to 3 minutes or until tender-crisp. Fluff couscous and spoon onto large platter; top with chicken and snap peas. Drizzle sauce over all. Garnish with citrus slices.

EACH SERVING: About 400 calories, 46g protein, 33g carbohydrate, 9g total fat (1g saturated), 6g fiber, 99mg cholesterol, 365mg sodium ☺ ♥ ▤

Chicken Parm Stacks

Chicken Parmesan goes healthy — with grilled rather than breaded chicken, and fresh veggies. Whole-wheat bread crumbs add great crunch with fewer calories.

Active time: 20 minutes
Total time: 30 minutes
Makes: 4 main-dish servings

1	slice whole-wheat bread
1	tablespoon plus 1 teaspoon olive oil
¼	cup packed fresh flat-leaf parsley leaves
1	garlic clove
⅜	teaspoon salt
⅜	teaspoon freshly ground black pepper
1	pound chicken-breast cutlets
1	pound yellow squash, cut into ½-inch-thick slices
1	pound ripe tomatoes, cut into ½-inch-thick slices
1	ounce Parmesan cheese

Basil leaves for garnish

1. Arrange oven rack 6 inches from broiler heat source. Preheat broiler. Line 18″ by 12″ jelly-roll pan with foil. Preheat large ridged grill pan or prepare outdoor grill for direct grilling over medium-high heat.

2. Tear bread into large chunks. In food processor with knife blade attached, pulse bread into fine crumbs. In small bowl, combine bread crumbs with 1 teaspoon oil.

3. To food processor, add parsley, garlic, ¼ teaspoon each salt and pepper, and remaining 1 tablespoon oil. Pulse until very finely chopped.

4. On large plate, rub half of parsley mixture all over chicken cutlets. Add chicken to hot grill pan or place on hot grill grate; cook 4 minutes. Turn chicken over and cook 3 to 4 minutes longer or until instant-read thermometer inserted horizontally into cutlet reaches 165°F.

5. Meanwhile, arrange squash in single layer in prepared pan. Toss with remaining parsley mixture. Broil 7 to 9 minutes or until squash is tender and browned. Transfer squash to serving platter in single layer. Place chicken on top.

6. In same pan, arrange tomato slices in single layer. Divide crumb mixture evenly over tomatoes. Sprinkle with remaining ⅛ teaspoon each salt and pepper. Broil 30 seconds or until crumbs are golden brown.

7. Arrange crumb-topped tomato slices on top of chicken. With vegetable peeler, shave paper-thin slices of Parmesan directly over tomatoes. Garnish with fresh basil leaves.

Each serving: About 250 calories, 29g protein, 12g carbohydrate, 10g total fat (3g saturated), 3g fiber, 69mg cholesterol, 415mg sodium ☺ ♥

Chicken with Tex-Mex Salsa

Fresh homemade salsa kicks up an easy summer standby like grilled chicken. Try our Classic Barbecued Chicken and Tangy Spicy Grilled Chicken variations. They're sure to leave no taste bud untouched!

ACTIVE TIME: 20 minutes
TOTAL TIME: 30 minutes
MAKES: 4 main-dish servings

½   cup finely chopped white onion
1   jalapeño chile
3   garlic cloves, in skins
1   can (14½ ounces) fire-roasted and diced tomatoes, drained well
¼   cup packed fresh cilantro leaves, chopped
1   tablespoon lime juice
1   teaspoon salt
½   teaspoon freshly ground black pepper
1   (3 to 3½ pounds) cut-up chicken (8 pieces)

1. Prepare outdoor grill for direct grilling over medium heat.

2. Prepare salsa: In small bowl, soak onion in cold water. Wrap jalapeño and garlic in foil. Grill 17 minutes or until vegetables are charred and blackened in spots. Cool. Remove stem, skin, and seeds from jalapeño. Peel and chop garlic. Transfer to food processor along with tomatoes, cilantro, lime juice, and ½ teaspoon salt. Pulse until finely chopped. Drain onion and stir into mixture.

3. Sprinkle remaining ½ teaspoon salt and pepper all over chicken. Place on grill, skin side down. Cover grill and cook 15 to 20 minutes or until instant-read thermometer inserted horizontally into thickest part of chicken reaches 165°F. (Smaller pieces will cook more quickly.)

4. Serve chicken with salsa.

EACH SERVING: About 425 calories, 43g protein, 7g carbohydrate, 24g total fat (7g saturated), 1g fiber, 134mg cholesterol, 870mg sodium ☺

CLASSIC BARBECUED CHICKEN: Proceed as described opposite, except omit salsa. In 3-quart saucepan, combine *⅓ cup tomato paste, ⅓ cup water, 2 tablespoons packed brown sugar, 2 tablespoons molasses, 2 tablespoons cider vinegar, 2 teaspoons Worcestershire sauce, 1 teaspoon soy sauce, 1 teaspoon Dijon mustard, ¼ teaspoon crushed red pepper,* and *¼ teaspoon each salt and pepper;* stir until well combined. Heat to boiling over high heat, then lower heat to maintain steady simmer. Cook, stirring occasionally, 30 minutes or until sauce has thickened. Immediately after chicken is cooked, transfer to large bowl with sauce. Toss until evenly coated.

EACH SERVING: About 475 calories, 43g protein, 20g carbohydrate, 24g total fat (7g saturated), 1g fiber, 134mg cholesterol, 875mg sodium

TANGY SPICY GRILLED CHICKEN: Proceed as described opposite, except omit salsa. In large bowl, stir *½ cup finely chopped red onion, ¼ cup honey, ¼ cup cayenne pepper sauce,* and *1 tablespoon cider vinegar.* Immediately after chicken is cooked, transfer to large bowl with sauce. Toss until evenly coated.

EACH SERVING: About 470 calories, 43g protein, 20g carbohydrate, 24g total fat (7g saturated), 1g fiber, 134mg cholesterol, 925mg sodium

EXPRESS-LANE INGREDIENT: CAYENNE PEPPER SAUCE

Cayenne pepper sauce adds instant heat to our Tangy Spicy Grilled Chicken and other grilled favorites, from ribs to burgers. It's made from a hot, red chile pepper, vinegar, and other flavorings, so be sure to serve cooling beverages alongside. But as addictive as it is, it isn't the only hot pepper sauce on the grocery store shelves. Experiment until you find a chile sauce that satisfies your flavor (and heat!) preferences. Consider chipotle chili pepper sauce, which adds a subtle smokiness to grilled foods, or sweet Thai Chile sauce, which is more sweet than hot.

Grilled Turkey Burgers

Flavor ground turkey with zucchini, onions, and Cajun seasoning before creating patties for the grill. Serve the burgers with lettuce, tomato, and a ketchup-and-hot-sauce mixture.

ACTIVE TIME: 15 minutes
TOTAL TIME: 25 minutes
MAKES: 4 main-dish servings

1	medium zucchini (6 ounces), shredded
2	tablespoons grated onion
1	teaspoon Cajun seasoning
1	pound ground turkey breast
4	ears corn, silk and husks removed
¼	cup ketchup
½	teaspoon hot pepper sauce
4	whole-wheat hamburger buns, split and toasted
4	leaves Boston lettuce
1	small ripe tomato, sliced

Pickle spears (optional)

1. Prepare outdoor grill for direct grilling over medium heat.

2. In medium bowl, combine zucchini, onion, and Cajun seasoning, stirring until blended. With hands, add ground turkey and mix until just blended. Shape into four ¾-inch-thick burgers, handling meat as little as possible for best texture.

3. Place burgers on hot grill grate and cook, turning once, 12 to 14 minutes or just until no longer pink throughout. (Instant-read thermometer inserted horizontally into center of burger should reach 165°F.)

4. After burgers have cooked 2 minutes, add corn to same grill grate. Cover and cook, turning occasionally, 10 to 12 minutes or until corn is browned in spots.

5. Prepare sauce: In small bowl, combine ketchup and hot sauce; set aside.

6. Serve burgers on buns with lettuce, tomato, and sauce. Serve with corn and pickle spears, if you like.

EACH SERVING: About 350 calories, 35g protein, 27g carbohydrate, 13g total fat (3g saturated), 3g fiber, 106mg cholesterol, 615mg sodium ☺

Prosciutto-Wrapped Turkey Cutlets with Basil-Melon Salsa

Italian ingredients — from prosciutto to fresh basil and cantaloupe — elevate grilling to a whole new level.

ACTIVE TIME: 5 minutes
TOTAL TIME: 25 minutes
MAKES: 4 main-dish servings

2   limes
1½   cups chopped cantaloupe
1½   cups chopped honeydew melon
1   small Kirby cucumber, shredded (½ cup)
1   jalapeño chile, seeded and finely chopped
¼   cup loosely packed fresh basil leaves, chopped
¼   teaspoon salt
4   turkey breast cutlets (1 pound total)
¼   teaspoon coarsely ground black pepper
4   ounces thinly sliced prosciutto

1. Grease grill rack. Prepare outdoor grill for direct grilling over medium heat.

2. From 1 lime, grate 1 teaspoon peel and squeeze 2 tablespoons juice. Cut remaining lime into 4 wedges and set aside. In medium bowl, combine lime juice, cantaloupe, melon, cucumber, jalapeño, basil, and salt. Makes about 3 cups.

3. Sprinkle turkey cutlets with lime peel and pepper. Wrap turkey cutlets with prosciutto, pressing prosciutto firmly onto turkey.

4. Place turkey on hot grill rack and cook, turning once, 5 to 7 minutes or until instant-read thermometer inserted horizontally into cutlet reaches 165°F. Transfer turkey to platter; serve with salsa and lime wedges.

EACH SERVING TURKEY: About 185 calories, 35g protein, 0g carbohydrate, 4g total fat (1g saturated), 0g fiber, 86mg cholesterol, 815mg sodium ☺

EACH ¼ CUP SALSA: About 10 calories, 0g protein, 3g carbohydrate, 0g total fat, 0g fiber, 0mg cholesterol, 50mg sodium ☺ ♥

TIP: When buying turkey cutlets for this recipe, make sure not to get the ones that are very thinly sliced for scaloppine.

Steak with Argentine Herb Sauce

Argentines are well known for their love of meat, and it's customary to serve grilled steaks and other meats with chimichurri sauce, a fresh blend with lots of green herbs, like the cilantro and parsley used in this recipe.

Active time: 15 minutes
Total time: 25 minutes
Makes: 6 main-dish servings

1	cup packed fresh flat-leaf parsley leaves
1	cup packed fresh cilantro leaves
1	garlic clove
3	tablespoons extra-virgin olive oil
2	tablespoons sherry vinegar
¼	teaspoon dried oregano
¼	teaspoon crushed red pepper
⅝	teaspoon kosher salt
⅝	teaspoon freshly ground black pepper
4	New York beef strip steaks, each 1 inch thick (2½ pounds total)

1. Prepare outdoor grill for direct grilling over medium-high heat. Fit wire rack into jelly-roll pan.

2. Prepare herb sauce: In food processor with knife blade attached, combine parsley, cilantro, and garlic; pulse until finely chopped. Add oil, vinegar, oregano, red pepper, and ⅛ teaspoon each salt and black pepper; pulse to blend.

3. Pat steaks dry. Sprinkle ½ teaspoon each salt and pepper all over steaks. Immediately place on grill; cook 7 to 8 minutes for medium-rare or until desired doneness, turning every 2 to 3 minutes. (Instant-read thermometer inserted horizontally into center of steak should reach 145°F.) Transfer to wire rack. Let stand 5 minutes.

4. Stir any meat juices into herb sauce. Slice steak; serve with sauce.

Each serving: About 445 calories, 38g protein, 1g carbohydrate, 31g total fat (10g saturated), 1g fiber, 136mg cholesterol, 285mg sodium

Rosemary-Lemon Steak: Omit herb sauce and salt and pepper for steaks. In bowl, combine *1 tablespoon minced fresh rosemary, 1½ teaspoons grated lemon peel, 2 teaspoons kosher salt,* and *½ teaspoon ground black pepper.* Cut *1 garlic clove* in half; rub cut sides all over steaks. Sprinkle rosemary mixture all over steaks; pat into meat. Grill as directed above.

Each serving: About 375 calories, 38g protein, 0g carbohydrate, 24g total fat (9g saturated), 0g fiber, 136mg cholesterol, 720mg sodium

Grilled Steak au Poivre: Omit herb sauce and salt and pepper for steaks. In mortar with pestle, or with heavy skillet, crush *2 tablespoons black peppercorns, 1 tablespoon coriander seeds,* and *1 teaspoon fennel seeds* until coarsely ground. Stir in *1 teaspoon kosher salt.* Sprinkle mixture all over steaks; pat into meat. Grill as directed above.

Each serving: About 385 calories, 38g protein, 2g carbohydrate, 24g total fat (9g saturated), 1g fiber, 136mg cholesterol, 400mg sodium

Seared Steak with Minted Watermelon

A dressing with lemongrass and lime brings Southeast Asian zing to this satisfying sirloin-and-rice-noodle salad.

ACTIVE TIME: 25 minutes
TOTAL TIME: 30 minutes
MAKES: 4 main-dish servings

8	ounces thin rice noodles
1	boneless beef sirloin steak, 1 inch thick (1 pound)
¼	teaspoon salt
¼	teaspoon freshly ground black pepper
1	shallot, finely chopped
1	stalk lemongrass, yellow and pale green part only, finely chopped
1	teaspoon sugar
¼	cup fresh lime juice
1	tablespoon reduced-sodium Asian fish sauce (see page 24)
½	small watermelon, rind removed, cut into ½-inch cubes (3 cups)
½	seedless (English) cucumber, cut in half and thinly sliced
½	cup packed fresh mint leaves, finely chopped

1. Prepare outdoor grill for direct grilling over medium heat.

2. Prepare noodles as label directs. Drain, rinse under cold water, and drain again.

3. Season steak with salt and pepper. Place steak on hot grill rack. Cover and cook, turning once, 12 to 13 minutes for medium-rare or until desired doneness. (Instant-read thermometer inserted horizontally into center of steak should reach 145°F.) Transfer steak to cutting board; let rest 10 minutes.

4. Meanwhile, in large bowl, stir together shallot, lemongrass, sugar, lime juice, and fish sauce until sugar dissolves. Thinly slice steak across the grain. Add to bowl, along with watermelon, cucumber, and mint. Toss gently until well mixed.

5. Divide noodles among serving plates. Top with steak mixture and accumulated juices.

EACH SERVING: About 430 calories, 26g protein, 64g carbohydrate, 8g total fat (3g saturated), 2g fiber, 75mg cholesterol, 435mg sodium ☺ ♥

QUICK TECHNIQUE: TESTING A STEAK FOR DONENESS

Here's a general formula for cooking a 1-inch steak over medium-high heat. To check the temperature, insert an instant-read thermometer horizontally into the thickest part of the steak.

Rare: 5 to 6 minutes per side (135°F)
Medium: 7 to 8 minutes per side (145°F)
Well-done: 9 to 10 minutes per side (160°F)

Note that these grill times are guidelines; check your steak earlier to avoid overcooking. And allow your steak to rest at least 3 minutes before serving. This allows time for the steak to finish cooking and for the succulent juices to be reabsorbed by the meat.

Anise Beef Kabobs

We like to buy a sirloin steak and cut it into chunks to ensure equal-size pieces for even grilling. But if you prefer, use precut beef cubes from your supermarket for the kabobs. The rub and meat can easily be doubled to feed a larger crowd. Serve with bowls of basmati rice, if you like.

ACTIVE TIME: 10 minutes
TOTAL TIME: 20 minutes plus 10 minutes marinating
MAKES: 4 main-dish servings

1	teaspoon anise seeds or fennel seeds
2	teaspoons olive oil
½	teaspoon salt
¼	teaspoon coarsely ground black pepper

Pinch crushed red pepper (optional)

1	boneless beef top sirloin steak, 1 inch thick (1 pound), cut into 1¼-inch chunks
4	(8-inch) metal skewers (see page 125)

1. Prepare outdoor grill for direct grilling over medium heat.

2. In mortar with pestle, or in resealable plastic bag with rolling pin, crush anise seeds. In medium bowl, combine anise seeds, oil, salt, black pepper, and crushed red pepper, if using. Add beef chunks, tossing until well coated. Cover and let beef stand 10 minutes at room temperature to marinate.

3. Loosely thread meat onto skewers. Place skewers on hot grill rack and cook, turning occasionally, 8 to 10 minutes for medium-rare or until desired doneness. (Instant-read thermometer inserted horizontally into center of beef should reach 145°F.)

EACH SERVING: About 220 calories, 21g protein, 0g carbohydrate, 14g total fat (5g saturated), 0g fiber, 68mg cholesterol, 340mg sodium ☺ ♥

TIP: *If you like, toss chunks of onion and bell peppers in 1 tablespoon olive oil and thread onto the skewers along with the meat.*

Burgers with French Onions

Rich and nutty, Gruyère cheese melts divinely and gives these burgers a French twist. Try our lip-smacking variation: Bacon-Wrapped Cheeseburgers with paprika ketchup.

ACTIVE TIME: 15 minutes
TOTAL TIME: 20 minutes
MAKES: 4 main-dish servings

⅓   cup light mayonnaise

¼   cup loosely packed fresh parsley leaves, finely chopped

1   small garlic clove, crushed with garlic press

½   teaspoon ground black pepper

2   teaspoons olive oil

1   medium red onion (6 to 8 ounces), cut in half, thinly sliced

4   ounces mushrooms, sliced

½   cup water

1   teaspoon sugar

½   teaspoon salt

1¼ pounds 85% lean ground beef

1   ounce Gruyère cheese, shredded (¼ cup)

4   brioche hamburger buns, toasted

4   leaves Boston lettuce

1. Prepare outdoor grill for direct grilling over medium heat.

2. In small bowl, stir together mayonnaise, parsley, garlic, and ¼ teaspoon pepper; set aside.

3. In 12-inch skillet, heat oil over medium-high heat. Add onion; cook, stirring occasionally, 3 to 4 minutes or until onion begins to soften. Add mushrooms, water, sugar, and ¼ teaspoon salt; cover and cook, stirring occasionally, 5 to 6 minutes or until mushrooms are tender.

4. Shape beef into four ¾-inch-thick burgers. Lightly sprinkle with remaining ¼ teaspoon each salt and pepper to season both sides.

5. Grill burgers, covered, 7 minutes for medium or until desired doneness, turning once. (Instant-read thermometer inserted horizontally into center of burger should reach 160°F.) Top each burger with ¼ cup onion mixture and 1 tablespoon cheese. Cover; cook 1 minute or until cheese has melted. Serve on buns with garlic mayonnaise and lettuce.

EACH SERVING: About 500 calories, 34g protein, 33g carbohydrate, 33g total fat (12g saturated), 2g fiber, 197mg cholesterol, 880mg sodium

BACON-WRAPPED CHEESEBURGERS: Proceed as described above, except omit garlic mayonnaise and onion mixture. In small bowl, stir together *⅓ cup ketchup* and *¼ teaspoon smoked paprika*. On plate, between paper towels, arrange *4 slices bacon* in single layer. Microwave on High 2 minutes or until some fat has rendered; transfer to cutting board. Let cool. Repeat with *4 more slices bacon.* Shape burgers as in step 4; wrap each with 2 strips bacon, crisscrossing over burger. Place, seam side down, on large plate. Grill burgers as in step 5, substituting *4 slices Cheddar cheese* for Gruyère. Serve on *4 hamburger buns*, toasted, with paprika ketchup.

EACH SERVING: About 555 calories, 40g protein, 27g carbohydrate, 31g total fat (12g saturated), 1g fiber, 124mg cholesterol, 1,150mg sodium

Grilled Pork Chops 'n' Peaches

Seared on the grill, just-picked juicy peaches gain a caramelized char — and become a mouthwatering match for these succulent chops. Coating the pork with a quickly made marinade of garlic and cilantro results in super-moist meat. For photo, see page 106.

ACTIVE TIME: 25 minutes
TOTAL TIME: 30 minutes
MAKES: 4 main-dish servings

3	small garlic cloves
½	cup packed cilantro stems and leaves
¼	teaspoon freshly ground black pepper
1	tablespoon reduced-sodium soy sauce
4	boneless pork chops, each ¾ inch thick
⅓	cup fresh lime juice
1	tablespoon dark brown sugar
¼	teaspoon crushed red pepper
6	peaches, ripe but firm
1	bunch green onions, roots trimmed, or 4 spring onions, halved

1. In food processor, combine garlic, cilantro, and pepper; pulse until very finely chopped. Add soy sauce and pulse to incorporate. Transfer to large resealable plastic bag and add pork chops. Rub garlic mixture all over chops, seal bag tightly, and refrigerate until ready to grill, or up to overnight.

2. In same processor (do not clean bowl), combine lime juice, brown sugar, crushed red pepper, and 2 peaches, pitted and cut into quarters; puree until smooth. Sauce can be refrigerated, covered, overnight.

3. Prepare grill for direct grilling over medium-high heat.

4. Cut remaining peaches into halves and remove pits; grill 5 to 7 minutes or until grill marks appear, turning occasionally. Grill chops, covered, 5 to 6 minutes or until cooked through, turning once. (Instant-read thermometer inserted horizontally into center of chop should reach 145°F.) Grill green onions 3 minutes or until softened, turning occasionally.

5. Drizzle sauce over chops and serve with peaches and green onions.

EACH SERVING: About 335 calories, 29g protein, 30g carbohydrate, 12g total fat (4g saturated), 5g fiber, 87mg cholesterol, 290mg sodium ☺ ♥ ⬜

Pineapple Pork Tacos

These zesty pork-and-pineapple tacos are the ideal summer dinner — they're quick, they're healthy, and they boast a perfect balance of sweet and spicy flavors.

Total time: 25 minutes
Makes: 4 main-dish servings

1	chipotle chile plus 2 tablespoons adobo sauce (from 1 can chiles in adobo)
3	tablespoons honey
2	garlic cloves, crushed with garlic press
½	small pineapple, peeled and cut into ½-inch-thick slices
½	teaspoon salt
½	teaspoon ground black pepper
1	pound boneless pork chops, each ¾ inch thick
½	small white onion, sliced
¼	cup chopped fresh cilantro leaves
8	corn tortillas, warmed

1. Prepare outdoor grill for direct grilling over medium heat.

2. In blender, puree chile, adobo sauce, honey, garlic, half of pineapple slices, and ¼ teaspoon each salt and pepper. Pour ⅓ cup sauce into pie plate; pour remainder into small bowl and set aside for serving.

3. Add pork chops to sauce in plate; turn to coat. Let stand. Grill onion and remaining pineapple until tender, 4 to 6 minutes, turning once. Transfer to cutting board.

4. Grill chops, thinly coated with sauce, 6 to 8 minutes or until meat just loses pink color throughout, turning once. (Instant-read thermometer inserted horizontally into center of chop should reach 145°F.)

5. Chop onion and pineapple; place in bowl. Stir in cilantro and ¼ teaspoon each salt and pepper. Cut pork into chunks; place in tortillas with pineapple mixture. Serve with reserved sauce.

Each serving: About 430 calories, 26g protein, 45g carbohydrate, 16g total fat (8g saturated), 4g fiber, 66mg cholesterol, 450mg sodium ☺

Cuban Grilled Pork

Sweet grilled pork tenderloin pairs beautifully with a black-bean-and-jicama side salad seasoned with cumin and plenty of fresh cilantro.

TOTAL TIME: 30 minutes
MAKES: 4 main-dish servings

3	limes
1	teaspoon olive oil
1	teaspoon cumin
1	garlic clove, crushed with garlic press
¾	teaspoon salt
1	pork tenderloin (1¼ pounds), cut crosswise into 8 slices, each flattened slightly
1	can (15 to 19 ounces) black beans, rinsed and drained
3	cups chopped jicama (1 pound)
¼	cup loosely packed fresh cilantro leaves, chopped
¼	teaspoon freshly ground black pepper

1. From 1 to 2 limes, grate 2 teaspoons peel and squeeze 3 tablespoons juice. Cut remaining lime into wedges. In small bowl, combine peel, oil, cumin, garlic, and ½ teaspoon salt; rub mixture on both sides of pork slices.

2. Spray large ridged grill pan with nonstick cooking spray; heat over medium heat. Cook pork, turning once, 11 to 14 minutes or until browned on outside and still slightly pink in center. (Instant-read thermometer inserted horizontally into center of pork should reach 145°F.)

3. In medium bowl, combine beans, jicama, lime juice, cilantro, remaining ¼ teaspoon salt, and pepper. Serve pork with bean salad and lime wedges.

EACH SERVING: About 310 calories, 36g protein, 30g carbohydrate, 7g total fat (2g saturated), 12g fiber, 89mg cholesterol, 785mg sodium ☺

Grilled Sausages with Mix-and-Match Toppings

Spicy grilled sausages topped with grilled veggies, sauerkraut, and relishes are a cookout staple and an easy way to satisfy a crowd.

ACTIVE TIME: 10 minutes
TOTAL TIME: 15 to 25 minutes
MAKES: 8 main-dish servings

8	sweet or hot Italian sausage links, 8 hot dogs, 2 large kielbasa sausage links, or 8 fully cooked bratwurst sausages
8	hot dog buns or Italian bread rolls, split

Choice of toppings (opposite)

1. Prepare outdoor grill for direct grilling over medium heat.

2. Grill Italian sausages, turning occasionally, 15 minutes (grill hot dogs 5 minutes, kielbasa 15 minutes, or bratwurst 10 minutes) or until browned and cooked through. Grill rolls or buns 1 to 2 minutes or until toasted. Serve sausages (kielbasa cut into 8 pieces) in toasted rolls with choice of toppings.

EACH SERVING ITALIAN SAUSAGE AND BUN WITHOUT TOPPING: About 405 calories, 20g protein, 25g carbohydrate, 25g total fat (8g saturated), 1g fiber, 47mg cholesterol, 1,208mg sodium ☺

Grilled Peppers and Onions

Active time: 15 minutes
Total time: 30 minutes
Makes: 5 cups

Prepare grill for direct grilling over medium heat. In large bowl, toss *1½ pounds thinly sliced peppers* (red, orange, and yellow), *1 thinly sliced medium onion, 2 tablespoons balsamic vinegar, 1 teaspoon extra-virgin olive oil, 1 teaspoon sugar, ¼ teaspoon dried oregano,* and *⅛ teaspoon each salt and pepper.* Transfer to large sheet of nonstick foil (or foil coated with nonstick cooking spray). Wrap foil around mixture, crimping edges to seal. Grill 15 to 18 minutes or until tender.

Each ½-cup serving: About 35 calories, 1g protein, 6g carbohydrate, 1g total fat (0g saturated), 1g fiber, 0mg cholesterol, 30mg sodium ☺ ♥

Red Pepper Relish

Active time: 10 minutes
Total time: 30 minutes plus cooling
Makes: 2 cups

In 2-quart saucepan, combine *½ cup red wine vinegar* with *¼ cup sugar* and heat to boiling over high heat. Add *2 finely chopped red peppers, ½ cup finely chopped sweet onion, 1 teaspoon mustard seeds,* and *¼ teaspoon salt.* Adjust heat to maintain simmer. Cook 20 minutes or until peppers are just tender. Cool slightly. Can be refrigerated, covered, up to 3 days.

Each ¼-cup serving: About 45 calories, 1g protein, 10g carbohydrate, 0g total fat, 1g fiber, 0mg cholesterol, 75mg sodium ☺ ♥ 🗑

Quick Sauerkraut

Active time: 10 minutes
Total time: 10 minutes plus standing
Makes: 6 cups

In large bowl, combine *8 cups very thinly sliced cabbage; 1 Granny Smith apple,* cut into thin matchsticks; *⅓ cup unseasoned rice vinegar; 1 teaspoon reduced-sodium fish sauce; ½ teaspoon caraway seeds;* and *1 teaspoon salt.* Let stand 3 hours, stirring occasionally. Can be refrigerated, covered, up to 3 days.

Each ½-cup serving: About 25 calories, 1g protein, 6g carbohydrate, 0g total fat, 2g fiber, 0mg cholesterol, 230mg sodium ☺ ♥ 🗑

Barbecued Shrimp and Peach Kabobs

The unexpectedly perfect pairing of sweet shrimp covered in spices and skewered with juicy peaches makes a tasty summer meal.

TOTAL TIME: 25 minutes
MAKES: 4 main-dish servings

12	(12-inch) metal or bamboo skewers
1	tablespoon packed dark brown sugar
1	teaspoon ancho chile powder
1	teaspoon sweet paprika
½	teaspoon ground cumin
¼	teaspoon cayenne (ground red) pepper
¼	teaspoon salt
¼	teaspoon freshly ground black pepper
1	pound shrimp (16 to 20 count), shelled and deveined
3	medium peaches, cut into 1-inch chunks
1	bunch green onions, dark green parts trimmed, cut into 2-inch pieces

Lime wedges for serving

1. If using bamboo skewers, soak skewers in cold water at least 30 minutes to prevent burning. Prepare outdoor grill for direct grilling over high heat.

2. In large bowl, combine brown sugar, chile powder, paprika, cumin, cayenne, salt, and black pepper. Add shrimp, peaches, and onions; toss until evenly coated.

3. Thread shrimp, peaches, and onion pieces alternately onto skewers.

4. Grill, turning once, 3 to 4 minutes or until all ingredients are browned and shrimp just become opaque throughout. Serve with lime wedges.

EACH SERVING: About 135 calories, 14g protein, 18g carbohydrate, 2g total fat (0g saturated), 3g fiber, 112mg cholesterol, 665mg sodium ☺

QUICK TECHNIQUE: SKEWER KNOW-HOW

Whether you're spearing chunks of chicken, steak, shrimp, or veggies, follow these tips for kabob success.

+ If you use metal skewers, look for the kind that are twisted or square—not round. Food twirls around when you try to flip kabobs on round skewers. (Wooden and bamboo skewers aren't so slippery, so their round shape is not a problem.)

+ Before using wooden or bamboo skewers, soak them in hot water for at least 30 minutes so they won't burn when exposed to the grill's heat and flames.

+ For even cooking, don't jam foods up against each other when assembling— leave a little space between each item on the skewer.

+ Combine foods with similar cooking times on the same skewer, and use two parallel skewers for unwieldy items, like large slices of onion.

Bacon-Wrapped Scallops

This luscious summer dish has an elegant appearance but it's easier to prepare than it looks!

TOTAL TIME: 30 minutes
MAKES: 4 main-dish servings

4   (12-inch) metal skewers (see page 125)
4   ears corn, husked
4   slices bacon
16   large sea scallops (see page 70)
¼   teaspoon ground black pepper
2   medium tomatoes, chopped
2   ripe nectarines, chopped
¼   cup chopped fresh basil leaves
2   tablespoons lemon juice
1   pinch cayenne (ground red) pepper
⅛   teaspoon salt

1. Prepare outdoor grill for direct grilling over medium heat.

2. Grill corn 10 minutes or until browned, turning occasionally. Meanwhile, on microwave-safe plate, place bacon between paper towels. Microwave on High 1 minute.

3. Press 4 scallops together, flat sides down, in a square; wrap with 1 slice bacon. Insert skewer through overlapping ends of bacon, pressing through to other side of scallops. Repeat with remaining scallops and bacon. Sprinkle black pepper on scallops.

4. Grill, covered, 5 to 7 minutes or until scallops are just opaque throughout, turning once.

5. Cut kernels off cobs and place in large bowl. Stir in tomatoes, nectarines, basil, lemon juice, cayenne, and salt. Serve with scallops.

EACH SERVING: About 215 calories, 16g protein, 30g carbohydrate, 5g total fat (1g saturated), 4g fiber, 25mg cholesterol, 290mg sodium ☺ ♥

Nantucket Seafood Packets

Grill mild-flavored scrod in individual foil packets with mussels, tomatoes, and lime butter.

Total time: 25 minutes
Makes: 4 main-dish servings

3   tablespoons butter or margarine, softened
1   teaspoon freshly grated lime peel
¾   teaspoon salt
½   teaspoon ground cumin
½   teaspoon ground coriander
½   teaspoon cayenne (ground red) pepper
4   scrod fillets (6 ounces each)
12   large mussels, scrubbed and debearded (see page 222)
2   ripe tomatoes, cut into 1½-inch pieces
1   cup loosely packed fresh cilantro, chopped

1. Prepare outdoor grill for direct grilling over medium heat. In small bowl, stir together butter, lime peel, salt, cumin, coriander, and cayenne.

2. Cut four 16" by 12" sheets heavy-duty foil; arrange on work surface. Place 1 fillet on half of each sheet. Dot fillets with butter mixture. Top each with 3 mussels and one-fourth of tomatoes. Bring up long sides of foil and fold over several times to seal well. Seal ends tightly.

3. Place packets on grill and cook, without turning, 10 minutes. With kitchen shears, cut X in top of each packet to let steam escape, then carefully pull back foil to open. Scrod should be opaque throughout and flake easily. Discard any mussels that have not opened. Sprinkle with cilantro.

Each serving: About 285 calories, 39g protein, 6g carbohydrate, 11g total fat (6g saturated), 103mg cholesterol, 826mg sodium ☺

Sweet and Smoky Salmon Kabobs

Just toss salmon chunks and zucchini slices in brown sugar and spices and thread them onto skewers for this easy main-dish grill recipe.

Active time: 10 minutes
Total time: 30 minutes
Makes: 8 main-dish servings

8   (12-inch) metal skewers (see page 125)
2   tablespoons packed dark brown sugar
1½   teaspoons smoked paprika
1   teaspoon chili powder
½   teaspoon cayenne (ground red) pepper
½   teaspoon freshly ground black pepper
¾   teaspoon salt
2¼   pounds skinless salmon fillet, cut into 1½-inch chunks
2   medium zucchini (8 ounces each), cut into ¼-inch-thick slices

1. Prepare outdoor grill for direct grilling over medium heat.

2. In large bowl, combine sugar, paprika, chili powder, cayenne, black pepper, and salt, breaking up any lumps. Add salmon and zucchini, tossing to evenly coat with spice mixture.

3. Thread zucchini slices, two at a time and alternating with salmon, onto skewers. Place on hot grill grate and cook, turning occasionally, 9 to 11 minutes or until salmon turns opaque throughout. (Instant-read thermometer inserted horizontally into center of salmon should reach 145°F.)

Each serving: About 205 calories, 26g protein, 6g carbohydrate, 8g total fat (1g saturated), 1g fiber, 70mg cholesterol, 280mg sodium ☺ ♥

Black Bean Burgers

This south-of-the-border burger proves that beef-free doesn't have to be bland: Spiced with coriander and cumin, and capped with chile-spiked Tex-Mex mayo, it's as fiery as it is filling.

ACTIVE TIME: 15 minutes
TOTAL TIME: 20 minutes
MAKES: 4 main-dish servings

¼   cup dried bread crumbs

¼   teaspoon ground cumin

¼   teaspoon ground coriander

3   cups cooked black beans or 2 cans (15 ounces each) reduced-sodium black beans, rinsed and drained

¼   cup light mayonnaise

¼   teaspoon salt

¼   teaspoon freshly ground black pepper

2   large stalks celery, finely chopped

1   chipotle chile in adobo, finely chopped

4   green-leaf lettuce leaves

4   whole-wheat hamburger buns, toasted

4   slices ripe tomato

1. In food processor with knife blade attached, pulse bread crumbs, cumin, coriander, two-thirds of beans, 2 tablespoons mayonnaise, salt, and pepper until well blended. Transfer to large bowl. Stir in celery and remaining whole beans until well combined. Divide into 4 portions and shape into patties.

2. Prepare outdoor grill for direct grilling over medium heat, or heat large ridged grill pan over medium heat. Add burgers and cook until lightly browned and heated through, 10 to 12 minutes, turning once.

3. Meanwhile, in small bowl, combine chipotle chile and remaining 2 tablespoons mayonnaise until well mixed. Place 1 lettuce leaf on bottom of each bun; top with patty, then tomato slice. Divide chipotle mayonnaise among burgers and replace tops of buns to serve.

EACH SERVING: About 370 calories, 18g protein, 59g carbohydrate, 8g total fat (1g saturated), 14g fiber, 5mg cholesterol, 725mg sodium ☺

Hoisin-Ginger Tofu and Veggies

A great hoisin-ginger glaze flavors tofu, zucchini, and red pepper. Be sure to buy extra-firm tofu; other varieties will fall apart while cooking.

TOTAL TIME: 30 minutes
MAKES: 4 main-dish servings

HOISIN-GINGER GLAZE

½   cup hoisin sauce
2   garlic cloves, crushed with garlic press
1   tablespoon vegetable oil
1   tablespoon reduced-sodium soy sauce
1   tablespoon grated, peeled fresh ginger
1   tablespoon seasoned rice vinegar
⅛   teaspoon cayenne (ground red) pepper

TOFU AND VEGGIES

1   package (15 ounces) extra-firm tofu (see page 100)
2   medium zucchini (10 ounces each), cut lengthwise into quarters and then crosswise in half
1   large red pepper, cut lengthwise into quarters, stem and seeds discarded
1   bunch green onions, trimmed
1   teaspoon vegetable oil

1. Prepare outdoor grill for direct grilling over medium heat.

2. Prepare hoisin-ginger glaze: In small bowl, with fork, mix hoisin sauce, garlic, oil, soy sauce, ginger, vinegar, and cayenne until well blended.

3. Prepare tofu and veggies: Cut tofu horizontally into 4 pieces, then cut each piece crosswise in half. Place pieces on paper towels; pat dry with additional paper towels. Arrange tofu on large plate and brush both sides with half of glaze. Spoon remaining half of glaze into medium bowl; add zucchini and red pepper. Gently toss vegetables to coat with glaze. On separate plate, rub green onions with oil.

4. Place tofu, zucchini, and red peppers on hot grill rack over medium heat. Grill tofu, 6 minutes, gently turning once with wide metal spatula. Transfer tofu to platter; keep warm. Continue cooking vegetables until tender and browned, about 5 minutes longer, transferring them to platter with tofu as they are done.

5. Add green onions to grill during last minute of cooking time; transfer to platter and serve.

EACH SERVING: About 245 calories, 15g protein, 22g carbohydrate, 11g total fat, (1g saturated), 5g fiber, 0mg cholesterol, 615mg sodium ☺

EXPRESS-LANE INGREDIENT: HOISIN SAUCE

Widely used in Chinese cooking, this thick, reddish-brown sauce adds sweet and spicy flavor to everything from poultry and pork to our Hoisin-Ginger Tofu and Veggies above. Made from a mixture of soybeans, garlic, chili peppers, and other spices, this versatile sauce can form the base for a more complex sauce. Or you can just brush it on your protein before cooking, or even put a bottle on the table to be used as a condiment. Refrigerate bottled hoisin sauce after opening.

Grilled Veggie Pizza

Everyone's favorite takeout gets a low-cal, high-fiber makeover with a heap of veggies — sweet from a turn on the grill — a whole-wheat crust, and a sprinkle of cheese.

TOTAL TIME: 30 minutes
MAKES: 4 main-dish servings

2	medium portobello mushroom caps, sliced
1	small red onion (4 to 6 ounces), sliced into rounds
1	small yellow summer squash, sliced
1	tablespoon olive oil
¼	teaspoon salt
¼	teaspoon ground black pepper
1	pound whole-wheat pizza dough
2	ripe plum tomatoes, thinly sliced
½	cup shredded smoked mozzarella (2 ounces)
¼	cup packed fresh basil leaves, sliced

1. Prepare outdoor grill for direct grilling over medium heat. Brush mushrooms, onion, and squash with oil; sprinkle with salt and pepper.

2. Grill vegetables, covered, 6 minutes or until tender and browned, turning once. Remove from grill and separate onion rings; set aside. Reduce heat on grill to medium-low.

3. Cover large cookie sheet with foil; spray with nonstick cooking spray. Stretch dough into 10″ by 14″ rectangle. Place on cookie sheet.

4. Lift dough and foil; place, dough side down, on grill, gently peeling off foil. Cover; cook 3 minutes or until bottom is crisp. Turn crust over. Quickly top with tomatoes, vegetables, and cheese. Cover; cook 2 minutes longer or until bottom is crisp. Slide onto cutting board; garnish with basil.

EACH SERVING: About 375 calories, 13g protein, 58g carbohydrate, 10g total fat (2g saturated), 9g fiber, 11mg cholesterol, 695mg sodium ☺

5

Fix It and Forget It

Nothing makes the preparation of dinner easier than the original fix-it-and-forget-it appliance—the slow cooker. Simply add your ingredients to the bowl first thing in the morning, and your home-cooked dinner will be waiting by the end of the day. Plus, slow-cooking allows even tough cuts of meat to become their most tender, vegetables to fully absorb stocks and spices, and flavors to develop to their fullest.

In this chapter, we share our most delicious—not to mention affordable—slow-cooker poultry recipes. Prepare French classics like Coq au Vin and Chicken Fricasee with ease. Or make our Red-Cooked Turkey Thighs with Leeks, plus baby carrots, all in a single pot. You can even make Tangy Barbecue Chicken in a slow cooker.

Roasts and even ribs cook up tender and juicy in a slow cooker: Recipes like Sweet and Tangy Braised Chuck Roast, Chipotle Pork Tacos (made from boneless pork shoulder), and Red Wine–Braised Short Ribs all make for satisfying family meals.

The slow cooker's versatility doesn't stop there. We've included creative recipes that allow you to make Spaghetti and Meatballs, Mediterranean Seafood Stew, and a barley risotto with butternut squash in your slow cooker. For tips on how to get the most from this convenient appliance, see "Slow-Cooker Success" on page 137.

Red Wine–Braised Short Ribs (recipe page 149)

Tangy Barbecue Chicken

This recipe makes more than enough barbecue for one family meal. The next day, use the leftover chicken to make our sweet-and-savory chicken-and-apple salad, below.

ACTIVE TIME: 15 minutes
SLOW-COOK TIME: 4 hours on High
MAKES: 4 main-dish servings

1	cup ketchup
2	tablespoons spicy brown mustard
2	tablespoons balsamic vinegar
2	teaspoons Worcestershire sauce
1	garlic clove, pressed with a garlic press
1/4	teaspoon smoked paprika (see Tip, page 135)
3/8	teaspoon freshly ground black pepper
1/2	teaspoon salt
4	bone-in chicken-breast halves (3 to 3 1/2 pounds total), skin removed
4	chicken drumsticks (1 1/2 pounds total), skin removed

1. Spray 6-quart slow-cooker bowl with non-stick cooking spray.

2. In medium bowl, whisk together ketchup, mustard, vinegar, Worcestershire sauce, garlic, smoked paprika, and 1/8 teaspoon pepper; transfer half of sauce to slow-cooker bowl.

3. Sprinkle chicken with salt and remaining 1/4 teaspoon pepper; add to slow-cooker bowl. Spoon remaining sauce over and around chicken to coat. Cover with lid and cook on High 4 hours or until chicken is cooked through.

4. Transfer 2 chicken breasts to container; refrigerate up to 3 days. Transfer remaining chicken to serving platter. Whisk cooking liquid until well mixed; drizzle over chicken (see Tip). Serve any remaining sauce on the side.

EACH SERVING: About 320 calories, 44g protein, 18g carbohydrate, 7g total fat (2g saturated), 0g fiber, 144mg cholesterol, 1,275mg sodium 🍲

TIP: *If you prefer a thicker sauce, transfer cooking liquid to a saucepan and boil until thickened.*

CHICKEN SALAD WITH APPLES AND CHEDDAR:
Remove and discard bones from *reserved chicken;* shred meat. In large bowl, whisk *3 tablespoons olive oil; 2 tablespoons cider vinegar; 2 teaspoons Dijon mustard;* and *1/4 teaspoon each salt and ground black pepper.* Add to same bowl: *1 head red leaf lettuce,* chopped, and *1 small red pepper,* very thinly sliced; toss until well combined. Divide among serving plates; top with *1 Granny Smith apple,* thinly sliced; *1/4 cup chopped walnuts,* toasted; and *2 ounces extra-sharp Cheddar cheese,* coarsely grated. Serves 4.

EACH SERVING: About 400 calories, 36g protein, 12g carbohydrate, 23g total fat (6g saturated), 3g fiber, 95mg cholesterol, 415mg sodium ☺

Chicken with Beans and Sweet Potatoes

This spicy, smoky Latin chicken dish boasts a good portion of your daily fiber and beta carotene, thanks to black beans and sweet potatoes. And with just fifteen minutes of prep, this slow-cooker meal is easy to throw together in the morning.

ACTIVE TIME: 15 minutes
SLOW-COOK TIME: 8 hours on Low or 4 hours on High
MAKES: 6 main-dish servings

3	pounds bone-in chicken thighs, skin and fat removed
2	teaspoons ground cumin
¼	teaspoon salt
¼	teaspoon freshly ground black pepper
1	teaspoon smoked paprika (see Tip) or ½ teaspoon chopped chipotle chiles in adobo sauce
½	teaspoon ground allspice
1	cup reduced-sodium chicken broth
½	cup salsa
3	large garlic cloves, crushed with garlic press
2	cans (15 to 19 ounces each) black beans, rinsed and drained
2	pounds sweet potatoes, peeled and cut into 2-inch pieces
1	jarred roasted red pepper, cut into strips (1 cup)
⅓	cup loosely packed fresh cilantro leaves, chopped

Lime wedges for serving

1. Sprinkle chicken thighs with ½ teaspoon ground cumin, salt, and black pepper. Heat nonstick 12-inch skillet over medium heat; add chicken and cook until well browned on all sides, about 10 minutes. Transfer chicken to plate. Remove skillet from heat.

2. In same skillet, with pan drippings, combine paprika, allspice, broth, salsa, garlic, and remaining 1½ teaspoons cumin.

3. In 6-quart slow cooker, combine beans and sweet potatoes. Place chicken on top of potato mixture in slow cooker; pour broth mixture over chicken. Cover slow cooker with lid and cook on Low 8 hours or on High 4 hours.

4. With tongs or slotted spoon, remove chicken pieces to large platter. Gently stir red pepper into potato mixture. Spoon mixture over chicken. Sprinkle with cilantro and serve with lime wedges.

EACH SERVING: About 415 calories, 36g protein, 61g carbohydrate, 6g total fat (1g saturated), 12g fiber, 107mg cholesterol, 875mg sodium ☺ 🧺

TIP: *Smoked paprika is highly prized for its pungent yet mellow flavor. Look for it in gourmet or spice shops, or use Hungarian hot paprika, available in most supermarkets.*

Speedy Coq au Vin

If you're an early riser with extra A.M. time, try our easy, make-ahead version of this French country classic. You can even cook extra bacon to munch on for breakfast.

ACTIVE TIME: 20 minutes
SLOW-COOK TIME: 8 hours on Low or 4 hours on High
MAKES: 4 main-dish servings

3	slices bacon, cut crosswise into ¾-inch pieces
1	package mushrooms (10 ounces), cut in half
2	cups frozen pearl onions
1	chicken (3½ to 4 pounds), cut into 8 pieces, skin removed from all but wings
½	teaspoon salt
¼	teaspoon freshly ground black pepper
1	medium onion, chopped
1	large carrot, chopped
4	garlic cloves, chopped
1	cup dry red wine
2	tablespoons tomato paste
1	bay leaf
¾	cup chicken broth

1. In nonstick 12-inch skillet, cook bacon over medium heat until browned. With slotted spoon, transfer bacon to paper towels to drain, leaving bacon fat in skillet; set aside.

2. Meanwhile, in 5- to 6-quart slow cooker, combine mushrooms and pearl onions; set aside.

3. Sprinkle chicken pieces with salt and pepper. In skillet with bacon fat, cook chicken (in two batches, if necessary) over medium-high heat until browned, about 10 minutes. Place chicken over vegetables in slow cooker.

4. Discard drippings from skillet. Reduce heat to medium; add onion and carrot, and cook, stirring frequently, 2 minutes or until onion softens. Stir in garlic and cook 1 minute. Add wine, tomato paste, and bay leaf; heat to boiling, stirring to dissolve tomato paste. Pour wine mixture and broth over chicken pieces. Cover slow cooker with lid and cook on Low 8 hours or on High 4 hours.

5. To serve, discard bay leaf. With large spoon, transfer chicken and sauce to deep platter; sprinkle with bacon.

EACH SERVING: About 400 calories, 52g protein, 20g carbohydrate, 13g total fat (4g saturated), 5g fiber, 156mg cholesterol, 690mg sodium ☺ 🍲

QUICK TECHNIQUE: SLOW-COOKER SUCCESS

The slow cooker is your ally for busy weeknight meal prep. It allows you to make homemade soups and stews and meltingly tender meat with a minimum of effort. Here are tips to ensure that you get the most from this convenient appliance.

✦ Prep the night before, and all you'll need do in the morning is toss your ingredients into the slow-cooker bowl and flip the switch. (Measure ingredients, cut veggies, and trim fat from meats, then refrigerate components separately in bowls or storage bags.)

✦ Less tender cuts of meat and poultry—such as pork shoulder, chuck roast, beef brisket, and poultry legs—are best suited for slow-cooking. Skim fat from cooking liquid when done. (Fish and other seafood aren't good options unless they're added in the last hour of cooking.)

✦ For richer flavor in stews, sprinkle meat and poultry with flour and brown it in a skillet before putting it in the slow cooker. (Be sure to scrape up the browned bits that stick to the bottom of the skillet and add them to the pot; they'll help thicken the sauce and enhance the flavor even more.)

✦ Resist the urge to take the lid off the cooker and stir the ingredients, especially in the early stages of warming—the pot will lose valuable heat.

✦ When you're cooking root vegetables, put them at the bottom of the pot—they cook more slowly than meat.

✦ Slow-cooking intensifies flavorful spices and seasonings such as chili powder and garlic, so use them conservatively.

✦ Dried herbs may lessen in flavor, so adjust seasonings by stirring a little more in at the end of cooking. When using fresh herbs, save some to toss in at the last minute for fresh flavor and color.

Chicken Fricassee

This rich slow-cooked chicken dinner with mushrooms, peas, and potatoes is perfect for an at-home dinner date.

ACTIVE TIME: 25 minutes
SLOW-COOK TIME: 5 hours on Low
MAKES: 6 main-dish servings

2½ pounds skinless, bone-in chicken thighs

½ teaspoon grated lemon peel

¼ teaspoon dried thyme

1 teaspoon salt

½ teaspoon ground black pepper

¾ cup chicken broth

1 teaspoon chicken-broth concentrate or demi-glace

1½ pounds small red potatoes, scrubbed and cut in half

8 ounces white mushrooms, cut in half

1 large shallot, chopped

2 garlic cloves, chopped

½ cup whole milk

1 tablespoon butter, melted

1½ cups frozen peas, thawed

⅓ cup light sour cream

Chopped fresh parsley for garnish

1. In gallon-size resealable plastic bag, combine chicken with lemon peel, thyme, and ½ teaspoon each salt and pepper; refrigerate overnight.

2. In 6- to 7-quart slow-cooker bowl, combine chicken broth, broth concentrate, potatoes, mushrooms, shallot, and garlic. Place chicken in slow-cooker bowl on top of vegetables.

3. Cover slow cooker with lid and cook 5 hours on Low or until chicken is cooked through. Transfer chicken to cutting board. Skim and discard fat from cooking liquid. Stir ¼ teaspoon salt into cooking liquid.

4. Transfer potatoes to large bowl; mash with milk, melted butter, and remaining ¼ teaspoon salt. Into chicken mixture, stir peas and sour cream. Serve over potatoes; garnish with chopped parsley.

EACH SERVING: About 380 calories, 33g protein, 28g carbohydrate, 15g total fat (6g saturated), 4g fiber, 110mg cholesterol, 600mg sodium ☺ 🍲

Creamy Chicken and Potatoes

Attention, potpie lovers! This comforting slow-cooker dish features chicken and vegetables bathed in a creamy, thyme-laced sauce.

ACTIVE TIME: 20 minutes
SLOW-COOK TIME: 8 hours on Low or 6 hours on High
MAKES: 6 main-dish servings

2	cups peeled baby carrots (about half of 16-ounce bag)
1	pound red potatoes, cut into quarters
1	small onion, coarsely chopped
1	garlic clove, crushed with garlic press
1	cut-up chicken (3½ to 4 pounds), skin removed from all pieces except wings
1	cup chicken broth
3	tablespoons cornstarch
½	teaspoon dried thyme
1	teaspoon salt
¼	teaspoon freshly ground black pepper
1	package (10 ounces) frozen peas, thawed
½	cup heavy or whipping cream

1. In 5- to 6-quart slow cooker, combine carrots, potatoes, onion, and garlic. Place chicken pieces on top of vegetables. In 2-cup liquid measuring cup, with fork, mix broth, cornstarch, thyme, salt, and pepper; pour mixture over chicken and vegetables. Cover slow cooker with lid and cook on Low 8 hours or on High 6 hours.

2. With tongs or slotted spoon, transfer chicken pieces to warm, deep platter. With slotted spoon, transfer vegetables to platter with chicken pieces. Cover platter to keep warm.

3. Stir peas and cream into cooking liquid to heat through. Spoon sauce over chicken and vegetables on platter.

EACH SERVING: About 380 calories, 36g protein, 30g carbohydrate, 12g total fat (6g saturated), 4g fiber, 127mg cholesterol, 680mg sodium ☺ 🍲

EXPRESS-LANE INGREDIENT: CANNED BROTHS

Homemade broth is wonderful to have on hand, but don't underestimate the convenience and quality of the canned variety. In addition to standard canned broths, supermarkets carry high-quality broths in vacuum-packed containers that rival homemade.

Many brands also offer reduced-sodium, no-salt-added, and fat-free options, but you can simulate these options yourself. To tame the saltiness of regular canned broth, dilute one 14½-ounce can of broth with ¾ cup water. To remove the fat from broth, freeze the unopened can for 2 hours or overnight; this will solidify a thin layer of surface fat. Open the can, lift off the fat, and discard it.

Red-Cooked Turkey Thighs with Leeks

Turkey takes a ride on the Orient Express with this Chinese-inspired dish, which features succulent meat simmered in a soy-and-fresh-ginger sauce.

ACTIVE TIME: 20 minutes
SLOW-COOK TIME: 8 hours on Low or 4 hours on High
MAKES: 6 main-dish servings

4	large leeks (2 pounds)
½	cup dry sherry
⅓	cup soy sauce
¼	cup packed brown sugar
2	tablespoons minced, peeled fresh ginger
1	teaspoon Chinese five-spice powder (see page 160)
3	small turkey thighs (1 pound each), skin removed
3	garlic cloves, crushed with garlic press
2	cups peeled baby carrots (about half of 16-ounce bag)

1. Cut off root and dark-green tops from leeks. Discard tough outer leaves. Cut each leek lengthwise in half, then crosswise in half. Rinse leeks in large bowl of cold water, swishing to remove sand. Transfer leeks to colander, leaving sand in bowl. Repeat several times, until no sand remains. Drain well.

2. In 4½- to 6-quart slow-cooker bowl, combine sherry, soy sauce, brown sugar, ginger, and five-spice powder. Add leeks, turkey, garlic, and carrots; toss to coat with soy mixture. Cover slow cooker with lid and cook on Low 8 to 10 hours or on High 4 to 5 hours.

3. Transfer turkey and vegetables to deep platter. Skim and discard fat from cooking liquid. Spoon cooking liquid over turkey and vegetables.

EACH SERVING: About 355 calories, 41g protein, 24g carbohydrate, 10g total fat (3g saturated), 2g fiber, 112mg cholesterol, 1,005mg sodium ☺ 🍲

Herbed Turkey Thighs and Orzo

This fragrant slow-cooked dish is infused with all the flavors of fall. Use leftover turkey to prepare our pita sandwiches.

ACTIVE TIME: 20 minutes
SLOW-COOK TIME: 7 hours on Low or 5 hours on High
MAKES: 4 main-dish servings

1	tablespoon olive oil
6	bone-in turkey thighs (6 to 8 pounds total), skin removed
½	teaspoon salt
½	teaspoon ground black pepper
1	cup reduced-sodium chicken broth
1	sprig fresh rosemary
4	garlic cloves, smashed
1	teaspoon cumin seeds
½	teaspoon dried oregano
1½	cups dry red wine
2	tablespoons freshly grated lemon peel
2	tablespoons chopped fresh dill
2	tablespoons chopped fresh parsley
1	cup orzo, cooked

1. In 12-inch skillet, heat oil over medium-high heat. Sprinkle turkey thighs with salt and pepper. In batches, add turkey to skillet; cook 7 to 8 minutes or until browned, turning once. Transfer to 6-quart slow-cooker bowl, along with broth and rosemary.

2. To same skillet, add garlic, cumin, and oregano. Cook 30 seconds, stirring. Add wine; cook 3 minutes or until wine is reduced by half, stirring and scraping up browned bits.

3. Pour contents of skillet into slow-cooker bowl. Cover slow cooker with lid and cook on Low 7 hours or on High 5 hours.

4. Meanwhile, combine lemon peel, dill, and parsley. Reserve half of herb mixture for turkey pitas; refrigerate in airtight container.

5. Transfer 2 turkey thighs to container; refrigerate up to 3 days. Divide remaining 4 turkey thighs among serving plates and garnish with remaining herb mixture. Transfer cooking liquid to fat separator; discard fat. In medium bowl, toss orzo with ½ *cup cooking liquid.* Serve turkey with orzo and remaining cooking liquid.

EACH SERVING: About 575 calories, 72g protein, 35g carbohydrate, 14g total fat (4g saturated), 2g fiber, 254mg cholesterol, 690mg sodium 🍲

TURKEY PITAS WITH CUCUMBER SALAD:

In medium bowl, combine *1 cup plain fat-free Greek yogurt* and *½ English (seedless) cucumber,* peeled and finely chopped. Stir in *1 tablespoon fresh lemon juice; 1 small garlic clove,* pressed; *reserved herb mixture;* and *¼ teaspoon salt.* Shred *reserved turkey* into chunks. Place in medium microwave-safe bowl; microwave on High 2 minutes. In large bowl, toss *12 ounces ripe tomatoes,* chopped; remaining *½ cucumber,* finely chopped; *½ small red onion,* finely chopped; *1 tablespoon fresh lemon juice; 2 teaspoons olive oil;* and *¼ teaspoon each salt and pepper.* Toast *4 pitas;* fill with turkey, cucumber salad, and *⅓ cup crumbled feta cheese.* Serves 4.

EACH SERVING: About 490 calories, 46g protein, 43g carbohydrate, 14g total fat (5g saturated), 3g fiber, 107mg cholesterol, 985mg sodium

Latin-Style Beef (*Ropa Vieja*)

The name of this braised beef translates literally as "old clothes," because the meat is cooked until it's so tender it can be shredded into what resembles a pile of rags.

ACTIVE TIME: 20 minutes
SLOW-COOK TIME: 9 hours on High or 6 hours on Low
MAKES: 10 main-dish servings

1   can (14½ ounces) diced tomatoes
1   tablespoon capers, drained
1   tablespoon ground cumin
½   teaspoon ground cinnamon
1   teaspoon salt
3   garlic cloves, sliced
2   large red, yellow, and/or green peppers, sliced
2   large pickled jalapeño chiles, sliced
1   medium onion, cut in half and sliced
1   fresh beef brisket (3 pounds)
Warm tortillas and/or cooked white rice with parsley (optional)

1. In 4½- to 6-quart slow-cooker bowl, combine tomatoes with their juice, capers, cumin, cinnamon, and salt. Add garlic, peppers, jalapeños, onion, and brisket; stir to coat brisket and vegetables with tomato mixture. Cover slow cooker with lid and cook on Low 9 to 10 hours or on High 6 hours to 6 hours 30 minutes, until meat is tender.

2. With slotted spoon, transfer brisket and vegetables to large bowl. With two forks, shred brisket with the grain into fine strips. Skim and discard fat from cooking liquid. Stir cooking liquid into brisket mixture. Serve brisket mixture with tortillas and/or rice, if you like.

EACH SERVING: About 400 calories, 35g protein, 7g carbohydrate, 25g total fat (9g saturated), 2g fiber, 109mg cholesterol, 690mg sodium ☺ 🍲

Beer-Braised Beef Stew

Pair this beef stew with a dark beer, and you'll have the perfect meal for a guys' night.

ACTIVE TIME: 30 minutes
SLOW-COOK TIME: 10 hours on Low
MAKES: 8 main-dish servings

1	boneless beef chuck roast (4 pounds), tied
¾	teaspoon salt
½	teaspoon ground black pepper
2	teaspoons vegetable oil
2	medium onions, sliced
2	pounds carrots, sliced
2	tablespoons water
1	bottle (12 ounces) dark beer (such as a brown ale)
⅓	cup distilled white vinegar
½	cup ketchup
⅓	cup golden raisins
3	tablespoons brown sugar

Steamed green beans for serving (optional)

1. Rub roast with ½ teaspoon each salt and pepper. In 12-inch skillet, heat oil over medium-high heat until very hot. Brown roast on all sides. Transfer to 6- to 7-quart slow-cooker bowl.

2. To skillet, add onions, carrots, water, and remaining ¼ teaspoon salt; cook over medium-high heat, stirring, 2 to 4 minutes or until slightly softened. Add beer and vinegar. Simmer 4 minutes, stirring. Transfer vegetables and liquids to slow-cooker bowl along with ketchup, raisins, and brown sugar.

3. Cover slow cooker with lid and cook 10 hours on Low or until roast is tender.

4. Skim and discard fat from cooking liquid. Slice meat; serve with vegetables and green beans, if desired. Drizzle with cooking liquid.

EACH SERVING: About 580 calories, 48g protein, 28g carbohydrate, 30g total fat (12g saturated), 4g fiber, 185mg cholesterol, 535mg sodium

QUICK TECHNIQUE: TYING A ROAST

It takes just a minute or two to tie a roast with kitchen twine. The payoff: The meat holds its shape so it cooks more evenly. Start by wrapping two strings lengthwise around the meat so it does not curl during cooking; knot and tie the strings. Then tie strings horizontally around the meat, at 2- to 3-inch intervals, until the roast forms a neat package. Snip off any excess string, and your roast is ready for the oven.

Pot Roast with Red Wine Sauce

Classic French flavors like thyme, pearl onions, and red wine season this easy slow-cooker meal. Use the leftovers to make our hearty pot-roast-and-black-bean chili, below.

ACTIVE TIME: 20 minutes
SLOW-COOK TIME: 10 hours on Low
MAKES: 6 main-dish servings

1	boneless beef chuck roast (4½ pounds), tied (see page 145)
¼	teaspoon salt
¼	teaspoon ground black pepper
1	teaspoon vegetable oil
1	pound carrots
1	pound frozen pearl onions
3	garlic cloves, crushed in a garlic press
½	teaspoon dried thyme
1	cup dry red wine
1	can (28 ounces) no-salt-added tomatoes, diced and drained
1	bay leaf

Fresh flat-leaf parsley leaves, chopped, for garnish

1. With paper towels, pat beef dry; season with salt and pepper.

2. In 12-inch skillet, heat oil over medium-high heat. Add beef and cook 10 to 13 minutes, turning to brown all sides. Transfer browned beef to 6-quart slow-cooker bowl.

3. While beef browns, peel carrots and cut into 2-inch chunks. Transfer to slow-cooker bowl.

4. To same skillet, add onions, garlic, and thyme. Cook 2 minutes or until golden, stirring often. Add wine; cook 3 minutes, stirring and scraping up browned bits. Transfer to slow-cooker bowl, along with tomatoes and bay leaf; cover and cook on Low 10 hours.

5. Transfer beef to cutting board; discard strings. Cut off one-third of beef; transfer to container along with one-third of vegetables. Refrigerate up to 3 days. Transfer remaining vegetables to serving platter; discard bay leaf.

6. Transfer cooking liquid from slow-cooker bowl to 8-cup liquid measuring cup; discard fat. Pour one-third of liquid into container; refrigerate up to 3 days.

7. Slice meat across grain and arrange on serving platter with vegetables. Pour remaining cooking liquid over all. Garnish with parsley.

EACH SERVING: About 515 calories, 47g protein, 11g carbohydrate, 30g total fat (12g saturated), 3g fiber, 181mg cholesterol, 205mg sodium ▭

POT ROAST CHILI: Chop *reserved beef and vegetables.* In 5-quart saucepot, heat *1 teaspoon vegetable oil* over medium heat. Add *2 garlic cloves,* crushed with garlic press; *4 teaspoons ground cumin;* and *1 teaspoon chili powder.* Stir in *2 cans (15 ounces each) no-salt-added black beans,* drained and rinsed; chopped beef and vegetables; *reserved cooking liquid;* and ¼ *teaspoon salt.* Heat to boiling, then reduce heat to simmer 10 minutes, stirring occasionally. Serve with *chopped fresh cilantro, sour cream, and lime wedges.*

EACH SERVING: About 380 calories, 31g protein, 26g carbohydrate, 16g total fat (6g saturated), 9g fiber, 91mg cholesterol, 225mg sodium ☺

Sweet and Tangy Braised Chuck Roast

The classic roast is given a sweet treatment here with gingersnap-cookie crumbs and raisins.

ACTIVE TIME: 10 minutes
SLOW-COOK TIME: 8 hours on Low or 6 hours on High
MAKES: 6 main-dish servings

6   (2-inch) gingersnap cookies, crushed into fine crumbs

2   cups peeled baby carrots (about half of 16-ounce bag)

2   large stalks celery, cut crosswise into 2-inch pieces

1   medium onion, cut into 1-inch pieces

1   cup dry red wine

2   tablespoons red wine vinegar

¼   cup dark seedless raisins

1   teaspoon salt

½   teaspoon ground black pepper

1   boneless beef chuck roast (2 pounds)

1. In 4½- to 6-quart slow-cooker bowl, combine gingersnap crumbs, carrots, celery, onion, wine, vinegar, raisins, salt, and pepper.

2. Place roast on top of vegetables. Cover slow cooker with lid and cook on Low 8 to 10 hours or on High 6 to 6½ hours, until roast is very tender.

3. Place roast on warm platter. Skim and discard fat from cooking liquid. Serve roast with vegetables and sauce.

EACH SERVING: About 360 calories, 25g protein, 17g carbohydrate, 21g total fat (8g saturated), 2g fiber, 83mg cholesterol, 540mg sodium ☺ 🧺

Red Wine-Braised Short Ribs

This rich and flavorful rib recipe is perfect for any dinner party or decadent night in. We like it tossed with egg noodles. For photo, see page 132.

ACTIVE TIME: 20 minutes
SLOW-COOK TIME: 10 hours on Low or 5 hours on High
MAKES: 8 main-dish servings

4   pounds bone-in beef short ribs
½   teaspoon salt
½   teaspoon ground black pepper
2   teaspoons vegetable oil
1½ cups Burgundy or pinot noir wine
1   tablespoon beef broth concentrate or demi-glace
2   tablespoons tomato paste
2   dried bay leaves
½   teaspoon dried thyme
1½ pounds carrots, cut into 2-inch sticks
8   ounces portobello mushroom caps, chopped
12 ounces cooked egg noodles (optional)
Chopped fresh parsley for serving

1. Sprinkle short ribs with salt and pepper on all sides. In 12-inch skillet, heat oil over medium-high heat until very hot. In batches, brown short ribs just on meaty sides.

2. Meanwhile, in 6- to 7-quart slow-cooker bowl, whisk together wine, broth, tomato paste, bay leaves, and thyme; add carrots and mushrooms. Transfer meat to slow-cooker bowl.

3. Cover slow cooker with lid and cook 5 hours on High or 10 hours on Low, or until very tender. Transfer meat to cutting board. Skim and discard fat from cooking liquid.

4. Transfer cooking liquid to 4-quart saucepot; heat to boiling over medium-high heat. Boil 5 to 10 minutes or until reduced by about half.

5. Remove and discard bay leaves. Serve meat and vegetables on top of egg noodles, if you like. Drizzle with reduced sauce and top with parsley.

EACH SERVING WITHOUT NOODLES: About 590 calories, 26g protein, 11g carbohydrate, 29g total fat (20g saturated), 3g fiber, 107mg cholesterol, 370mg sodium

Spaghetti and Meatballs

Use the leftover meatballs from this slow-cooked family favorite to make our hearty subs. They're topped with melted mozzarella and served on toasted Italian rolls.

ACTIVE TIME: 15 minutes
SLOW-COOK TIME: 6 hours on Low or 3 hours on High
MAKES: 4 main-dish servings

1½	pounds 85% lean ground beef chuck
½	pound ground pork
¼	cup dry bread crumbs
¼	cup grated Parmesan cheese, plus additional for serving
¼	cup very finely chopped fresh flat-leaf parsley leaves
1	large egg, lightly beaten
3	garlic cloves, 2 crushed with garlic press, 1 thinly sliced
1	tablespoon olive oil
1	teaspoon salt
½	teaspoon freshly ground black pepper
1	can (28 ounces) whole tomatoes, drained
1	can (14½ ounces) tomato puree
2	sprigs fresh basil
¼	teaspoon crushed red pepper
12	ounces spaghetti

1. In large bowl, with hands, combine beef, pork, bread crumbs, Parmesan, parsley, egg, crushed garlic, oil, ½ teaspoon salt, and ¼ teaspoon black pepper until well mixed. Form into 24 (1½-inch) meatballs. Meatballs can be refrigerated overnight.

2. Crush tomatoes into bits and place in 6-quart slow-cooker bowl (see Tip). Stir in tomato puree, basil, crushed red pepper, sliced garlic, and remaining ½ teaspoon salt and ¼ teaspoon black pepper. Gently stir in meatballs.

3. Cover slow cooker with lid and cook on Low 6 hours or on High 3 hours.

4. Prepare spaghetti as label directs. Divide among serving dishes. Transfer 12 meatballs and half of sauce to container; refrigerate up to 3 days. Top spaghetti with remaining meatballs and sauce; serve with additional Parmesan.

EACH SERVING: About 665 calories, 36g protein, 74g carbohydrate, 24g total fat (9g saturated), 5g fiber, 104mg cholesterol, 765mg sodium 🍲

TIP: *In true Italian tradition, we suggest crushing the tomatoes with your hands. (It's quick, it's surprisingly unmessy, and it makes a juicier sauce.) If you prefer, you can snip the tomatoes into small bits with scissors instead.*

MEATBALL SUBS: Arrange oven rack 6 inches from broiler heat source. Preheat broiler. Line baking pan with foil. In 4-quart saucepan, heat *reserved meatballs and sauce* over medium-high heat 5 minutes or until heated through. Split *4 (5-inch-long) Italian rolls* in half. Slice *1 garlic clove* in half and rub onto cut sides of rolls. Place rolls on prepared pan, cut sides facing up, and broil 2 to 3 minutes or until just golden. Divide reserved meatballs and sauce among rolls. Top with *4 ounces fresh mozzarella cheese,* thinly sliced. Broil 2 minutes or until cheese melts. Serves 4.

EACH SERVING: About 615 calories, 36g protein, 47g carbohydrate, 31g total fat (13g saturated), 3g fiber, 126mg cholesterol, 1,200mg sodium

Chinese Red-Cooked Pork Shoulder

This fragrant, Asian-style stew is simmered for hours in a combination of soy sauce, dry sherry, fresh ginger, and orange peel.

ACTIVE TIME: 30 minutes
TOTAL TIME: 8 hours on Low
MAKES: 10 main-dish servings

¼ cup packed brown sugar

¼ cup dry sherry

¼ cup seasoned rice vinegar

¼ cup plus 1 tablespoon reduced-sodium soy sauce

1 medium onion, chopped

1 piece (2 inches) fresh ginger, peeled and thinly sliced into rounds

2 garlic cloves, crushed with garlic press

2 strips (3" by ¾" each) fresh orange peel

1 stick cinnamon

1 whole star anise

1 bag (1 pound) peeled baby carrots

4 pounds well-trimmed boneless pork shoulder, cut into 1½-inch chunks (see Tip)

2 packages (10 ounces each) frozen broccoli flowerets, thawed

1. In 6- to 6½-quart slow-cooker bowl, combine brown sugar, sherry, rice vinegar, and ¼ cup soy sauce. Stir in onion, ginger, garlic, orange peel, cinnamon, star anise, and carrots. Top with pork; do not stir. Cover slow cooker with lid and cook on Low 8 hours.

2. Open lid and stir in thawed broccoli. Cover and continue to cook until broccoli is heated through, about 10 minutes.

3. Discard cinnamon and star anise. Skim and discard fat from cooking liquid. Stir in remaining 1 tablespoon soy sauce and serve.

EACH SERVING: About 335 calories, 38g protein, 16g carbohydrate, 13g total fat (4g saturated), 2g fiber, 121mg cholesterol, 645mg sodium ☺ 🍱

TIP: *If the pork is not well trimmed when you buy it, purchase 5 pounds and cut away the excess fat and skin in order to get 4 pounds of solid meat.*

Chipotle Pork Tacos

Prepare the meat in the morning and come home to tasty, spicy tacos with this easy make-ahead meal.

ACTIVE TIME: 25 minutes
SLOW-COOK TIME: 7 hours on High or 10 hours on Low
MAKES: 12 main-dish servings

3   tablespoons chopped chipotles in adobo
2   teaspoons chili powder
1   teaspoon grated lime peel
¾   teaspoon salt
¾   teaspoon ground black pepper
1   boneless pork shoulder (Boston butt; 4 to 5 pounds)
½   cup ketchup
¼   cup orange juice
2   tablespoons Worcestershire sauce
¼   teaspoon ground cinnamon
1   medium onion, chopped
2   garlic cloves, chopped
Flour tortillas (soft-taco size), shredded green cabbage, sliced radishes, chopped fresh cilantro, and lime wedges for serving

1. In small bowl, combine chipotles, chili powder, lime peel, and ½ teaspoon each salt and pepper. Cut pork shoulder into 4 equal pieces. Season with rub mixture.

2. In 6- to 7-quart slow-cooker bowl, whisk together ketchup, orange juice, Worcestershire sauce, cinnamon, and remaining ¼ teaspoon each salt and pepper; add onion and garlic. Place meat on top of vegetables in slow-cooker bowl.

3. Cover slow cooker with lid and cook 7 hours on High or 10 hours on Low or until very tender. Transfer meat to cutting board. Skim and discard fat from cooking liquid.

4. With hands, shred meat (discard fat and gristle). Return meat to slow-cooker bowl with sauce. Serve meat with tortillas, cabbage, radishes, cilantro, and lime wedges.

EACH SERVING: About 410 calories, 31g protein, 31g carbohydrate, 18g total fat (6g saturated), 2g fiber, 100mg cholesterol, 730mg sodium ☺ 🛒

Low 'n' Slow Ribs with Asian Cucumber Salad

Just twenty minutes of prep time yields delectable teriyaki-glazed ribs — and a side of Asian-style slaw — come dinnertime.

ACTIVE TIME: 20 minutes
SLOW-COOK TIME: 8 hours on Low or 4 hours on High
MAKES: 8 main-dish servings

3½ pounds pork spareribs
1 cup teriyaki glaze
1 English (seedless) cucumber (12 to 14 ounces), peeled and thinly sliced
1 bag (10 ounces) shredded carrots
¼ cup seasoned rice vinegar

1. In 4½- to 6-quart slow-cooker bowl, place ribs and teriyaki glaze, spreading teriyaki to coat ribs on all sides. Cover slow cooker with lid and cook on Low 8 hours or on High 4 hours.

2. Meanwhile, in medium bowl, stir cucumber, carrots, and rice vinegar until blended. Cover and refrigerate until ready to serve. Makes 4 cups salad.

3. To serve, transfer ribs to cutting board; cut into portions. Skim and discard fat from cooking liquid. Arrange ribs and salad on dinner plates. Spoon remaining liquid over ribs.

EACH SERVING: About 390 calories per serving, 26g protein, 18g carbohydrate, 22g total fat (9g saturated), 1g fiber, 89mg cholesterol, 1,185mg sodium ☺ 🍲

EXPRESS-LANE INGREDIENT: TERIYAKI SAUCE

This luscious Japanese sauce is a made from soy sauce, sake (or sherry), sugar, ginger, and other seasonings. It's a handy ingredient to have in your pantry for marinating beef, pork, or chicken; the sugar in the teriyaki caramelizes as the meat cooks, forming a nice glaze. For the Low 'n' Slow Ribs above, we got the most luscious, stick-to-your-ribs results using a thick teriyaki glaze (such as Kikkoman's Teriyaki Baste & Glaze).

Mediterranean Seafood Stew

Slow-cooking the liquid and vegetable base for this stew loads it with flavor, and throwing the seafood in toward the end keeps it sweet and tender. We like this served with crusty dinner rolls to soak up the juices. For a second tasty dinner, use leftovers to prepare the paella recipe below.

ACTIVE TIME: 20 minutes
SLOW-COOK TIME: 3 hours 30 minutes on High
MAKES: 4 main-dish servings

2   large leeks, white and pale-green parts only

1½   pounds fennel bulbs (about 2), trimmed and finely chopped

2¼   pounds ripe tomatoes, chopped

2   garlic cloves, chopped

1   teaspoon salt

½   teaspoon freshly ground black pepper

4   sprigs fresh thyme

8   sprigs fresh flat-leaf parsley, stems and leaves separated

1   pound mussels, beards removed, well scrubbed (see page 222)

1   pound peeled and deveined shrimp (16 to 20 count)

12   ounces skinless cod fillet, cut into 4-inch pieces

2   teaspoons extra-virgin olive oil

1. Cut root ends from leeks. Cut each leek lengthwise in half, then into ¼-inch-thick slices. Place in large bowl of cold water. With hands, swish leeks to remove grit. Repeat process, changing water several times. Drain.

2. Transfer leeks to 6-quart slow-cooker bowl along with fennel, tomatoes, garlic, salt, and pepper. With kitchen twine, tie thyme and parsley stems together. Bury in vegetable mixture.

3. Cover slow cooker with lid and cook on High 3 hours. Stir in mussels and shrimp, and lay fish on top. Immediately cover and cook 30 to 40 minutes longer or until mussels open and shrimp and fish turn opaque throughout.

4. Divide mussels among serving dishes. Discard herb bundle. Transfer 3 cups stew to container; refrigerate overnight. Divide remaining stew among serving dishes. Drizzle oil over stew. Chop reserved parsley leaves; sprinkle over stew.

EACH SERVING: About 375 calories, 32g protein, 46g carbohydrate, 7g total fat (1g saturated), 6g fiber, 112mg cholesterol, 1,250mg sodium ☺ 🍲

PAELLA: Preheat oven to 400°F. In 5-quart Dutch oven or other oven-safe heavy pot, heat *1 tablespoon olive oil* over medium-high heat. Add *4 ounces dry-cured Spanish chorizo,* cut into ¼-inch-thick half-moons. Cook, stirring, 2 to 3 minutes or until browned. Add *1½ cups Arborio rice;* cook, stirring, 2 minutes or until toasted. Stir in *reserved seafood stew; 1 can (14½ ounces) reduced-sodium chicken broth;* and *¼ cup fresh flat-leaf parsley leaves,* finely chopped. Heat to boiling and cook 5 minutes. Transfer to oven; bake 15 minutes. Cover; bake 5 minutes longer. Let stand 5 minutes. Garnish with *additional parsley;* serve with *lemon wedges.* Serves 4.

EACH SERVING: About 485 calories, 23g protein, 63g carbohydrate, 15g total fat (5g saturated), 4g fiber, 77mg cholesterol, 1,005mg sodium

Butternut Squash Barley Risotto

A slow cooker makes this creamy, comforting barley-based risotto blissfully convenient to prepare. This is a generous recipe—use the leftovers to make risotto cakes with a fresh tomato salad, opposite.

ACTIVE TIME: 15 minutes
SLOW-COOK TIME: 3 hours 30 minutes on High
MAKES: 9 main-dish servings

2	tablespoons butter or margarine
2	shallots, thinly sliced
2	sprigs fresh thyme
2	cups pearl barley
1	carton (32 ounces) vegetable broth
2	cups water
1	large butternut squash (2½ pounds), peeled, seeded, and cut into ½-inch cubes (see Tip)
1½	teaspoons salt
⅔	cup freshly grated Parmesan cheese
¼	teaspoon ground black pepper
2	tablespoons chopped fresh flat-leaf parsley leaves

1. In 12-inch skillet, melt 1 tablespoon butter over medium-high heat. Add shallots and cook, stirring frequently, 2 minutes or until golden. Add thyme; cook 30 seconds. Add barley and cook, stirring frequently, 2 minutes or until toasted and golden.

2. Transfer barley mixture to 6-quart slow-cooker bowl, along with broth, water, squash, and ½ teaspoon salt. Cover slow cooker with lid and cook on High 3 hours 30 minutes to 4 hours or until liquid is absorbed and squash is tender.

3. Discard thyme, then add Parmesan, remaining 1 tablespoon butter, 1 teaspoon salt, and pepper. Gently stir until butter and Parmesan melt. Transfer risotto to serving plates and garnish with parsley. Leftovers can be stored, covered, in refrigerator up to 3 days.

EACH SERVING: About 235 calories, 7g protein, 45g carbohydrate, 4g total fat (1g saturated), 10g fiber, 3mg cholesterol, 670mg sodium ☺ 🍲

TIP: Want to cut 5 minutes from your prep time? Purchase already peeled and chopped butternut squash from the supermarket.

Risotto Cakes with Tomato Salad: In large bowl, combine *2 1/4 pounds ripe tomatoes,* seeded and chopped; *1 small garlic clove,* crushed in garlic press; *1 tablespoon balsamic vinegar; 1 tablespoon olive oil; 1/4 teaspoon salt;* and *1/8 teaspoon ground black pepper.* Stir in *1/4 cup fresh basil leaves,* torn. In a separate large bowl, combine *3 1/2 cups leftover risotto; 1 large egg; 1/4 cup freshly grated Pecorino-Romano cheese; 1/4 cup fresh basil leaves,* finely chopped; and *1/4 teaspoon ground black pepper.* Using 1/3-cup measuring cup, form mixture into 12 patties about 3/4 inch thick. In nonstick 12-inch skillet, heat *1 teaspoon vegetable oil* over medium heat 1 minute. Add 6 patties. Cook 8 minutes or until golden brown, turning patties over once halfway through. Repeat with remaining mixture. Serve with tomato salad.

Each serving (2 patties): About 220 calories, 8g protein, 29g carbohydrate, 9g total fat (2g saturated), 7g fiber, 39mg cholesterol, 490mg sodium ☺

White Chili with Black Beans

Perfect for a cold winter day, this vegetarian slow-cooker recipe will please everyone.

Active time: 20 minutes
Slow-cook time: 6 hours on High or 9 hours on Low
Makes: 8 main-dish servings

2	teaspoons vegetable oil
1	medium onion, chopped
2	garlic cloves chopped
1	teaspoon chili powder
1/4	teaspoon salt
1	package (20 ounces) peeled butternut squash chunks, cut into quarters
1	can (15 ounces) reduced-sodium black beans, rinsed and drained
2	cups dried lentils, rinsed
5	cups reduced-sodium chicken or vegetable broth
1	jar (16 ounces) salsa verde
1	can (4 ounces) chopped green chiles

Shredded Cheddar cheese and lime wedges for serving (optional)

1. In 12-inch skillet, heat oil over medium heat. Add onion, garlic, chili powder, and salt. Cook, stirring frequently, 1 to 3 minutes or until slightly softened. Transfer to 6- to 7-quart slow-cooker bowl.

2. To slow-cooker bowl, add squash, black beans, lentils, broth, salsa verde, and chiles.

3. Cover slow cooker with lid and cook 6 hours on High or 9 to 10 hours on Low, or until lentils are tender. Serve with shredded Cheddar and lime wedges, if desired.

Each serving: About 285 calories, 17g protein, 50g carbohydrate, 3g total fat (0g saturated), 15g fiber, 0mg cholesterol, 885mg sodium ☺ ▦

6

Hot from the Oven

This chapter is full of hearty fare that will satisfy your whole family. Whether you choose to make baked chicken, mac and cheese, or a roast, once the dish is in the oven, you can go about your business until the kitchen timer goes off, then serve a piping-hot dinner with ease.

If you're like most family cooks, you probably prepare chicken a couple of nights a week. We hope you'll enjoy sampling new options like Chicken Tenders with Five-Spice BBQ Sauce and Deviled Chicken Thighs with Mashed Sweet Potatoes; both are sure kid pleasers. Or bake up our cheesy Turkey Enchiladas, made with roasted boneless turkey breast from the deli counter to save you time.

Pork tenderloin is quick roasting and so satisfying that we've included two recipes: one made with a sweet and savory marinade, the other with roasted grapes. Ground beef and packaged mashed potatoes allow you to make a cozy shepherd's pie in just twenty minutes.

Oven-baked fish could not be easier to prepare, or more healthful. Try our Greek-Style Tilapia with orzo and tomatoes or Tarragon-Citrus-Crusted Salmon, which includes a quick coleslaw. Meatless mains like Artichoke and Goat Cheese Pizza and Black Bean and Corn Tortilla Pie will be popular with meat eaters and vegetarians alike. Or try our baked mac and cheese, which sneaks in some tomatoes to ensure everyone is eating their vegetables.

Tarragon-Citrus-Crusted Salmon (recipe page 174)

Chicken Tenders with Five-Spice BBQ Sauce

These succulent, oven-fried chicken tenders are jazzed up with sesame seeds and Chinese five-spice powder, an indispensable blend of seasonings that showcases the five basic flavors of Chinese cuisine — sweet, sour, bitter, savory, and salty. More good news: Oven-frying keeps the saturated fat in check.

TOTAL TIME: 30 minutes
MAKES: 4 main-dish servings

¾   cup panko (Japanese-style bread crumbs)
2   tablespoons sesame seeds
1   large egg white
1   teaspoon Chinese five-spice powder
½   teaspoon salt
1   pound chicken-breast tenders
1   tablespoon olive oil
1   small onion (4 to 6 ounces), chopped
½   cup ketchup
1   tablespoon brown sugar
1½   teaspoons cider vinegar
1½   teaspoons Worcestershire sauce

1. Preheat oven to 475°F. In 10-inch skillet, toast bread crumbs and sesame seeds over high heat, stirring frequently, about 5 minutes or until golden. Transfer crumb mixture to plate.

2. In medium bowl, with wire whisk or fork, mix egg white, ½ teaspoon five-spice powder, and salt until foamy. Dip tenders in egg-white mixture, then in crumb mixture to coat. Place tenders on cookie sheet. Bake tenders, without turning, 13 to 15 minutes or until cooked through (165°F).

3. Meanwhile, in same skillet, heat oil over medium heat. Add onion and cook 8 to 10 minutes or until soft and lightly browned. Remove skillet from heat; stir in ketchup, sugar, vinegar, Worcestershire sauce, and remaining ½ teaspoon five-spice powder. Pour sauce into small bowl; serve with tenders.

EACH SERVING: About 280 calories, 30g protein, 23g carbohydrate, 8g total fat (1g saturated), 66mg cholesterol, 775mg sodium ☺

EXPRESS-LANE INGREDIENT: FIVE-SPICE POWDER

To add complex layers of flavor fast, try the power of five spices. A staple in Chinese cuisine, five-spice powder is a fragrant blend of seasonings. The usual mix is star anise, cinnamon, Szechuan peppercorns, fennel seeds, and cloves. You could buy all of these spices to grind and combine them yourself, but with store-bought five-spice powder, it's as easy as shaking it on. Just be sure to do so sparingly—this mix is slightly sweet but very pungent. We love it stirred into soy sauce and honey to make a quick glaze for everything from pork to poultry.

Crispy Sesame-Panko Chicken

Using panko rather than regular bread crumbs keeps the coating light so all the flavors can shine through.

Active time: 20 minutes
Total time: 30 minutes
Makes: 4 main-dish servings

1   large egg
½   teaspoon garlic powder
2   teaspoons mustard powder
1¾   teaspoons ground ginger
½   teaspoon ground black pepper
1   cup panko (Japanese-style bread crumbs)
3   tablespoons sesame seeds
1¼   pounds thin chicken cutlets
Nonstick cooking spray
1   pound cabbage, shredded
1   green onion, thinly sliced
1   teaspoon sugar
2   tablespoons plus 2 teaspoons cider vinegar
1   tablespoon plus ½ teaspoon reduced-
      sodium soy sauce
¼   teaspoon salt
¾   cup ketchup
1   teaspoon Worcestershire sauce
⅛   teaspoon cayenne (ground red) pepper

1. Preheat oven to 450°F. Place rack in 18" by 12" jelly-roll pan lined with foil. Spray with nonstick cooking spray.

2. In shallow dish, whisk egg, garlic powder, 1 teaspoon mustard powder, 1 teaspoon ginger, and ¼ teaspoon black pepper. In another dish, mix panko and sesame seeds.

3. Dip chicken into egg, then panko mix. Place on rack. Spray chicken with cooking spray; bake 15 to 20 minutes or until cooked through. (Instant-read thermometer inserted horizontally into center of chicken should reach 165°F.)

4. Meanwhile, toss cabbage with onion, sugar, 2 tablespoons vinegar, ½ teaspoon soy sauce, and ¼ teaspoon each salt and black pepper.

5. In bowl, mix ketchup, Worcestershire, cayenne pepper, and remaining 1 tablespoon soy sauce, 2 teaspoons vinegar, 1 teaspoon mustard powder, and ¾ teaspoon ginger. Serve chicken with sauce and slaw.

Each serving: About 435 calories, 38g protein, 42g carbohydrate, 12g total fat (1g saturated), 3g fiber, 137mg cholesterol, 1,070mg sodium ☺

Almond-Crusted Chicken and Slaw

These quick-cooking cutlets get their oven-crisped coating from chopped almonds. Carrots, red cabbage, oranges, and yellow peppers combine to create a colorful, crunchy slaw.

ACTIVE TIME: 20 minutes
TOTAL TIME: 30 minutes
MAKES: 4 main-dish servings

2	medium oranges
4	cups red cabbage (12 ounces), thinly sliced
2	large carrots, cut into thin matchsticks
1	large yellow pepper, very thinly sliced
2	tablespoons snipped chives
3	tablespoons white wine vinegar
4	teaspoons canola oil
½	teaspoon salt
½	teaspoon freshly ground black pepper
1	tablespoon all-purpose flour
½	cup almonds, very finely chopped
1	large egg white
¼	teaspoon ground cumin
¼	teaspoon no-salt-added chili powder
4	skinless, boneless chicken-breast cutlets (4 ounces each)

1. Arrange oven rack in lowest position; place 15" by 10" jelly-roll pan on rack. Preheat oven to 450°F.

2. Cut peel and white pith from oranges; discard trimmings. Cut oranges into segments; transfer, with their juices, to large bowl. Add cabbage, carrots, yellow pepper, chives, vinegar, 1 teaspoon oil, and ¼ teaspoon each salt and pepper. Toss well; let slaw stand.

3. Spread flour on medium plate; spread almonds on separate plate. In pie plate, beat egg white until foamy.

4. Sprinkle cumin, chili, and remaining ¼ teaspoon each salt and pepper over chicken. Press one side of 1 piece chicken in flour; shake off excess. Dip same side in egg white; press into nuts. Repeat with remaining chicken.

5. Remove hot pan from oven; brush with remaining oil. Add chicken, nut side down; roast 10 to 12 minutes or until chicken just loses its pink color throughout. (An instant-read thermometer inserted horizontally into cutlet should register 165°F.) Serve with slaw.

EACH SERVING: About 350 calories, 30g protein, 28g carbohydrate, 15g total fat (2g saturated), 7g fiber, 63mg cholesterol, 425mg sodium ☺ ♥

Deviled Chicken with Mashed Sweet Potatoes

These crispy, spicy chicken strips owe their devilish quality to healthy doses of cayenne pepper and garlic. Served atop velvety mashed sweet potatoes, this meal will please all.

Total time: 30 minutes
Makes: 4 main-dish servings

¼	cup Dijon mustard
2	tablespoons Worcestershire sauce
¼	teaspoon cayenne (ground red) pepper
1	garlic clove, crushed with garlic press
⅓	cup panko (Japanese-style bread crumbs)
¼	cup loosely packed fresh parsley leaves, chopped
2	pound skinless, boneless chicken thighs, cut into 1-inch-wide strips
4	medium sweet potatoes (12 ounces each), not peeled
1	tablespoon butter or margarine
¼	teaspoon salt
¼	teaspoon freshly ground black pepper

1. Position rack 5 to 7 inches from heat source and preheat broiler. Grease 15½" by 10½" jelly-roll pan.

2. In large bowl, mix mustard, Worcestershire, cayenne, and garlic until blended. On waxed paper, combine bread crumbs and parsley.

3. Toss chicken with mustard mixture; place in jelly-roll pan. Broil chicken, 5 to 7 inches from source of heat, 8 minutes. Remove pan from broiler, and sprinkle chicken with crumbs (do not turn chicken). Broil 2 minutes longer or until crumbs are browned and juices run clear when thickest part of thigh is pierced with knife.

(Instant-read thermometer inserted horizontally into center of chicken should reach 165°F.)

4. Meanwhile, place potatoes in microwave-safe large bowl; cover with vented plastic wrap. Microwave on High 5 minutes. Rearrange potatoes and cook 5 minutes longer or until tender. Cool potatoes 5 minutes. Cut each potato lengthwise in half and scoop flesh from skin into same bowl; discard skin. With potato masher, coarsely mash potatoes with butter, salt, and black pepper. Serve with chicken strips.

Each serving: About 580 calories, 46g protein, 52g carbohydrate, 20g total fat (7g saturated), 156mg cholesterol, 837mg sodium

Apricot Chicken Hash

Glaze roasted chicken thighs with sweet apricot jam and serve atop a potato and red pepper hash.

TOTAL TIME: 30 minutes
MAKES: 4 main-dish servings

8	skinless, boneless chicken thighs (1¾ pounds)
1	tablespoon reduced-sodium soy sauce
1	pound red potatoes, not tpeeled
1	large red pepper (8 to 10 ounces)
3	tablespoons apricot jam
1	tablespoon fresh lemon juice
1½	teaspoons vegetable oil
4	green onions, thinly sliced
¼	teaspoon salt

1. Preheat oven to 425°F. In large bowl, combine chicken and soy sauce; let stand. Cut potatoes and red pepper into ½-inch pieces. In small bowl, mix jam and lemon juice until blended.

2. In large microwave-safe bowl, combine potatoes with *¼ cup water*. Cover with vented plastic wrap and microwave on High 5 minutes or until potatoes are just tender. Drain.

3. Meanwhile, spread chicken on foil-lined 18" by 12" jelly-roll pan; brush with jam mixture. Roast 15 to 17 minutes or until instant-read thermometer registers 165°F.

4. Meanwhile, in nonstick 12-inch skillet, heat oil over medium heat 1 minute. Add red pepper and cook 3 minutes, stirring. Stir in potatoes, green onions, and salt. Cook, stirring, 5 to 7 minutes. Skim and discard fat from pan juices; serve chicken and hash with juices.

EACH SERVING: About 435 calories, 43g protein, 44g carbohydrate, 9g total fat (2g saturated), 5g fiber, 164mg cholesterol, 435mg sodium ☺

Chicken and Orzo Pilaf

Fresh vegetables and goat cheese round out this tasty meal. For photo, see page 13.

TOTAL TIME: 30 minutes
MAKES: 4 main-dish servings

1	lemon
1	pint cherry tomatoes, cut in half
1	medium orange pepper (8 ounces), chopped
3	garlic cloves, crushed with garlic press
2	tablespoons extra-virgin olive oil
¼	teaspoon dried oregano
¼	teaspoon salt
¼	teaspoon freshly ground black pepper
1	pound skinless, boneless chicken breasts, cut into 1-inch chunks
1	cup whole-wheat orzo pasta
4	stalks celery, thinly sliced at angle
2	ounces goat cheese, crumbled (½ cup)

1. Preheat oven to 450°F. Heat saucepan of *water* to boiling over high heat. From lemon, grate 1 teaspoon peel and squeeze 2 tablespoons juice.

2. On one side of 18" by 12" jelly-roll pan, toss tomatoes and orange pepper with garlic, 1 tablespoon oil, and ⅛ teaspoon each oregano, salt, and black pepper. On other side of pan, toss chicken with lemon peel, remaining 1 tablespoon oil, and remaining ⅛ teaspoon each oregano, salt, and black pepper. Roast 13 minutes or until chicken is cooked through (165°F).

3. Meanwhile, cook orzo as label directs. Drain well and transfer to large bowl. Add chicken and vegetables to orzo, along with celery and lemon juice. Toss until well mixed. Top with goat cheese.

EACH SERVING: About 420 calories, 34g protein, 41g carbohydrate, 14g total fat (4g saturated), 7g fiber, 79mg cholesterol, 325mg sodium ☺ ♥

Turkey Enchiladas

Roasted turkey breast from the deli counter and canned enchilada sauce are the secrets to these zesty enchiladas, a satisfying meal the whole family will enjoy.

ACTIVE TIME: 10 minutes
TOTAL TIME: 30 minutes
MAKES: 5 main-dish servings

12 ounces roasted boneless turkey breast (from deli), chopped

1 can (8¾ ounces) no-salt-added corn, drained

1 container (8 ounces) reduced-fat sour cream

1½ cups shredded reduced-fat (2%) Mexican cheese blend

2 tablespoons chopped fresh cilantro leaves

10 (6-inch) corn tortillas, warmed to soften

1 can (10 ounces) enchilada sauce

1 cup mild salsa

1. Preheat oven to 400°F. Spray 13″ by 19″ baking dish with nonstick cooking spray.

2. In large bowl, combine turkey, corn, sour cream, ¾ cup cheese, and 1 tablespoon cilantro.

3. Place about ⅓ cup turkey mixture on each tortilla and roll up tightly. Arrange in prepared baking dish, seam side down. Repeat with remaining tortillas and filling.

4. In bowl, stir enchilada sauce with salsa; pour over tortillas to cover. Top with remaining ¾ cup cheese. Bake 15 to 20 minutes or until cheese melts and enchiladas are heated through. Sprinkle with remaining 1 tablespoon cilantro.

EACH SERVING: About 445 calories, 34g protein, 42g carbohydrate, 16g total fat (7g saturated), 6g fiber, 98mg cholesterol, 725mg sodium ☺

EXPRESS-LANE INGREDIENT: VISIT THE DELI CASE

Leftover roast turkey, chicken, and beef make a convenient start to a quick weeknight meal when you have them. When you don't, visit the deli case at your local supermarket. There, you can buy roasted boneless turkey breast, as we did to make these Turkey Enchiladas. Or purchase a small smoked chicken breast, salami, or slices of roast beef and add them to salad for a hearty meal in a bowl. You only need a small amount of protein to make a meal—and the payoff is less time in the kitchen.

Upside-Down Shepherd's Pie

This casserole was originally created as a way to use up the leftovers from Sunday dinners, but thanks to ground beef and packaged mashed potatoes you can have it anytime. The prep time for this recipe has been slashed to a bare minimum too.

TOTAL TIME: 20 minutes
MAKES: 4 main-dish servings

1	package (20 ounces) refrigerated mashed potatoes (see Tip)
1	pound 90% lean ground beef
1	tablespoon butter or margarine
1	cup chopped onion
1/3	cup ketchup
1	teaspoon dried dill weed
1/2	cup loosely packed fresh parsley leaves, chopped
1/3	cup reduced-fat sour cream

1. Preheat oven to 450°F. Spray 1½-quart ceramic or glass baking dish or deep-dish pie plate with nonstick cooking spray. Press cold mashed potatoes onto bottom and up side of casserole. Bake potato crust 20 minutes or until edge is golden.

2. Meanwhile, heat 10-inch skillet over medium-high heat. Add ground beef and cook 4 to 5 minutes or until beef is no longer pink, breaking it up with side of spoon. Spoon beef into bowl lined with paper towels to drain.

3. In same skillet, melt butter over medium heat. Add onion and cook, stirring occasionally, 6 to 7 minutes or until tender and golden. Return beef to skillet. Stir in ketchup and dill. Reduce heat to low; stir in parsley and sour cream.

4. To serve, spoon ground-beef mixture into mashed-potato crust.

EACH SERVING: About 490 calories, 26g protein, 31g carbohydrate, 29g total fat (12g saturated), 94mg cholesterol, 945mg sodium 🍲

TIP: *For a change of pace, replace half of the mashed potatoes with an equal amount of cooked mashed parsnips or carrots.*

Pork Tenderloin with Roasted Grapes

Roasted grapes are absolutely delicious and a perfect match for the sweetness of pork. A side of mashed potatoes and kale — made quickly in the microwave — completes the meal.

ACTIVE TIME: 15 minutes
TOTAL TIME: 30 minutes
MAKES: 4 main-dish servings

1	teaspoon fennel seeds, crushed
¾	teaspoon salt
½	teaspoon coarsely ground black pepper
1	pork tenderloin (1 pound)
4	teaspoons extra-virgin olive oil
3	cups seedless red and green grapes (1 pound)
½	cup canned chicken broth
1½	pounds Yukon gold potatoes
1	garlic clove, crushed with garlic press
1	bag (16 ounces) ready-to-cook chopped kale
⅓	cup water
¾	cup low-fat (1%) milk, warmed

1. Preheat oven to 475°F. In cup, with fork, stir fennel seeds, salt, and pepper. Rub mixture all over pork.

2. In 12-inch skillet with oven-safe handle, heat oil over medium-high until very hot. Add pork and cook 5 minutes, turning to brown all sides.

3. Add grapes and broth to skillet; heat to boiling. Cover and place in oven. Roast until instant-read thermometer inserted in center of roast reaches 145°F, 15 to 18 minutes. Transfer pork to warm platter; set grapes and pan juices aside.

4. Meanwhile, place potatoes in microwave-safe bowl; cover and microwave on High 12 minutes or until fork tender. In 6-quart saucepot, heat remaining 2 teaspoons oil with garlic over medium-high heat 1 minute. Add kale and water. Reduce heat to medium; cover and cook 8 minutes or until kale wilts. Coarsely mash potatoes with milk and remaining ¼ teaspoon salt.

5. Just before serving, heat grape mixture to boiling over high heat; boil until liquid has thickened slightly, about 1 minute. Slice pork; serve with grapes, pan juices, and potatoes and kale.

EACH SERVING: About 465 calories, 35g protein, 63g carbohydrate, 9g total fat (2g saturated), 6g fiber, 77mg cholesterol, 692mg sodium

SAUSAGES AND ROASTED GRAPES: In step 1, omit the fennel seeds, salt, and pepper rub. In step 2, instead of the pork tenderloin, add 2 teaspoons extra-virgin olive oil plus 1 pound sweet Italian turkey or pork sausage links to 12-inch skillet and cook for 5 minutes, turning to brown all sides. Continue with steps 3 and 4. When the sausages and grapes are done, stir 1 tablespoon balsamic vinegar into the pan juices in skillet. Serve sausages with grapes, pan juices, and potatoes and kale. Serves 4.

EACH SERVING: About 530 calories, 30g protein, 65g carbohydrate, 19g total fat (1g saturated), 5g fiber, 70mg cholesterol, 926mg sodium

Roasted Pork and Chard Sauté

Hearty as a Sunday dinner but weeknight-fast, ultra-lean tenderloin pairs up with vitamin-packed veggies. Serve with your favorite whole-grain side for extra fiber.

TOTAL TIME: 30 minutes
MAKES: 4 main-dish servings

1 pork tenderloin (1 pound)
1 teaspoon reduced-sodium soy sauce
1 tablespoon plus 1 teaspoon olive oil
$^1/_4$ teaspoon ground cardamom
$^3/_8$ teaspoon salt
$^1/_4$ teaspoon freshly ground black pepper
2 medium carrots
2 garlic cloves
2 bunches Swiss chard

1. Preheat oven to 475°F.

2. Place pork in baking pan, tucking in the tapered end for even cooking. Rub soy sauce and 1 teaspoon oil all over pork, then sprinkle with $^1/_8$ teaspoon cardamom, $^1/_4$ teaspoon salt, and $^1/_8$ teaspoon pepper. When oven is hot, roast 20 to 25 minutes or until pork is barely pink in center and instant-read thermometer inserted horizontally into center reaches 145°F.

3. Meanwhile, thinly slice carrots at an angle and finely chop garlic. Discard stems of Swiss chard, then slice leaves.

4. In 12-inch skillet, heat remaining 1 tablespoon oil over medium heat. Add carrots and cook, stirring occasionally, 4 to 5 minutes or until just tender. Add garlic; cook 1 minute, stirring. Add Swiss chard and remaining $^1/_8$ teaspoon each salt and pepper. Cook, stirring frequently, 6 to 8 minutes or until tender. Stir in remaining $^1/_8$ teaspoon cardamom and cook 1 minute, stirring. Remove from heat.

5. Cut pork into slices crosswise. Place vegetable mixture on serving plates. Top with sliced pork.

EACH SERVING: About 200 calories, 25g protein, 8g carbohydrate, 8g total fat (2g saturated), 3g fiber, 62mg cholesterol, 575mg sodium ☺

Summer Squash, Ham, and Mozzarella Crepes

Light but satisfying, this dish is a great way to get your family to eat their vegetables. The filling is especially tasty made with sun-ripened summer tomatoes, but you can also use well-drained canned peeled plum tomatoes. If you can't find refrigerated crepes in your supermarket, substitute small flour tortillas.

ACTIVE TIME: 20 minutes
TOTAL TIME: 30 minutes
MAKES: 4 main-dish servings

2	teaspoons olive oil
1	garlic clove, crushed with garlic press
1	pound plum tomatoes, seeded and chopped
3	zucchini (8 ounces each), each cut lengthwise in half, then crosswise into ¼-inch-thick slices
1	small red pepper, thinly sliced
½	cup loosely packed fresh basil leaves, thinly sliced
½	teaspoon salt
¼	teaspoon coarsely ground black pepper
1	package (4½ ounces) refrigerated crepes (ten 7-inch crepes)
10	thin slices baked ham (6 ounces total)
1½	cups shredded part-skim mozzarella cheese (6 ounces)

1. Preheat oven to 400°F. In nonstick 12-inch skillet, heat oil over medium heat. Add garlic; cook, stirring, 1 minute. Add tomatoes, zucchini, and red pepper; cover and cook, stirring occasionally, until tender, about 7 minutes.

2. Stir in basil, salt, and black pepper; cook, uncovered, until all liquid has evaporated, about 5 minutes. Reserve 1 cup zucchini mixture; keep warm.

3. Place crepes on work surface. Top each crepe with 1 ham slice, then about ⅓ cup zucchini mixture; sprinkle with mozzarella. Fold each crepe over to enclose filling. Place crepes, seam side up, in two 13" by 9" baking pans. Bake crepes until golden, about 6 minutes. To serve, top with reserved zucchini mixture.

EACH SERVING: About 305 calories, 23g protein, 27g carbohydrate, 13g total fat (5g saturated), 57mg cholesterol, 1,160mg sodium ☺

Greek-Style Tilapia

This healthy Mediterranean fish dish requires just five ingredients — and thirty minutes of your time.

ACTIVE TIME: 20 minutes
TOTAL TIME: 30 minutes
MAKES: 4 main-dish servings

2   lemons
1½   pounds tilapia fillets
1   tablespoon fresh oregano leaves, chopped, plus additional sprigs for garnish
¼   teaspoon salt
¼   teaspoon freshly ground black pepper
1   pint grape tomatoes, cut lengthwise in half
8   ounces orzo

1. Preheat oven to 400°F. From lemons, grate ½ teaspoon peel and squeeze ¼ cup juice.

2. In 13″ by 9″ glass or ceramic baking dish, arrange tilapia. Evenly sprinkle fillets with lemon juice and peel, chopped oregano, salt, and pepper. Add tomatoes to baking dish around tilapia; cover with foil and roast 16 to 18 minutes or until tilapia is opaque throughout and tomatoes are tender. (Instant-read thermometer inserted horizontally into center of fillet should reach 145°F.)

3. Meanwhile, cook orzo in *boiling salted water* as label directs. Drain well.

4. Serve tilapia, tomatoes, and orzo with juices from baking dish.

EACH SERVING: About 395 calories, 36g protein, 50g carbohydrate, 6g total fat (0g saturated), 2g fiber, 0mg cholesterol, 310mg sodium ☺ ♥

Roasted Salmon with Summer Squash

Moist and flavorful, this no-fuss fish doesn't need much enhancement—or complicated cooking. Just pop it in the oven for fifteen minutes and pair it with tarragon-tossed seasonal veggies for a feed-'em-fast supper.

ACTIVE TIME: 15 minutes
TOTAL TIME: 30 minutes
MAKES: 4 main-dish servings

1	lemon
4	pieces skinless salmon fillet (6 ounces each)
½	teaspoon salt
¼	teaspoon freshly ground black pepper
4	medium summer squash (8 ounces each), each cut diagonally into ½-inch-thick slices
1	tablespoon chopped fresh tarragon leaves, plus additional sprigs for garnish

1. Preheat oven to 400°F. From lemon, grate ½ teaspoon peel and squeeze 3 tablespoons juice.

2. Place salmon in 13" by 9" glass or ceramic baking dish. Sprinkle with lemon peel, 1 tablespoon lemon juice, ¼ teaspoon salt, and ⅛ teaspoon pepper. Roast salmon 14 to 16 minutes or until just opaque throughout. (Instant-read thermometer inserted horizontally into center of fillet should reach 145°F.)

3. Meanwhile, in 4-quart saucepan, place steamer basket and *1 inch water*. Heat water to boiling over high heat. Add squash; cover and reduce heat to medium. Steam vegetables 8 minutes or until tender. Transfer to bowl and toss with tarragon, remaining ¼ teaspoon salt, ⅛ teaspoon pepper, and 2 tablespoons lemon juice.

Arrange squash and salmon on dinner plates; garnish salmon with tarragon sprigs.

EACH SERVING: About 275 calories, 37g protein, 8g carbohydrate, 11g total fat (2g saturated), 3g fiber, 93mg cholesterol, 375mg sodium ☺ ♥

QUICK TECHNIQUE: REMOVING PIN BONES

Salmon and other fish fillets, especially thick ones, may still contain a few small bones, which you don't want to serve to your family or guests. Before cooking, run your fingers over the flesh, and if you find any stray pin bones, use tweezers to remove them.

Tarragon-Citrus-Crusted Salmon

Baked — not fried, this salmon dish features a deliciously light and crispy coating of panko (Japanese bread crumbs). For photo, see page 158.

ACTIVE TIME: 20 minutes
TOTAL TIME: 25 minutes
MAKES: 4 main-dish servings

1	lemon
3	navel oranges
1	tablespoon Dijon mustard
1	tablespoon extra-virgin olive oil
1/8	teaspoon sugar
1/2	teaspoon salt
1	English (seedless) cucumber, cut in half lengthwise and thinly sliced
8	ounces red cabbage, very thinly sliced (4 cups)
1/4	cup panko (Japanese-style bread crumbs)
2	green onions, finely chopped
1	tablespoon packed fresh tarragon leaves, finely chopped, plus leaves for garnish
1/4	teaspoon freshly ground black pepper
4	pieces skinless center-cut salmon fillet (4 ounces each)
4	teaspoons plain fat-free Greek yogurt

1. Preheat oven to 400°F. Line 18" by 12" jelly-roll pan with foil. From lemon, grate 1 teaspoon peel and squeeze 3 tablespoons juice. From oranges, grate 1½ teaspoons peel; set aside. Cut off peel and white pith from oranges and discard trimmings. Cut oranges into ½-inch-thick slices. Arrange orange slices, slightly overlapping, into center of prepared pan.

2. In large bowl, stir together mustard, oil, sugar, lemon juice, and ¼ teaspoon salt. Add cucumber and cabbage; toss to coat. Set aside.

3. In small bowl, stir together lemon peel, orange peel, panko, green onions, tarragon, and ¼ teaspoon each salt and pepper.

4. Arrange salmon on orange slices, skin side down; spread 1 teaspoon yogurt on each fillet. Top with panko mixture, pressing gently so that crust adheres.

5. Bake salmon 10 to 13 minutes or until opaque throughout. (Instant-read thermometer inserted horizontally into center of salmon should reach 145°F.) Transfer fillets with orange slices to serving plates; garnish with tarragon leaves. Serve with cabbage mixture.

EACH SERVING: About 330 calories, 29g protein, 26g carbohydrate, 13g total fat (2g saturated), 5g fiber, 72mg cholesterol, 470mg sodium ☺ ♥

Sesame Salmon with Bok Choy

Salmon sings with the classic Asian combination of sesame and soy sauce. Plus, this dish is low-carb and filled with flavor.

TOTAL TIME: 30 minutes
MAKES: 4 main-dish servings

4	pieces skinless salmon fillet (6 ounces each), skin removed
¼	teaspoon salt
⅛	teaspoon freshly ground black pepper
3	tablespoons black and/or white sesame seeds
¼	cup reduced-sodium soy sauce
1	garlic clove, crushed with side of chef's knife
1	teaspoon grated, peeled fresh ginger
½	teaspoon Asian sesame oil (see page 33)
1	pinch crushed red pepper
2	bunches bok choy (1½ pounds total), cut crosswise into thirds and root ends cut into quarters
1	teaspoon butter (no substitutions)

1. Preheat oven to 375°F. On waxed paper, sprinkle salmon with salt and pepper to season all sides. Coat one side of each salmon fillet with sesame seeds.

2. Heat oven-safe 12-inch skillet over medium-high heat. Add fillets, seeded sides down, and cook 2 minutes, without turning. Transfer skillet to oven and bake salmon 10 to 12 minutes or just until salmon turns opaque in center. (Instant-read thermometer inserted horizontally into center of fillet should reach 145°F.)

3. Meanwhile, in 5½- to 6-quart saucepot, combine soy sauce, garlic, ginger, sesame oil, and crushed red pepper. Add bok choy to soy-sauce mixture; with tongs, toss to combine. Cover and heat to boiling over high heat. Reduce heat to medium and cook, covered, 8 minutes, stirring occasionally. Uncover and cook 3 minutes longer or until bok choy is tender.

4. Remove pot from heat. With tongs, transfer bok choy to dinner plates; discard garlic. Whisk butter into soy-sauce mixture until blended. Place fillets, seeded sides up, on plates with bok choy; drizzle with soy-sauce mixture.

EACH SERVING: About 330 calories, 39g protein, 7g carbohydrate, 16g total fat (3g saturated), 96mg cholesterol, 870mg sodium ☺

Horseradish Salmon

Horseradish Salmon

This dinner is low calorie and heart healthy, too.

TOTAL TIME: 25 minutes
MAKES: 4 main-dish servings

1   English (seedless) cucumber, cut in half lengthwise and then into ¼-inch-thick half-moons
2   tablespoons distilled white vinegar
2   tablespoons chopped fresh dill
2   tablespoons olive oil
¼   teaspoon salt
¼   teaspoon ground black pepper
½   cup panko (Japanese-style bread crumbs)
2   tablespoons prepared horseradish, drained
4   skinless, boneless salmon fillets (5 to 6 ounces each)
6 ounces baby spinach

1. Preheat oven to 475°F. Line large cookie sheet with foil.

2. In large bowl, toss cucumber, vinegar, 1 tablespoon dill, 1 tablespoon oil, and ⅛ teaspoon each salt and pepper.

3. In small bowl, combine panko, horseradish, and remaining ⅛ teaspoon each dill and oil. Sprinkle salmon with remaining ⅛ teaspoon each salt and pepper; place on cookie sheet, smooth side up. Press panko mixture evenly on top of fillets. Bake salmon 8 minutes or until golden brown on top and opaque throughout. (Instant-read thermometer inserted horizontally into center of salmon should reach 145°F.)

4. Toss spinach with cucumber mixture in bowl; serve with salmon.

EACH SERVING: About 345 calories, 36g protein, 8g carbohydrate, 18g total fat (3g saturated), 5g fiber, 93mg cholesterol, 300mg sodium ☺ ♥

Asian Flounder Bake

A flatfish prized for its fine texture and delicate flavor, flounder is often called sole, even though only imported Dover sole is true sole. Here, the fillets are tossed with an Asian-inspired marinade, then layered with grated carrots and baby spinach and baked.

TOTAL TIME: 20 minutes
MAKES: 4 main-dish servings

¼   cup reduced-sodium soy sauce
2   tablespoons dry sherry
1   teaspoon sugar
1   teaspoon grated, peeled fresh ginger
1   teaspoon Asian sesame oil (see page 33)
1   bag (10 ounces) shredded carrots
1   bag (5 to 6 ounces) baby spinach
4   flounder or sole fillets (5 ounces each)
1   green onion, thinly sliced
1   tablespoon sesame seeds, toasted (optional)

1. Preheat oven to 450°F.

2. Meanwhile, in cup, with fork, mix soy sauce, sherry, sugar, ginger, and sesame oil.

3. In 13" by 9" baking pan, spread carrots in even layer. Top with even layer of spinach, then top with fillets. Pour soy-sauce mixture evenly over flounder. Bake just until fish turns opaque throughout, 12 to 14 minutes. (Instant-read thermometer inserted into center of fillet should reach 145°F.) To serve, sprinkle with green onion and top with sesame seeds, if you like.

EACH SERVING: About 200 calories, 30g protein, 11g carbohydrate, 3g total fat (1g saturated), 6g fiber, 68mg cholesterol, 735mg sodium ☺

Vegetable and Mozzarella Kabobs

Here's a deliciously different choice when you're in the mood for kabobs — summer veggies, chunks of mozzarella that get brown and melty under the broiler, and garlic croutons to soak up all the tasty dressing and the juices from the tomatoes. Double or even triple the yield to serve the whole gang.

ACTIVE TIME: 20 minutes
TOTAL TIME: 35 minutes
MAKES: 2 main-dish servings

3	large ripe plum tomatoes
1	small zucchini (6 ounces)
1	small yellow squash (6 ounces)
6	jumbo mushrooms
6	ounces part-skim mozzarella cheese
1	small loaf Italian bread
2	tablespoons minced oil-packed sun-dried tomatoes
2	tablespoons balsamic vinegar
3/4	teaspoon salt
1/4	teaspoon ground black pepper
4	tablespoons olive oil
1 to 2 bunches fresh parsley for garnish	
1	small garlic clove, minced
5	(15-inch) metal skewers (see page 125)

1. Set rack 5 inches from heat source and preheat broiler. Line 15½" by 10½" jelly-roll pan with foil.

2. Cut each plum tomato crosswise in half; cut zucchini and squash into 1½-inch chunks. Trim tough ends from mushrooms. Cut mozzarella into 6 chunks. Cut six 1½-inch cubes from bread; reserve remaining bread for another use.

3. In large bowl, mix sun-dried tomatoes, vinegar, salt, pepper, and 2 tablespoons oil. Add plum tomatoes, zucchini, yellow squash, mushrooms, and mozzarella to vinegar dressing and toss until well coated. Let stand 10 minutes. Meanwhile, line large platter with parsley.

4. In small bowl, mix garlic and remaining 2 tablespoons oil. Brush bread cubes with garlic oil.

5. On one skewer, alternately thread yellow squash and zucchini. On another skewer, thread mushrooms; on another skewer, thread tomato halves; on another skewer, thread mozzarella chunks; and on remaining skewer, thread chunks of bread. Reserve any dressing remaining in bowl.

6. Arrange all except bread kabob in prepared jelly-roll pan. Broil cheese kabob until cheese cubes are just heated through and slightly melted, about 5 minutes; broil remaining kabobs until vegetables are tender-crisp, about 10 minutes, turning once and basting with reserved dressing. Remove kabobs to parsley-lined platter as they are done.

7. Discard foil and place bread kabob in same jelly-roll pan. Broil until lightly toasted, turning once. Place on platter with vegetable and cheese kabobs. Remove skewers before serving.

EACH SERVING: About 615 calories, 32g protein, 28g carbohydrate, 44g total fat (13g saturated), 5g fiber, 45mg cholesterol, 1,505mg sodium

Macaroni and Cheese with Tomatoes

Predictable: Our classic mac and cheese, with its 1¼ pounds of cheese, has 640 calories and 30 fat grams per serving. Surprising: Our revamped whole-wheat rotini version, with reduced-fat cheese and low-fat milk, is still creamy and flavorful but has only 420 calories and 12 fat grams. We top it with tomato slices and bread crumbs to add color and crunch.

ACTIVE TIME: 15 minutes
TOTAL TIME: 30 minutes
MAKES: 4 main-dish servings

8	ounces whole-wheat rotini pasta (2½ cups)
4	teaspoons cornstarch
2	cups low-fat (1%) milk
½	teaspoon Dijon mustard
¼	teaspoon salt
¼	teasoon ground black pepper
4	ounces reduced-fat (2%) pasteurized process cheese spread, cut into ½-inch cubes
2	ounces extra-sharp Cheddar cheese, shredded (½ cup)
⅓	cup freshly grated Pecorino-Romano cheese
2	tablespoons plain dried bread crumbs
1	ripe tomato, thinly sliced

1. Set rack 6 inches from heat source and preheat broiler. Grease shallow 1½-quart broiler-safe baking dish with nonstick cooking spray.

2. Cook rotini in *boiling salted water* as package label directs.

3. Meanwhile, in 2-quart saucepan, whisk cornstarch into milk; heat to boiling over medium heat, whisking occasionally. Boil 1 minute. Remove saucepan from heat; whisk in mustard, salt, and pepper. Stir in cheese spread, Cheddar, and ¼ cup Romano. (Cheese does not need to melt completely.) In small bowl, combine bread crumbs with remaining Romano.

4. When pasta is done, drain and return to saucepot. Stir cheese sauce into pasta; spoon into prepared baking dish. Arrange tomato slices on top; sprinkle with crumb mixture.

5. Broil casserole 2 to 3 minutes or until top is lightly browned. Let stand 5 minutes to set slightly for easier serving.

EACH SERVING: About 420 calories, 23g protein, 59g carbohydrate, 12g total fat (7g saturated), 5g fiber, 37mg cholesterol, 920mg sodium ☺ 🍴

Artichoke and Goat Cheese Pizza

Delicate layers of phyllo form the crust of this easy but sophisticated pizza. If you'll be using frozen phyllo, leave the unwrapped package in the refrigerator for a full day. A gradual thaw will produce sheets that are pliable and less likely to stick together or tear.

ACTIVE TIME: 10 minutes
TOTAL TIME: 25 minutes
MAKES: 4 main-dish servings

6   sheets (16" by 12" each) fresh or frozen (thawed) phyllo

2   tablespoons butter or margarine, melted

4   ounces soft, mild goat cheese, such as Montrachet

1   jar (6 ounces) marinated artichoke hearts, drained and cut into pieces

1½ cups grape or cherry tomatoes, each cut in half

1. Preheat oven to 450°F. Place 1 sheet of phyllo on ungreased large cookie sheet; brush phyllo with some melted butter. Repeat layering with remaining phyllo and butter, but do not brush top layer.

2. Crumble cheese over phyllo; top with artichokes and tomatoes. Bake until golden brown around edges, 12 to 15 minutes.

3. Transfer pizza to large cutting board. With pizza cutter or knife, cut pizza lengthwise in half, then cut each half crosswise into 4 pieces.

EACH SERVING (2 PIECES): About 240 calories, 9g protein, 20g carbohydrate, 16g total fat (8g saturated), 2g fiber, 28mg cholesterol, 366mg sodium ☺

Black Bean and Corn Tortilla Pie

Not really a pie per se, this Mexican main dish more closely resembles a triple-decker quesadilla: flour tortillas layered with salsa, a black-bean-and-corn mixture, and Monterey Jack cheese.

ACTIVE TIME: 10 minutes
TOTAL TIME: 20 minutes
MAKES: 4 main-dish servings

1   jar (11 to 12 ounces) medium-hot salsa

1   can (8 ounces) no-salt-added tomato sauce

1   can (15 to 16 ounces) no-salt-added black beans, rinsed and drained

1   can (15 to 16 ounces) no-salt-added whole-kernel corn, drained

½   cup packed fresh cilantro leaves

4   (10-inch) low-fat flour tortillas

6   ounces shredded reduced-fat Monterey Jack cheese (1½ cups)

Reduced-fat sour cream (optional)

1. Preheat oven to 500°F. Spray 15½" by 10½" jelly-roll pan with nonstick cooking spray.

2. In small bowl, mix salsa and tomato sauce. In medium bowl, mix black beans, corn, and cilantro.

3. Place 1 tortilla in jelly-roll pan. Spread one-third of salsa mixture over tortilla. Top with one-third of bean mixture and one-third of cheese. Repeat layering two more times, then place last tortilla on top. Bake pie until cheese melts and filling is hot, 10 to 12 minutes. Serve with sour cream, if you like.

EACH SERVING: About 440 calories, 25g protein, 65g carbohydrate, 11g total fat (5g saturated), 13g fiber, 30mg cholesterol, 820mg sodium ☺

Black Bean and Corn Tortilla Pie

7

Wrap It Up

When weeknights get busy, wrap up the day with one of our tasty recipes for pitas, burritos, gyros, or sandwiches. Just keep a stash (in your freezer or fridge) of flour and corn tortillas, pitas, and other favorite breads and you've got dozens of options. Fill them with everything from pulled pork to grilled shrimp to beans and veggies. Some of our recipes, like Turkey and Cucumber Salad Wraps, require no cooking at all.

Stuff pitas with curried chicken salad or grilled chicken tossed in a creamy Caesar dressing. Or skip the bread altogether and wrap a gingery chicken stir-fry in crisp Boston lettuce leaves. Or take advantage of supermarket rotisseries chicken and prepare our chicken tostadas topped with a luscious avocado sauce. (See "Express-Lane Ingredient: Rotisserie Chicken" on page 190 for details.)

Tacos are always a popular dinner: Choose our fish and zucchini version or Queso Blanco Soft Tacos, stuffed with a refreshing salad and mild Mexican cheese. Or wrap up our Quick Mu Shu Pork filling with coleslaw in flour tortillas.

If you're looking for something heartier, Chipotle Steak Sandwiches on toasted ciabatta bread are just the thing. Or try sweet and tangy Pulled Pork Sandwiches or our Greek lamb burgers served in pitas with sliced cucumbers and a minty yogurt sauce.

Our Falafel Sandwiches are easy to make from canned garbanzos, while Turkey and Spicy Hummus Clubs are stacked high with store-bought hummus, deli turkey, bacon, and tomatoes.

Flank Steak Fajitas (recipe page 193)

Curried Chicken Pitas

This curry-spiced chicken salad packs extra-sweet flavor with the addition of cantaloupe. Stuff in toasted pitas for a light, casual summer meal.

TOTAL TIME: 20 minutes
MAKES: 4 main-dish servings

¼ cup packed fresh cilantro leaves, finely chopped

¼ cup reduced-fat sour cream

2 tablespoons reduced-fat mayonnaise

1 tablespoon fresh lime juice

1 teaspoon grated, peeled fresh ginger

¼ teaspoon curry powder

¼ teaspoon ground coriander

⅛ teaspoon salt

2 cups chopped, cooked chicken-breast meat

5 radishes, each cut into ¼-inch-thick half-moons

1½ cups chopped cantaloupe (8 ounces)

¼ small red onion, finely chopped

3 tablespoons roasted cashews, chopped

4 pitas, toasted and cut in half

1. In small bowl, whisk cilantro, sour cream, mayonnaise, lime juice, ginger, curry powder, coriander, and salt until well blended. If making ahead, cover and refrigerate up to 24 hours.

2. In bowl, combine chicken, radishes, cantaloupe, and onion. If making ahead, cover and refrigerate up to 24 hours.

3. To serve, toss chicken mixture with half of dressing. Sprinkle with cashews. Serve in pitas with remaining dressing.

EACH SERVING: About 380 calories, 29g protein, 45g carbohydrate, 9g total fat (3g saturated), 3g fiber, 65mg cholesterol, 535mg sodium ☺ 🍱

EXPRESS-LANE INGREDIENT: CURRY POWDER

Widely used in Indian cooking, curry powders vary greatly in heat intensity. The mixes can contain up to twenty different spices, including tumeric, cardamom, red chiles, black pepper, and cumin, so premixed blends are a time saver. Madras-style curry powder, available in most supermarkets, is moderately spicy and a good choice for the recipes in this book that call for curry powder.

Spicy Ginger Chicken in Lettuce Cups

For a heartier option, add some cooked rice to these light and luscious wraps.

TOTAL TIME: 30 minutes
MAKES: 4 main-dish servings

3   tablespoons reduced-sodium soy sauce
1   tablespoon grated, peeled fresh ginger
1   teaspoon honey
2   teaspoons Asian sesame oil
1½ pounds chicken tenders, cut into ¼-inch chunks
1   cup frozen shelled edamame (soybeans)
2   medium stalks celery, chopped
12 large Boston lettuce leaves

1. In cup, whick together soy sauce, ginger, and honey; set aside.

2. In nonstick 12-inch skillet, heat oil on medium 1 minute. Add chicken and cook 3 minutes, stirring occasionally.

3. Add edamame to chicken in skillet and cook 2 minutes, stirring occasionally. Stir in celery; cook 2 minutes longer. Add soy sauce mixture; cook 1 to 2 minutes or until chicken is cooked through (165°F), stirring occasionally to coat chicken with sauce.

4. Arrange three lettuce leaves on each dinner plate. Divide chicken mixture among lettuce leaves, using a generous ¼ cup per leaf. Fold leaves over chicken mixture and eat out of hand.

EACH SERVING: About 260 calories, 40g protein, 9g carbohydrate, 7g total fat (1g saturated), 3g fiber, 82mg cholesterol, 565mg sodium ☺

QUICK TECHNIQUE: PEELING AND GRATING FRESH GINGER

Use the edge or tip of a spoon, not a vegetable peeler, to scrape away ginger's delicate skin. You'll find that a spoon is easier to maneuver around the rhizome's knobby ends. It also removes a thinner layer of skin than a grater, leaving more useable ginger.

To finely grate fresh ginger, a Microplane grater, available at kitchenware stores, is the best tool. Originally created as a tool for woodworkers, its razor-sharp teeth, which allow grating in both directions, has proven to be an indispensable tool for cooks.

Note: You can freeze any extra unpeeled ginger, wrapped well in plastic wrap, for up to six months.

Turkey and Spicy Hummus Clubs

Adding Sriracha (Thai-style chili sauce) to hummus is an easy way to make a delicious spicy condiment, one that pairs perfectly with this turkey club. It's available at Asian markets and in the Asian section of many grocery stores.

TOTAL TIME: 20 minutes
MAKES: 4 main-dish servings

1	container (8 to 10 ounces) hummus
1	tablespoon Sriracha or other Asian chili sauce
¼	cup light mayonnaise
¼	teaspoon smoked paprika (see Tip, page 135)
8	slices reduced-sodium bacon
12	slices multi-grain bread, lightly toasted
8	ounces reduced-sodium deli smoked turkey, thinly sliced
2	cups arugula
2	ripe tomatoes, sliced

1. In small bowl, stir together hummus and chili sauce. In separate small bowl, stir together mayonnaise and smoked paprika.

2. Place 4 slices bacon on microwave-safe plate lined with paper towels. Cover slices with paper towel. Microwave on High 3 to 4 minutes or until crisp. Repeat with remaining 4 slices bacon and clean paper towels. Let bacon cool completely; crumble.

3. Spread 1 tablespoon mayonnaise on one side of 4 bread slices. Spread 2 tablespoons hummus on one side of remaining bread slices.

4. For each sandwich: Place one-fourth of turkey on 1 bread slice with hummus. Top with 1 bread slice with mayonnaise, with mayonnaise facing up. Layer 2 slices bacon, one-fourth of arugula, and one-fourth of tomatoes on top of mayonnaise. Top with another bread slice with hummus and serve.

EACH SERVING: About 585 calories, 35g protein, 60g carbohydrate, 25g total fat (3g saturated), 12g fiber, 53mg cholesterol, 1,500mg sodium

Turkey and Cucumber Salad Wraps

These turkey wraps make a simple and tasty on-the-go lunch.

Total time: 30 minutes
Makes: 4 main-dish servings

¼ cup mayonnaise

¼ cup mango chutney

⅛ teaspoon freshly ground black pepper

2 cups chopped cantaloupe (½ medium)

½ small English (seedless) cucumber, chopped

½ cup packed fresh cilantro leaves

4 (12-inch) flour tortillas or wraps

2 cups mixed greens

1 pound reduced-sodium deli smoked turkey, thinly sliced

1. In large bowl, stir together mayonnaise, chutney, and pepper. Add cantaloupe, cucumber, and cilantro; toss to combine.

2. Working with 1 tortilla at a time, place about ¾ cup cantaloupe mixture, ½ cup greens, and 4 ounces turkey into center of tortilla. Fold in sides and roll tightly around filling. Serve immediately, or wrap tightly in foil or plastic wrap and refrigerate up to 3 hours.

Each serving: About 570 calories, 37g protein, 60g carbohydrate, 22g total fat (6g saturated), 3g fiber, 66mg cholesterol, 1,540mg sodium

Chicken Gyros

We replaced the traditional minced lamb with chicken breasts for an equally yummy Greek-style sandwich that's topped with a fresh tomato salad and lemony yogurt sauce.

Total time: 25 minutes
Makes: 4 main-dish servings

1	teaspoon olive oil
1½	pounds skinless, boneless chicken-breast halves, cut into 1-inch chunks
½	teaspoon dried oregano
½	teaspoon salt
½	teaspoon freshly ground black pepper
¼	cup tahini
¼	cup water
3	tablespoons nonfat plain yogurt
1	tablespoon fresh lemon juice
1	garlic clove, crushed with garlic press
¼	cup fresh cilantro leaves, chopped
¼	teaspoon cayenne (ground red) pepper
4	(6-inch) pitas
2	cups romaine lettuce, sliced
½	English (seedless) cucumber, chopped
1	large ripe tomato, chopped
2	green onions, sliced

1. In nonstick 12-inch skillet, heat oil over medium heat 1 minute. Sprinkle chicken with oregano and ¼ teaspoon each salt and black pepper, and toss to coat. Add chicken to skillet and cook 5 to 7 minutes or until chicken is no longer pink throughout (165°F). Transfer chicken to plate or bowl; cover with foil to keep warm.

2. Meanwhile, make tahini sauce: In small bowl, with wire whisk, combine tahini, water, yogurt, lemon juice, and garlic. Stir in cilantro, cayenne, and remaining ¼ teaspoon each salt and black pepper. Makes about ¾ cup.

3. To serve, cut off one-fourth of each pita and save for another use. Carefully open each pita pocket and fill with one-fourth each of romaine, cucumber, tomato, chicken, and green onions. Top with tahini sauce; serve gyros with any additional sauce on the side.

Each serving: About 360 calories, 34g protein, 41g carbohydrate, 6g total fat (1g saturated), 4g fiber, 64mg cholesterol, 695mg sodium ☺

Chicken Tostadas with Avocado Sauce

Rotisserie chicken makes this yummy meal a cinch to pull together. The tangy avocado sauce is simply mixed in a blender.

ACTIVE TIME: 25 minutes
TOTAL TIME: 30 minutes
MAKES: 4 main-dish servings

1	avocado, peeled and pitted
½	cup packed fresh cilantro leaves
1	garlic clove, crushed with garlic press
½	cup reduced-fat sour cream
¼	cup fresh lime juice
3	tablespoons water
⅝	teaspoon salt
1	head romaine lettuce, shredded
½	small red onion, thinly sliced
1	small orange pepper, seeded and finely chopped
4	corn tortillas
3	cups coarsely shredded chicken meat
4	ripe plum tomatoes, sliced
¼	cup crumbled fresh Mexican cheese, such as queso fresco, or feta cheese

Lime wedges for garnish

1. Prepare avocado sauce: In blender, puree avocado, cilantro, garlic, sour cream, lime juice, water, and ½ teaspoon salt until very smooth. If making ahead, cover and refrigerate up to 24 hours.

2. In large bowl, combine lettuce, onion, and pepper. Cover and refrigerate up to 24 hours.

3. To serve, place 1 tortilla between two paper towels. Microwave on High about 1 minute or until golden and crisp. Repeat with remaining tortillas. Place 1 tortilla on each serving plate.

4. In medium bowl, toss shredded chicken with ¾ cup avocado sauce. In bowl with lettuce mixture, toss ⅛ teaspoon salt and remaining sauce.

5. Divide chicken among tortillas. Top with lettuce mixture, then tomato slices. Sprinkle cheese over tomatoes. Garnish with lime wedges.

EACH SERVING: About 445 calories, 28g protein, 28g carbohydrate, 21g total fat (6g saturated), 6g fiber, 110mg cholesterol, 700mg sodium ☺ 🍱

EXPRESS-LANE INGREDIENT: ROTISSERIE CHICKEN

Want a quick and tasty meal on a busy weeknight? Start with a supermarket rotisserie chicken. Its meat makes a succulent base for many tasty meals—from wraps to salads to pastas—and saves you precious time and effort.

A 2½-pound chicken will yield about 4 cups white and dark meat. That's enough to make these yummy Chicken Tostadas, with leftovers for a chicken salad the next day. Sure, it will cost you a bit more than roasting your own chicken, but for five to seven dollars, you'll have the base for two delicious meals, which is a lot cheaper than ordering two takeout dinners for a family of four.

Quick Mu Shu Pork

Like Chinese-style soft tacos, this quick dish of sautéed ready-to-use coleslaw mix and tender ground pork will become a fun family favorite.

ACTIVE TIME: 15 minutes
TOTAL TIME: 20 minutes
MAKES: 4 main-dish servings

1	pound ground pork
1	tablespoon dry sherry
2	tablespoons reduced-sodium soy sauce
1/8	teaspoon freshly ground black pepper
1	tablespoon vegetable oil
2	garlic cloves, crushed with garlic press
1/4	teaspoon crushed red pepper
1	cup diced jicama
1	bag (14 ounces) coleslaw mix
2	tablespoons water
3	green onions, thinly sliced, plus additional for garnish
1	teaspoon sugar
8	soft taco-size (8-inch) flour tortillas
8	teaspoons hoisin sauce (see page 130)

1. In medium bowl, combine pork, sherry, 1 tablespoon soy sauce, and black pepper.

2. In 12-inch skillet, heat oil over medium-high heat. Add pork mixture in single layer and cook 1 minute without stirring. Cook, stirring, 1 minute longer or until pork just loses its pink color (160°F). Transfer pork to large bowl.

3. To same skillet, add garlic and red pepper and cook 10 seconds. Add jicama, coleslaw, and water. Cook, stirring occasionally, 2 to 4 minutes or until vegetables are just tender.

4. Add green onions, sugar, pork, and remaining 1 tablespoon soy sauce and cook, stirring, 1 minute longer.

5. Wrap tortillas in damp paper towels and microwave on High 1 minute or until tortillas are warm and pliable.

6. To serve, spread 1 teaspoon hoisin on each tortilla, divide pork mixture among tortillas, and fold to eat out of hand.

EACH SERVING: About 570 calories, 26g protein, 42g carbohydrate, 32g total fat (10g saturated), 6g fiber, 82mg cholesterol, 940mg sodium

Chipotle Steak Sandwiches

Pump up a flatiron-steak sandwich with chipotle-spiced mayonnaise. Serve with a gingery cucumber salad.

Total time: 30 minutes
Makes: 4 main-dish servings

¼ cup light mayonnaise
¼ teaspoon chipotle chile powder
1 pound beef shoulder top blade steak (flatiron), 1 inch thick
¼ teaspoon ground black pepper
⅜ teaspoon salt
1 sweet onion (6 to 8 ounces), thinly sliced
1 tablespoon water
1 large English (seedless) cucumber (1 pound), peeled and thinly sliced
1 tablespoon fresh lemon juice
½ teaspoon grated, peeled fresh ginger
2 ciabatta rolls, halved and toasted

1. In small bowl, combine mayonnaise and chile powder. Set aside.

2. Heat 10-inch cast-iron or other heavy skillet over medium-high heat until very hot. Season steak with pepper and ⅛ teaspoon salt; cook, turning once, 15 minutes for medium or until desired doneness. (Instant-read thermometer inserted horizontally into center of steak should reach 145°F.) Transfer to cutting board.

3. To same skillet, add onion, water, and ⅛ teaspoon salt. Reduce heat to medium-low; cook, stirring, 5 to 7 minutes or until tender.

4. Meanwhile, in medium bowl, toss cucumber, lemon juice, ginger, and remaining ⅛ teaspoon salt until well mixed.

5. Slice steak across grain. Spread chile mayonnaise on rolls; top with steak and onion. Serve with cucumber salad.

Each serving: About 315 calories, 25g protein, 24g carbohydrate, 14g total fat (4g saturated), 2g fiber, 65mg cholesterol, 615mg sodium ☺

EXPRESS-LANE INGREDIENT: CHIPOTLES IN ADOBO

Chipotle chiles in adobo are dried, smoked red jalapeño peppers canned in a thick chile puree. These chiles with their sauce are very hot and can burn your skin; wear plastic gloves when handling them. They are found in Latin-American markets and many supermarkets. In these spicy steak sandwiches, we call for chipotle chile powder, a dried and ground version of these peppers that adds great smoky flavor to any dish.

Leftover chipotles in adobo can be frozen. Freeze individual chiles with some sauce on a cookie sheet lined with waxed paper until firm, then remove the waxed paper and store in a heavy-duty resealable plastic bag for up to three months.

Flank Steak Fajitas

Use a cast-iron skillet to achieve the perfect doneness for the steaks and vegetables in these delicious fajitas. (For photo, see page 182).

ACTIVE TIME: 15 minutes
TOTAL TIME: 30 minutes
MAKES: 4 main-dish servings

2	garlic cloves, chopped
1	pound beef flank steak
1	bunch radishes (10 ounces), trimmed and cut into quarters
3/8	teaspoon salt
2	limes
1/2	cup reduced-fat sour cream
8	fajita-size (6-inch) flour tortillas
1/4	teaspoon freshly ground black pepper
2	teaspoons vegetable oil
3	poblano peppers, stems and seeds removed, thinly sliced
1	medium onion (6 to 8 ounces), thinly sliced
1/4	cup water

1. Rub garlic all over steak, and let stand at room temperature. In small colander or sieve, toss radishes with 1/8 teaspoon salt. Place colander over bowl, cover, and refrigerate. Into small bowl, grate peel from 1 lime and cut lime into quarters; set aside. Stir sour cream into lime peel. Cover bowl and refrigerate.

2. Preheat toaster oven to 300°F. Wrap tortillas in foil and heat in toaster oven 15 minutes or until warm and pliable.

3. Heat 12-inch cast-iron or other heavy skillet over medium-high heat until very hot. Brush garlic off steak and discard. Squeeze juice from lime quarters all over steak, then sprinkle with remaining 1/4 teaspoon salt and black pepper to season both sides. Add 1 teaspoon oil to skillet, then add steak. Cook, turning once, 10 minutes for medium-rare or until desired doneness. (Instant-read thermometer inserted horizontally into steak should reach 145°F.) Transfer steak to cutting board; reduce heat to medium.

4. Add remaining 1 teaspoon oil to skillet; add peppers and onion. Cook, stirring occasionally, 2 to 3 minutes or until onion browns. Add water and cook, stirring occasionally, 5 minutes longer or until vegetables are tender.

5. Cut steak across grain into thin slices. Cut remaining lime into wedges. Divide steak and vegetables among tortillas; top with lime sour cream. Serve with radish salad and lime wedges.

EACH SERVING: About 525 calories, 34g protein, 51g carbohydrate, 21g total fat (8g saturated), 4g fiber, 60mg cholesterol, 625mg sodium

Pulled Pork Sandwich

Finger-lickin' flavor: That's what you expect from pulled pork — and that's what we pulled off with our recipe redo. The iconic sandwich, reinvented with spice-rubbed lean pork tenderloin and topped with a vinegary slaw, is still delectable — but with 88 percent less fat! Plus, salt-free chili powder keeps the sodium under control.

ACTIVE TIME: 15 minutes
TOTAL TIME: 30 minutes
MAKES: 4 main-dish servings

1½	teaspoons salt-free chili powder
1	teaspoon smoked paprika (see Tip, page 135)
1	teaspoon mustard powder
³⁄₈	teaspoon salt
¼	teaspoon freshly ground black pepper
1	pound pork tenderloin, cut into 2-inch-thick medallions
3	cups shredded cabbage mix for coleslaw
2	tablespoons plus 1 teaspoon cider vinegar
2	tablespoons snipped fresh chives
1	tablespoon plus 2 teaspoons spicy brown mustard
⅓	cup barbecue sauce
1	tablespoon water
4	soft whole-wheat hamburger buns, lightly toasted

1. Fill 6-quart saucepot with *1 inch water* and add steamer insert. Cover; heat over high heat to boiling. Reduce heat to medium.

2. In small bowl, combine chili powder, paprika, mustard powder, ¼ teaspoon salt, and pepper. Rub spices all over pork. Place pork in steamer; cover and steam, turning once, 18 to 20 minutes or until instant-read thermometer inserted horizontally into center of pork reaches 145°F.

3. Meanwhile, in medium bowl, toss cabbage mix with 2 tablespoons vinegar, chives, 1 tablespoon mustard, and remaining ⅛ teaspoon salt; set aside.

4. Transfer pork to plate. Discard water in pot; remove steamer. When cool enough to handle, shred pork into bite-size pieces.

5. Return pork to saucepot. Stir in barbecue sauce, water, and remaining 1 teaspoon vinegar and 2 teaspoons mustard. Cook over medium heat, stirring frequently, until heated through. Divide pork and slaw among buns.

EACH SERVING: About 300 calories, 27g protein, 33g carbohydrate, 6g total fat (2g saturated), 5g fiber, 60mg cholesterol, 690mg sodium ☺ 🍱

Lamb Burgers with Minted Yogurt Sauce

Grilling is a great way to cook juicy and flavorful ground lamb, whether you cook it outdoors or indoors on a grill pan. Try adding the chopped walnuts to the meat — they give it great texture. If you can't find ground lamb at the supermarket, you can make these burgers with ground beef or poultry.

ACTIVE TIME: 20 minutes
TOTAL TIME: 25 minutes
MAKES: 4 main-dish servings

1	ripe plum tomato, chopped
¼	cup plain low-fat yogurt
2	tablespoons light mayonnaise
¾	cup loosely packed fresh mint leaves, coarsely chopped
1	teaspoon salt
¼	teaspoon ground black pepper
1¼	pounds ground lamb
¼	cup walnuts, chopped (optional)
1	garlic clove, crushed with garlic press
2	teaspoons ground cumin
4	(6-inch) pita breads
1	medium Kirby (pickling) cucumber, not peeled, sliced

1. Prepare outdoor grill for direct grilling over medium heat, or lightly spray ridged grill pan with nonstick cooking spray, then heat on medium until hot.

2. In small bowl, stir tomato, yogurt, mayonnaise, 2 tablespoons mint, ¼ teaspoon salt, and pepper until blended; set sauce aside. Makes about ¾ cup.

3. In medium bowl, combine lamb, walnuts (if using), garlic, cumin, remaining ¾ teaspoon salt, and remaining mint just until blended but not overmixed.

4. Shape lamb mixture into four ¾-inch-thick burgers, handling meat as little as possible.

5. Place burgers on hot grill rack or pan; cook, turning once, 10 to 12 minutes for medium or until desired doneness (160°F.)

6. To serve, cut off one-third from side of each pita. Place burgers in pitas; top with sauce and cucumber.

EACH SERVING: About 485 calories, 32g protein, 31g carbohydrate, 25g total fat (10g saturated), 3g fiber, 105mg cholesterol, 985mg sodium

Fish and Zucchini Tacos

This quick and easy recipe uses roasted fish for a healthier take on the usual fried-fish taco. Serve it with salsa on the side for a fun, light meal the whole family will enjoy.

ACTIVE TIME: 10 minutes
TOTAL TIME: 24 minutes
MAKES: 4 main-dish servings

2	medium zucchini
1	tablespoon vegetable oil
¼	teaspoon chipotle chile powder (see page 192)
½	teaspoon salt
2	limes
1	pound skinless red snapper or other firm white fish fillets
½	cup packed fresh cilantro leaves, chopped, plus sprigs for garnish
8	(6-inch) corn tortillas
1	ripe avocado, halved, pitted, peeled, and cut into ¼-inch slices (see Tip)
½	cup chunky salsa

1. Preheat oven to 400°F. Trim zucchini, then cut each crosswise into 2-inch pieces. Cut each piece lengthwise through center into eight wedges. On 18″ by 12″ jelly-roll pan, combine zucchini, oil, chile powder, and ¼ teaspoon salt until well mixed. Roast 10 minutes.

2. From 1 lime, squeeze 1 tablespoon juice. Cut remaining lime into wedges; set aside. Push zucchini to one side of pan. Arrange fish in single layer on other side. Sprinkle fish with lime juice, then 2 tablespoons cilantro and remaining ¼ teaspoon salt. Roast 8 to 10 minutes or until fish is just opaque throughout. (Instant-read thermometer inserted horizontally into center of fish should reach 145°F.)

3. Meanwhile, wrap tortillas in damp paper towels and place in glass or ceramic pie plate. Microwave on High 1 minute or until just warm and pliable.

4. Break fish into large chunks. Divide fish and zucchini among tortillas. Top with avocado and remaining cilantro. Garnish with cilantro sprigs and serve with lime wedges and salsa.

EACH SERVING: About 365 calories, 29g protein, 35g carbohydrate, 14g total fat (2g saturated), 8g fiber, 42mg cholesterol, 570mg sodium ☺

TIP: *For the richest flavor and creamiest texture, select a Hass avocado (one of the two commonly available varieties) with dark, rough skin that yields slightly to gentle pressure. Avoid any that feel mushy.*

Shrimp Taco Pockets

These Mexican-inspired shrimp "tacos" use pita pockets instead of traditional taco shells or tortillas for an interesting twist.

TOTAL TIME: 30 minutes
MAKES: 4 main-dish servings

12	ounces medium shrimp (26 to 30 count), cooked and peeled
½	cup salsa verde
½	cup pickled jalapeño chiles, drained and finely chopped
¼	cup sour cream
1½	cups chopped romaine lettuce
1	cup fresh corn kernels (see page 234)
1	small orange pepper (6 ounces), chopped
1	small tomato (4 ounces), chopped
¼	cup cilantro leaves, plus additional for garnish
4	pitas, each cut in half (see Tip)
½	cup queso fresco or mild feta cheese, crumbled

1. In medium bowl, toss shrimp with salsa.

2. In large bowl, mix jalapeños and sour cream. Add romaine, corn, pepper, tomato, and cilantro. Toss until well coated.

3. Open each pita pocket. Divide shrimp and vegetable mixtures among pitas. Top each taco with cheese and garnish with cilantro. Serve immediately.

EACH SERVING: About 400 calories, 33g protein, 49g carbohydrate, 8g total fat (3g saturated), 3g fiber, 188mg cholesterol, 980mg sodium ☺

TIP: *If pitas are dry and in danger of cracking, wrap them in damp paper towels and microwave on High 15 seconds to make them more pliable.*

Queso Blanco Soft Tacos

Queso blanco is a tangy white Mexican frying cheese that's firmer than mozzarella, so it holds its shape when melted. It's a delicious counterpoint to a mix of crisp veggies and fresh cilantro—all wrapped up in soft tortillas.

TOTAL TIME: 20 minutes
MAKES: 4 main-dish servings

3	green onions, thinly sliced
3	plum tomatoes, cut into ½-inch pieces
1	ripe avocado, pitted, peeled, and cut into ½-inch pieces
¼	small head romaine lettuce, thinly sliced (2 cups)
¼	cup loosely packed fresh cilantro leaves
1	cup mild or medium-hot salsa
1	package (12 ounces) queso blanco (see Tip), cut into 12 slices
12	(6-inch) corn tortillas, warmed
1	lime, cut into 4 wedges

1. On platter, arrange green onions, tomatoes, avocado, lettuce, and cilantro. Pour salsa into serving bowl.

2. Heat nonstick 12-inch skillet over medium heat. Add cheese and heat until dark brown in spots, 2 to 3 minutes, turning once.

3. Place 1 slice cheese in each tortilla and fold in half. Serve immediately with platter of vegetable accompaniments, salsa, and lime wedges.

EACH SERVING: About 545 calories, 26g protein, 49g carbohydrate, 29g total fat (13g saturated), 9g fiber, 60mg cholesterol, 1,300mg sodium

TIP: *If you can't find queso blanco, a Mexican frying cheese, in your supermarket's dairy case, use shredded Monterey Jack. Sprinkle some cheese on half of each tortilla, then fold the other half over. Place the tortillas on a cookie sheet and heat in a 400°F oven until the cheese has melted, 4 to 5 minutes.*

Zucchini and Mixed Bean Burritos

Here's a quick version of the sort of flavorful vegetarian burritos restaurants serve. Cinnamon adds an unexpected touch of sweetness to the zucchini. A simple carrot slaw would make a nice side dish.

ACTIVE TIME: 15 minutes
TOTAL TIME: 25 minutes
MAKES: 4 main-dish servings

2	teaspoons vegetable oil
4	medium zucchini (5 ounces each), cut lengthwise in half, then sliced crosswise
¼	teaspoon salt
¼	teaspoon ground cinnamon
1	can (15 ounces) Spanish-style red kidney beans
1	can (15 to 19 ounces) black beans, rinsed and drained
4	(10-inch) flour tortillas
1	cup shredded Monterey Jack cheese (optional)
½	cup loosely packed fresh cilantro leaves
1	jar (16 ounces) chunky-style salsa
1	heart romaine lettuce, chopped
¼	cup salsa verde
2	avocados, pitted and peeled
2	tablespoons fresh lime juice

1. In 12-inch skillet, heat oil over medium-high heat. Add zucchini, salt, and cinnamon; cook until zucchini is tender-crisp, about 5 minutes.

2. Meanwhile, in 2-quart saucepan, heat kidney beans with their sauce and black beans over medium heat just to simmering; keep warm.

3. Microwave tortillas, on plate between paper towels, on High 1 to 2 minutes or until heated through. Allow each person to assemble burrito, using a warm tortilla, zucchini and bean mixtures, cheese, if desired, and cilantro. Pass salsa to serve with burritos.

EACH SERVING: About 480 calories, 19g protein, 80g carbohydrate, 10g total fat (2g saturated), 20g fiber, 0mg cholesterol, 953mg sodium

Falafel Sandwiches

Serve these small Middle-Eastern chickpea patties in pita pockets with lettuce, tomatoes, cucumbers, and tangy yogurt.

ACTIVE TIME: 10 minutes
TOTAL TIME: 25 minutes
MAKES: 4 main-dish servings

4	green onions, cut into ½-inch pieces
2	garlic cloves, each cut in half
½	cup packed fresh flat-leaf parsley leaves
2	teaspoons dried mint
1	can (15 to 19 ounces) garbanzo beans, rinsed and drained
½	cup plain dried bread crumbs
1	teaspoon ground coriander
1	teaspoon ground cumin
1	teaspoon baking powder
½	teaspoon salt
¼	teaspoon cayenne (ground red) pepper
¼	teaspoon ground allspice

Nonstick olive-oil cooking spray

4	(6- to 7-inch) whole-wheat pitas

Accompaniments: sliced romaine lettuce, sliced ripe tomatoes, sliced cucumber, sliced red onion, nondairy plain yogurt (optional)

1. In food processor with knife blade attached, finely chop green onions, garlic, parsley, and mint. Add beans, bread crumbs, coriander, cumin, baking powder, salt, cayenne, and all-spice; blend until a coarse puree forms.

2. Shape bean mixture, by scant ½ cups, into eight 3-inch round patties and place on waxed paper. Coat both sides of patties with nonstick cooking spray.

3. Heat nonstick 10-inch skillet over medium-high heat. Add half of patties and cook until dark golden brown, about 8 minutes, turning once. Transfer patties to paper towels to drain. Repeat with remaining patties.

4. Cut off top third of each pita to form a pocket. Place two warm patties in each pita. Serve with choice of accompaniments.

EACH SERVING WITHOUT ACCOMPANIMENTS: About 365 calories, 14g protein, 68g carbohydrate, 5g total fat (1g saturated), 10g fiber, 0mg cholesterol, 1,015mg sodium ☺

Grilled Eggplant Sandwiches

Fresh tomato, basil, and mozzarella are a classic Italian combination — add luscious grilled eggplant for a "meaty" new twist.

TOTAL TIME: 20 minutes
MAKES: 4 main-dish servings

1	medium eggplant, cut into ½-inch slices and salted (see box)
2	tablespoons plus 2 teaspoons balsamic vinegar
2	tablespoons olive oil
½	teaspoon salt
¼	teaspoon ground black pepper
1	medium tomato (6 to 8 ounces each), sliced
4	ounces fresh mozzarella cheese, sliced
1	small bunch fresh basil, leaves removed
1	(12-inch) loaf ciabatta or other Italian bread, split horizontally

1. Toss eggplant slices with 2 tablespoons vinegar, olive oil, salt, and pepper.

2. Grill eggplant over medium-high heat 5 to 7 minutes or until very tender, turning once.

3. Layer eggplant, tomato, mozzarella, and basil on bottom of ciabatta. Drizzle with remaining 2 teaspoons vinegar; replace top. Cut into servings.

EACH SERVING: About 255 calories, 12g protein, 60g carbohydrate, 15g total fat (5g saturated), 4g fiber, 22mg cholesterol, 878mg sodium ☺

QUICK TECHNIQUE: SALTING EGGPLANT

To keep eggplant from absorbing too much cooking oil (and reduce bitterness), place the slices in a colander set over a bowl, sprinkle them generously with salt, and let them stand while you prepare the rest of the ingredients. The salt will extract excess water. No need to rinse the eggplant before you proceed with cooking.

8

Toss It All Together

Main-dish salads are an easy way to get supper on the table fast— and throw in lots of healthful ingredients. Crisp greens, an abundance of vitamin-rich vegetables, and proteins like grilled chicken or steak, canned tuna or shrimp, and hard-boiled eggs or beans can all be part of the mix. Just add some crusty bread, and dinner is served.

Hearty options like Barbecue Chicken Chopped Salad and Tex-Mex Turkey Cobb Salad will satisfy even the biggest appetites. Asian Chicken Salad and Zucchini and Ham Ribbons are also substantial: The first is served over vermicelli rice noodles, while the second is paired with goat-cheese toasts. Our Grilled Steak Salad tosses a trio of chargrilled ingredients—flank steak, sweet potatoes, and cherry tomatoes— in a luscious balsamic and soy sauce dressing.

For easy elegance, serve our Red, White, and Green Salad, which combines strawberries, baby greens, and goat cheese with shredded chicken. Or opt for seafood: Mussels Marinière with Bacon Frisée Salad or Seared Scallop Salad with Basil Vinaigrette will appeal to grown-up palates.

Spinach Salad with Tuna and Avocado includes white beans for a protein- and vitamin-packed dinner. And, of course, we haven't forgotten to include whole grains: Get your fiber fix from Sesame Soba Noodles with Poached Salmon or Tomato Couscous with Olives and Green Beans, which makes whole-wheat couscous its base.

Layered Tuna and Tomatoes (recipe page 216)

Mushroom and Chicken Salad with Bacon

Win your family over to the salad-as-stand-alone-meal idea with this bistro mainstay: The filling combo of poultry and bacon tossed with arugula and frisée is both easy and flavorful.

ACTIVE TIME: 25 minutes
TOTAL TIME: 30 minutes
MAKES: 4 main-dish servings

4   slices (3 ounces) bacon, cut into ½-inch pieces

Olive oil, if needed

1½   pounds skinless, boneless chicken-breast halves, cut into ½-inch-wide strips

¼   teaspoon salt

1   medium shallot (2 ounces), finely chopped

1   pound cremini mushrooms, sliced

1   cup reduced-sodium chicken broth

2   tablespoons balsamic vinegar

1   bag (5 to 6 ounces) baby arugula

1   small head frisée (3 ounces), stem ends trimmed and discarded

1. In 12-inch skillet, cook bacon over medium heat, stirring occasionally, 5 to 6 minutes or until browned. With slotted spoon, transfer bacon to paper towels to drain; remove fat from skillet and reserve 4 teaspoons. (If you do not have 4 teaspoons bacon fat, add enough olive oil to equal 4 teaspoons.)

2. To same skillet, return 2 teaspoons reserved bacon fat and heat over medium heat. Add chicken and salt; cook, stirring occasionally, 7 to 8 minutes or until browned outside and no longer pink inside (165°F). Transfer chicken to bowl.

3. To same skillet, add remaining 2 teaspoons bacon fat and shallot; cook 1 minute, stirring. Add mushrooms; cover and cook 5 minutes. Remove cover and cook over medium-high heat, stirring frequently, 4 to 5 minutes longer or until mushrooms are browned and tender and most liquid has evaporated. Add broth and vinegar; heat to boiling. Remove skillet from heat.

4. In large bowl, combine arugula and frisée; add chicken and mushroom mixture and toss until well combined. Top with reserved bacon.

EACH SERVING: About 330 calories, 48g protein, 9g carbohydrate, 10g total fat (3g saturated), 4g fiber, 108mg cholesterol, 535mg sodium ☺

Asian Chicken Salad

Fish sauce, lime juice, cilantro, and peanuts give this salad its Thai-inspired flavor.

ACTIVE TIME: 20 minutes
TOTAL TIME: 25 minutes
MAKES: 4 main-dish servings

4½ ounces vermicelli rice noodles

¼ cup reduced-sodium Asian fish sauce (see page 24)

3 tablespoons fresh lime juice

2 tablespoons packed light brown sugar

¼ teaspoon crushed red pepper

2 cups shredded skinless rotisserie chicken meat (see page 190)

4 cups thinly sliced Napa cabbage (from 1 small head)

2 cups shredded carrots

½ cup loosely packed fresh mint leaves

½ cup loosely packed fresh cilantro leaves

½ cup unsalted roasted peanuts, chopped

1. In 8-cup glass measuring cup, microwave *6 cups water* on High 10 minutes. Add rice noodles; cook on High 1 to 2 minutes or until noodles are tender. Drain.

2. Meanwhile, in large bowl, combine fish sauce, lime juice, brown sugar, and crushed red pepper. Add chicken, cabbage, carrots, mint, and cilantro; toss to coat.

3. Divide noodles among dinner plates; top with chicken mixture. Sprinkle with peanuts to serve.

EACH SERVING: About 350 calories, 27g protein, 30g carbohydrate, 15g total fat (3g saturated), 7g fiber, 63mg cholesterol, 990mg sodium ☺

QUICK TECHNIQUE: CHOPPING FRESH HERBS

There's nothing like a sprinkling of fresh herbs to brighten a dish. To chop parsley, cilantro, mint, or other small leaves, strip the leaves from the stems and pile them on a cutting board. Using a sharp chef's knife, chop the herbs into small pieces by holding the tip of the blade against the board and rocking the handle up and down. Continue until the herbs are chopped as coarsely or finely as you want.

To slice basil, sage, or other herbs with large leaves, stack the leaves on a cutting board, then tightly roll them up lengthwise, cigar style. Cut crosswise with a sharp chef's knife into thin or thick slices. This is sometimes referred to as chiffonade.

Barbecue Chicken Chopped Salad

Full of robust flavor and fresh ingredients, this hearty main-dish salad will please kids and adults alike.

ACTIVE TIME: 15 minutes
TOTAL TIME: 25 minutes
MAKES: 4 main-dish servings

1	cup corn kernels (from 2 ears corn; see page 234)
1	teaspoon vegetable oil
3	skinless, boneless chicken-breast halves
¼	teaspoon salt
¼	teaspoon freshly ground black pepper
1	tablespoon barbecue sauce
2	limes
¼	cup light ranch dressing
2	hearts romaine lettuce, coarsely chopped
¾	cup loosely packed fresh cilantro leaves, chopped
½	small jicama (10 to 12 ounces), peeled and cut into ¼-inch chunks
1	can (15 ounces) pink or pinto beans, rinsed and drained
1	ripe tomato, chopped
1	cup shredded Monterey Jack cheese
1	cup crushed tortilla chips

1. In microwave-safe small bowl, combine corn and 2 tablespoons water; cover with vented plastic wrap. Microwave on High 1 minute; drain and refrigerate.

2. Brush large ridged grill pan with oil; heat over medium heat. Place chicken between two sheets plastic wrap. With flat side of meat mallet, pound chicken to even ½-inch thickness. Sprinkle with salt and pepper to season both sides. Working in batches if necessary, cook chicken, turning once, 12 to 14 minutes or until juices run clear when pierced with tip of knife. (Instant-read thermometer inserted horizontally into center of chicken should reach 165°F.) Transfer to cutting board; brush with barbecue sauce. Cool slightly; cut into 1-inch chunks.

3. Into small bowl, from 1 lime, squeeze 1 tablespoon juice. Cut remaining lime into 4 wedges and reserve. With fork, whisk ranch dressing into lime juice. In large bowl, toss lettuce and cilantro with half of lime dressing until evenly coated; place on serving platter. Top lettuce with corn, jicama, beans, tomato, cheese, chips, and chicken. Drizzle remaining dressing all over, and serve with reserved lime wedges.

EACH SERVING: About 580 calories, 43g protein, 52g carbohydrate, 23g total fat (8g saturated), 13g fiber, 91mg cholesterol, 920mg sodium

Red, White, and Green Salad

Strawberries are the red, goat cheese the white, and baby greens and herbs the green in this tasty summer salad.

TOTAL TIME: 10 minutes plus 10 minutes standing
MAKES: 4 main-dish servings

1	pound strawberries, hulled and sliced
2	tablespoons balsamic vinegar
¼	teaspoon salt
¼	teaspoon ground black pepper
1	package (5 ounces) baby-greens-and-herbs mix
3	cups coarsely shredded cooked chicken
4	ounces herbed goat cheese, crumbled

1. In large bowl, combine strawberries, vinegar, salt, and pepper. Let stand 10 minutes to marinate, stirring often.

2. Add greens and chicken; toss to combine.

3. Divide salad among serving plates. Top with goat cheese.

EACH SERVING: About 300 calories, 32g protein, 11g carbohydrate, 14g total fat (6g saturated), 2g fiber, 109mg cholesterol, 355mg sodium ☺

Tex-Mex Turkey Cobb Salad

Southwestern accents give this classic a fresh new attitude.

TOTAL TIME: 30 minutes
MAKES: 4 main-dish servings

¼	cup fresh lime juice
2	tablespoons chopped fresh cilantro leaves
4	teaspoons olive oil
1	teaspoon sugar
¼	teaspoon ground cumin
¼	teaspoon salt
¼	teaspoon coarsely ground black pepper
1	medium head romaine lettuce (1¼ pounds), trimmed, leaves cut into ½-inch-wide strips
1	pint cherry tomatoes, cut into quarters
12	ounces cooked skinless roast turkey meat, cut into ½-inch pieces (2 cups)
1	can (15 to 19 ounces) black beans, rinsed and drained
2	small cucumbers (6 ounces each), peeled, seeded, and sliced ½ inch thick

1. Prepare dressing: In small bowl, with wire whisk, combine lime juice, cilantro, oil, sugar, cumin, salt, and pepper.

2. Place lettuce in large serving bowl. Arrange tomatoes, turkey, beans, and cucumbers in rows over lettuce and present the salad. Just before serving, toss salad with dressing.

EACH SERVING: About 310 calories, 39g protein, 32g carbohydrate, 7g total fat (1g saturated), 13g fiber, 71mg cholesterol, 505mg sodium ☺

Thai Beef Salad

Roast beef from the deli counter makes this herb-packed salad easy to prepare. You could swap in leftover grilled flank steak, cooked shrimp, or rotisserie chicken for the roast beef.

TOTAL TIME: 30 minutes
MAKES: 4 main-dish servings

THAI DRESSING

¼ cup seasoned rice vinegar

¼ cup fresh lime juice (from 2 to 3 limes)

3 tablespoons vegetable oil

2 tablespoons grated, peeled fresh ginger

1 tablespoon Asian fish sauce (see page 24)

⅛ teaspoon cayenne (ground red) pepper

SALAD

8 ounces thinly sliced deli roast beef, cut into ½-inch-wide strips

2 medium carrots, cut into 2" by ¼" matchstick strips

1 small red pepper, cut into 2" by ¼" matchstick strips

2 green onions, thinly sliced on angle

1 large head Boston lettuce (10 ounces)

1½ cups loosely packed fresh cilantro leaves

1½ cups loosely packed fresh basil leaves

1½ cups loosely packed fresh mint leaves

1. Prepare dressing: In large bowl, with wire whisk, mix together vinegar, lime juice, oil, ginger, fish sauce, and cayenne pepper.

2. Prepare salad: Add roast beef, carrots, red pepper, and green onions to dressing in bowl; toss to coat.

3. To serve, separate 4 large leaves from head of lettuce and reserve. Tear remaining lettuce into bite-size pieces. Add torn lettuce, cilantro, basil, and mint to bowl with beef; toss again. Place 1 reserved lettuce leaf on each dinner plate; fill with salad mixture.

EACH SERVING: About 275 calories, 19g protin, 17g carbohydrate, 15g total fat (2g saturated), 5g fiber, 46mg cholesterol, 880mg sodium ☺

Grilled Steak Salad

Cherry tomatoes and sweet potatoes are made even sweeter by a turn on the grill. Pair them with juicy chargrilled flank steak and you have the king of steak salads.

TOTAL TIME: 30 minutes
MAKES: 4 main-dish servings

4	medium sweet potatoes (2 to 3 pounds total), scrubbed and cut into ½-inch slices
4	pints (24 ounces) cherry tomatoes
3	tablespoons reduced-sodium soy sauce
2	tablespoons balsamic vinegar
1	tablespoon maple syrup
³⁄₈	teaspoon freshly ground black pepper
¼	teaspoon salt
1	pound beef flank steak
2	bags (10 ounces each) chopped romaine lettuce

1. Prepare outdoor grill for direct grilling on medium-high heat. In large microwave-safe bowl, combine sweet potatoes and *½ cup water*. Cover with vented plastic wrap and microwave on High 10 to 12 minutes or until tender. Drain.

2. Meanwhile, fold 30″ by 12″ sheet heavy-duty foil crosswise in half. Place tomatoes on double thickness of foil; bring long sides of foil up and fold several times to seal well. Fold over ends of foil to seal in juices.

3. In small bowl, whisk together soy sauce, vinegar, syrup, and ⅛ teaspoon pepper.

4. Sprinkle remaining ¼ teaspoon each salt and pepper all over steak; place on hot grill grate with tomato packet and sweet potatoes. Grill steak, turning once, 10 minutes for medium-rare (when instant-read thermometer inserted horizontally into center reaches 145°F); grill tomatoes 10 minutes, turning once; grill sweet potatoes 5 minutes, turning once.

5. In large bowl, toss lettuce with one-third of dressing until evenly coated. Divide lettuce among serving plates. Top with steak, tomatoes, sweet potatoes, and remaining dressing.

EACH SERVING: About 390 calories, 30g protein, 51g carbohydrate, 8g total fat (3g saturated), 11g fiber, 65mg cholesterol, 950mg sodium ☺

Zucchini and Ham Ribbons

Shave summer zucchini into thin ribbons for this no-cook summer salad, flavored with a fresh pistachio pesto.

TOTAL TIME: 20 minutes
MAKES: 4 main-dish servings

2	pounds small zucchini, ends trimmed
4	slices deli ham (1 ounce each), sliced into ½-inch ribbons
1	lemon
⅔	cup salted pistachios, shelled
⅓	cup packed fresh basil leaves
⅓	cup packed fresh mint leaves
1	garlic clove
⅛	teaspoon salt
3	tablespoons extra-virgin olive oil
2	tablespoons water
8	slices whole-wheat baguette, toasted
1½	ounces goat cheese, softened
⅛	teaspoon freshly ground black pepper

1. With vegetable peeler, peel zucchini into wide ribbons. Transfer ribbons to large bowl and add ham. If making ahead, cover and refrigerate up to 24 hours.

2. From lemon, grate 1 teaspoon peel and squeeze 2 tablespoons juice. Cover and refrigerate lemon peel.

3. Prepare pesto: In food processor with knife blade attached, pulse pistachios until finely chopped. Add basil, mint, garlic, lemon juice, and salt. Process until finely chopped. With machine running, slowly drizzle in oil and water. Puree until smooth, scraping down sides if necessary. If making ahead, transfer pesto to bowl, cover, and refrigerate up to 24 hours. If serving right away, proceed to next step.

4. To serve, spread each baguette slice with about 1 teaspoon goat cheese. Sprinkle reserved lemon peel and pepper over toasts. Add pesto to bowl with zucchini and ham; toss until well combined. Serve with goat-cheese toasts.

EACH SERVING: About 380 calories, 15g protein, 25g carbohydrate, 27g total fat (5g saturated), 3g fiber, 20mg cholesterol, 650mg sodium ☺ 🍱

Layered Tuna and Tomatoes

Try mixing red beefsteak tomatoes and green heirloom tomatoes in this salad for lots of color. Green heirloom tomatoes are fully ripe, despite their color. If you can't locate them at your local market, use any other variety. (For photo, see page 204.)

TOTAL TIME: 20 minutes
MAKES: 4 main-dish servings

2	slices whole-wheat bread
3	tablespoons olive oil
⅛	teaspoon salt
1	tablespoon capers, rinsed, drained, and finely chopped
2	tablespoons red wine vinegar
1	teaspoon Dijon mustard
¼	teaspoon freshly ground black pepper
1	can (15 ounces) no-salt-added white kidney (cannellini) beans, rinsed and drained
2	large beefsteak tomatoes, chopped
2	large green heirloom tomatoes, chopped
1	can (5 to 6 ounces) tuna in olive oil, drained and flaked
1	hard-cooked egg, finely chopped
1	tablespoon packed fresh flat-leaf parsley leaves, finely chopped

1. In food processor with knife blade attached, pulse bread until coarse crumbs form. In 12-inch skillet, heat 1 tablespoon oil over medium heat. Add crumbs and salt. Cook, stirring occasionally, 5 minutes or until crumbs are crisp and toasted. Transfer to large sheet of waxed paper to cool. If making ahead, transfer crumbs to airtight container and set aside at room temperature up to 24 hours.

2. Prepare dressing: In small bowl, with wire whisk, mix capers, vinegar, mustard, pepper, and remaining oil until well blended. In medium bowl, toss beans with 1 tablespoon dressing. Cover and refrigerate remaining dressing up to 2 days.

3. On large platter, arrange tomatoes in one layer. Top with beans, tuna, and egg. Cover and refrigerate up to 24 hours.

4. To serve, spoon remaining dressing over entire mixture on platter and sprinkle with bread crumbs and parsley.

EACH SERVING: About 365 calories, 17g protein, 36g carbohydrate, 17g total fat (3g saturated), 8g fiber, 71mg cholesterol, 590mg sodium ☺ 🍱

QUICK TECHNIQUE: HARD-COOKED EGG

Here's a foolproof way to hard-boil eggs: Place the eggs in a saucepan with enough *cold water* to cover by at least 1 inch; heat to boiling over high heat. Immediately remove the saucepan from heat and cover tightly; let stand fifteen minutes. Pour off the hot water and run cold water over the eggs to cool them. Don't peel off the shells until you're ready to eat the eggs.

Spinach Salad with Tuna and Avocado

Got fifteen minutes? Pull together this satisfying main-dish tuna salad. It's tossed with a luscious avocado dressing and finished with still more avocado.

TOTAL TIME: 15 minutes
MAKES: 4 main-dish servings

3	tablespoons fresh lemon juice
1	tablespoon extra-virgin olive oil
1	tablespoon water
1	teaspoon Dijon mustard
1	ripe Hass avocado, cut in half, pitted, and peeled
1	pinch cayenne (ground red) pepper
¼	teaspoon salt
2	tablespoons fresh flat-leaf parsley leaves, finely chopped
2	tablespoons snipped fresh chives
1	package (5 ounces) baby spinach
2	stalks celery, thinly sliced
1	medium red pepper, thinly sliced
1	can (15 ounces) white kidney (cannellini) beans, rinsed and drained
2	cans (5 ounces each) tuna packed in water, drained well

1. In blender, combine lemon juice, oil, water, mustard, half of avocado, cayenne pepper, and salt. Puree until smooth, scraping container occasionally. Stir in parsley and chives.

2. In large bowl, toss spinach, celery, red pepper, beans, and tuna with dressing. Divide among serving plates.

3. Thinly slice remaining avocado and arrange slices on top of salads.

EACH SERVING: About 280 calories, 20g protein, 26g carbohydrate, 11g total fat (2g saturated), 10g fiber, 24mg cholesterol, 645mg sodium ☺

Mediterranean Swordfish Salad

Crisp cucumber, juicy grape tomatoes, salty feta cheese, and the grilled meaty goodness of swordfish make a delicious nod to Greece.

Total time: 20 minutes
Makes: 4 main-dish servings

3   tablespoons olive oil
1   swordfish steak, 1 inch thick (1¼ pounds)
¼   teaspoon ground black pepper
¾   teaspoon salt
2   tablespoons fresh lemon juice
1½ teaspoons chopped fresh oregano leaves or ½ teaspoon dried oregano
1   English (seedless) cucumber (12 ounces), cut into ½-inch pieces
1   pint grape or cherry tomatoes, cut in half
1⅓ ounces feta cheese, crumbled (⅓ cup)

1. In 10-inch skillet, heat 1 tablespoon oil over medium-high heat until very hot. Pat swordfish dry with paper towels. Add swordfish to skillet. Sprinkle with pepper and ½ teaspoon salt and cook until swordfish is browned on both sides and just opaque throughout, 10 to 12 minutes, turning once. (Instant-read thermometer inserted horizontally into center of fish should reach 145°F.)

2. Meanwhile, in large bowl, with fork, mix lemon juice, oregano, and remaining 2 tablespoons oil and ¼ teaspoon salt.

3. When swordfish is done, with wide metal spatula, transfer to cutting board; trim and discard skin. Cut swordfish into 1-inch cubes. Add swordfish, cucumber, and tomatoes to dressing in bowl; toss gently to coat. Just before serving, sprinkle with feta.

Each serving: About 315 calories, 32g protein, 8g carbohydrate, 17g total fat (5g saturated), 2g fiber, 68mg cholesterol, 720mg sodium ☺

Shrimp and Tomato Summer Salad

Want to enjoy this light but satisfying dinner salad year-round? Swap in plum tomatoes or use 1½ pints cherry tomatoes, halved. For photo, see page 5.

TOTAL TIME: 25 minutes
MAKES: 6 main-dish servings

2	tablespoons olive oil
2	tablespoons red wine vinegar
¾	teaspoon salt
¼	teaspoon coarsely ground black pepper
½	cup loosely packed fresh parsley leaves, chopped
¼	cup loosely packed fresh mint leaves, thinly sliced
1	pound cooked shelled and deveined large shrimp
2½	pounds ripe tomatoes, cut into 1-inch pieces
1	English (seedless) cucumber or 4 Kirby cucumbers, each cut lengthwise into quarters, then cut crosswise into 1-inch pieces
1	small red onion, chopped
2	ounces feta cheese, crumbled (½ cup)

In serving bowl, with wire whisk, mix oil, vinegar, salt, and pepper until blended; stir in parsley and mint. Add shrimp, tomatoes, cucumber, and onion to dressing in bowl; stir to combine. Sprinkle salad with feta and serve at room temperature, or cover and refrigerate to serve later.

EACH SERVING: About 200 calories, 20g protein, 13g carbohydrate, 8g total fat (2g saturated), 3g fiber, 156mg cholesterol, 585mg sodium ☺ 🍲

QUICK TECHNIQUE: CHOPPING FRESH TOMATOES

Have you ever tried to slice a ripe tomato and ended up sawing it into a pulpy mess? Unless you have a razor-sharp edge on a chef's knife, you're better off using a serrated knife, which will glide through the skin and flesh without crushing the tomato. To retain the juice inside the tomato, slice from stem to blossom end. If you want smaller pieces, cut these slices crosswise.

Shrimp, Watermelon, and Feta Salad

You'll be able to serve this fresh, protein-rich summer salad in just twenty minutes.

ACTIVE TIME: 10 minutes
TOTAL TIME: 20 minutes
MAKES: 4 main-dish servings

4   tablespoons prepared lemon-and-chive dressing
1   pound shelled and deveined large shrimp
1   bag (5 to 6 ounces) mixed baby greens
3   cups diced (1½-inch chunks) seedless watermelon (from 1½ pounds with rind)
2   ounces feta cheese, crumbled (½ cup)

1. In nonstick 12-inch skillet, heat 1 tablespoon dressing over medium heat 1 minute. Add shrimp and cook, stirring occasionally, 6 to 8 minutes or until shrimp are opaque throughout.

2. Meanwhile, in large bowl, toss mixed greens, watermelon, and remaining 3 tablespoons dressing until evenly coated.

3. Divide salad among serving plates and top with shrimp and crumbled feta.

EACH SERVING: About 280 calories, 27g protein, 12g carbohydrate, 14g total fat (3g saturated), 1g fiber, 185mg cholesterol, 415mg sodium ☺

Sesame Soba Noodles with Poached Salmon

Japanese soba noodles are made with buckwheat flour and have a nutty flavor. They are excellent served cool with our Micro-Poached Salmon. Or swap in leftover grilled chicken breasts or flank steak, cut into thin strips.

ACTIVE TIME: 20 minutes
TOTAL TIME: 25 minutes
MAKES: 4 main-dish servings

8   ounces dried soba noodles
1   teaspoon salt
1   large carrot, shredded
8   ounces snow peas, strings removed, cut in half
½   cup Soy Vinaigrette (recipe opposite)
2   green onions, thinly sliced
2   tablespoons toasted sesame seeds
6   ounces mixed baby greens
Micro-Poached Salmon (recipe opposite), flaked with fork into 1-inch chunks

1. Fill 4-quart saucepan with enough *water* to cover noodles and heat to boiling over high heat. Add noodles and salt and cook 3 minutes. Add carrot and cook 1 minute longer. Add snow peas and cook 2 minutes longer. Drain and rinse under cold water until noodles are cool. Drain well again.

2. Transfer mixture to large bowl and toss with soy vinaigrette, green onions, and sesame seeds.

3. Divide baby greens among serving plates. Top with soba mixture, then salmon.

EACH SERVING: About 540 calories, 44g protein, 56g carbohydrate, 15g total fat (2g saturated), 7g fiber, 93mg cholesterol, 825mg sodium

Soy Vinaigrette

In medium bowl, stir together *⅓ cup soy sauce, ¼ cup fresh lime juice, 3 tablespoons rice wine vinegar*, and *1 tablespoon sugar* until sugar dissolves. Cover and refrigerate up to 3 days. Makes about ¾ cup dressing.

Each 2-tablespoon serving: About 30 calories, 0g protein, 5g carbohydrate, 0g total fat, 0g fiber, 0mg cholesterol, 480mg sodium ☺ 🍱

Micro-Poached Salmon

In an 8-inch-square glass baking dish, arrange thin slices of *1 lemon* in single layer. Place *4 skinless center-cut salmon fillets* (6 ounces each) on top of lemon slices. Sprinkle with *¼ teaspoon salt*. Add *¼ cup water* to dish. Cover with vented plastic wrap and microwave on High 8 minutes or until fish just turns opaque throughout. (Instant-read thermometer inserted horizontally into center of fish should reach 145°F.) With slotted spatula, transfer salmon to paper towels to drain. Let cool to room temperature, about 15 minutes. Serves 4.

Each serving: About 240 calories, 34g protein, 0g carbohydrate, 11g total fat (2g saturated), 0g fiber, 93mg cholesterol, 220mg sodium ☺

Mussels Marinière with Bacon Frisée Salad

Planning a romantic dinner for two? This savory mussels dish with bacon frisée salad and a fresh baguette is just the thing.

TOTAL TIME: 20 minutes
MAKES: 2 main-dish servings

2   slices thick-cut bacon, cut into ½-inch pieces

2   tablespoons sherry vinegar

1   small head frisée (4 to 5 ounces), leaves separated

⅛   teaspoon freshly ground black pepper

1   tablespoon olive oil

1   tablespoon butter or margarine

1   medium onion (6 to 8 ounces), finely chopped

2   garlic cloves, crushed with garlic press

1   cup dry white wine

3   pounds mussels, beards removed, well washed (see box)

½   cup packed fresh parsley leaves, finely chopped

1   small baguette (7 ounces), cut in half and toasted

1. In 12-inch skillet, cook bacon over medium heat 6 to 8 minutes or until crisp and browned. With slotted spoon, transfer to plate lined with paper towel; set aside. To drippings in skillet, add vinegar and cook 1 minute over medium heat. Pour liquid into medium bowl (do not scrape browned bits from bottom of pan); add frisée and pepper. Toss to coat.

2. In wide 8-quart saucepot, heat oil and butter over medium-high heat until butter melts. Add onion and garlic and cook, stirring, 2 minutes or until almost translucent. Add wine and heat to boiling. Add mussels, stir once, cover sauce pot, and cook 1 minute. Stir again, cover, and cook 1 to 2 minutes longer or just until mussels open; do not overcook.

3. Immediately divide mussels and cooking liquid between two large serving bowls and top with parsley. Divide salad between two serving plates and top with reserved bacon. Serve mussels and salad with baguette.

EACH SERVING: About 790 calories, 33g protein, 73g carbohydrate, 39g total fat (11g saturated), 8g fiber, 66mg cholesterol, 1,420mg sodium

QUICK TECHNIQUE: SCRUBBING AND DEBEARDING MUSSELS

Scrub mussels well under cold running water. To debeard, grab the hairlike beard firmly with your thumb and forefinger and pull it away, or scrape it off with a knife. (Cultivated mussels usually do not have beards.)

Seared Scallop Salad with Basil Vinaigrette

For a simple and refreshing dinner, toss pan-fried scallops and white beans with our fresh and flavorful basil-and-lemon vinaigrette.

TOTAL TIME: 10 minutes
MAKES: 4 main-dish servings

1	can (15 to 19 ounces) white kidney beans (cannellini), rinsed and drained
2	tablespoons fresh lemon juice
½	cup loosely packed fresh basil leaves, chopped
3	tablespoons olive oil
¾	teaspoon salt
1	pound sea scallops (see Tip)
¼	teaspoon coarsely ground black pepper
1	bag (4 to 5 ounces) mesclun or baby salad greens

1. In large bowl, toss beans with lemon juice, basil, 2 tablespoons oil, and ¼ teaspoon salt; set bean mixture aside.

2. In 12-inch skillet, heat remaining 1 tablespoon oil over medium-high heat until very hot but not smoking. Meanwhile, pull tough crescent-shaped muscle from side of each scallop.

3. Add scallops to skillet; sprinkle with pepper and remaining ½ teaspoon salt. Cook scallops until just opaque throughout, 4 to 5 minutes, turning once.

4. To serve, toss mesclun with bean mixture and arrange on dinner plates; top with scallops.

EACH SERVING: About 300 calories, 25g protein, 23g carbohydrate, 12g total fat (2g saturated), 6g fiber, 37mg cholesterol, 795mg sodium ☺

TIP: When selecting scallops, choose those that are creamy pink in color; avoid scallops that are very white and plump—they may have been soaked in a preservative solution. Soaked scallops tend to expel a lot of liquid while cooking and won't brown nicely.

Crab Cobb Salad

You can keep the bacon in this lightened version of the Cobb salad, thanks to a low-cal yogurt dressing. Serve with a whole-wheat baguette.

TOTAL TIME: 30 minutes
MAKES: 4 main-dish servings

3	slices center-cut bacon
1	cup plain low-fat yogurt
¼	cup loosely packed snipped fresh chives
1	tablespoon Dijon mustard
¼	teaspoon salt
¼	teaspoon freshly ground black pepper
2	hearts of romaine lettuce, torn
8	ounces lump crabmeat, picked over
2	large tomatoes, seeded and chopped (see Tip)
1	ripe avocado, pitted, peeled, and chopped

1. On microwave-safe plate, between paper towels, arrange bacon in single layer. Microwave on High 3 minutes or until crisp. When cool, crumble.

2. In small bowl, with wire whisk, stir together yogurt, chives, mustard, salt, and pepper.

3. In large bowl, toss romaine with half of dressing. In small bowl, gently stir half of remaining dressing into crabmeat.

4. Divide romaine among serving plates. Arrange tomatoes, avocado, bacon, and crabmeat in rows over romaine. Spoon remaining dressing over salads.

EACH SERVING: About 200 calories, 18g protein, 15g carbohydrate, 8g total fat (2g saturated), 5g fiber, 64mg cholesterol, 615mg sodium ☺

TIP: *For speedy seeding, halve tomatoes crosswise and gently dig seeds out with your fingers.*

Black Bean and Avocado Salad

Summer veggies, romaine, and black beans are tossed with a creamy cilantro-lime dressing.

TOTAL TIME: 30 minutes
MAKES: 4 main-dish servings

2	limes
¼	cup light mayonnaise
½	cup packed fresh cilantro leaves
2	tablespoons reduced-fat sour cream
½	teaspoon ground cumin
¼	teaspoon sugar
⅛	teaspoon salt
⅛	teaspoon coarsely ground black pepper
1	small head romaine lettuce (1 pound), cut into ¾-inch pieces (8 cups)
2	ripe tomatoes, cut into ½-inch pieces
2	Kirby cucumbers (4 ounces each), not peeled, each cut lengthwise into quarters, then crosswise into ¼-inch pieces
1	ripe avocado, pitted, peeled, and cut into ½-inch pieces
1	can (15 to 19 ounces) black beans, rinsed and drained

1. From limes, grate ½ teaspoon peel and squeeze 3 tablespoons juice. In blender, puree lime peel and juice, mayonnaise, cilantro, sour cream, cumin, sugar, salt, and pepper until smooth. Makes about ½ cup.

2. In large serving bowl, toss lettuce, tomatoes, cucumbers, avocado, and beans with dressing until well coated. Serve as soon as possible so that avocado has no time to discolor.

EACH SERVING: About 230 calories, 9g protein, 34g carbohydrate, 10g total fat (2g saturated), 12g fiber, 3mg cholesterol, 520mg sodium ☺

Tomato Couscous with Olives and Green Beans

Large pearl couscous, also called Israeli couscous, adds dimension to this simple, healthy Mediterranean salad of fresh and sun-dried tomatoes, green beans, and olives.

ACTIVE TIME: 25 minutes
TOTAL TIME: 30 minutes
MAKES: 4 main-dish servings

¼ cup sun-dried tomatoes (not oil-packed), finely chopped

12 ounces green beans, trimmed

1 cup Israeli (pearl) couscous

1 pint grape tomatoes

½ cup pitted Kalamata olives

½ cup packed fresh flat-leaf parsley leaves

1 lemon

2 tablespoons champagne vinegar

1 tablespoon extra-virgin olive oil

1 teaspoon sugar

½ teaspoon salt

½ teaspoon freshly ground black pepper

1 can (15 to 19 ounces) no-salt-added pinto beans, rinsed and drained

1. In small bowl, cover sun-dried tomatoes with *hot water*. Let stand.

2. Fill large covered saucepot with *water* and heat to boiling over high heat. Fill large bowl with ice and water. Add green beans to boiling water. Cook until crisp-tender, 4 to 5 minutes; transfer to ice water. When cool, drain well. Cut into 1-inch pieces.

3. Cook couscous as label directs. Drain, rinse with cold water, and drain again.

4. Meanwhile, cut grape tomatoes in half and chop olives and parsley.

5. Into large bowl, from lemon, grate 1 teaspoon peel; squeeze 2 tablespoons juice. Stir in vinegar, oil, sugar, and ¼ teaspoon each salt and pepper. Drain sun-dried tomatoes well; stir into mixture. Add beans, couscous, grape tomatoes, olives, parsley, and remaining ¼ teaspoon each salt and pepper. Stir until well mixed.

EACH SERVING: About 340 calories, 12g protein, 56g carbohydrate, 8g total fat (1g saturated), 10g fiber, 0mg cholesterol, 630mg sodium ☺

Caesar Pasta Salad

Perfect for a summer picnic: The vegetarian Caesar dressing is sure to please everyone.

TOTAL TIME: 30 minutes
MAKES: 6 main-dish servings

1	pound farfalle pasta
1	large lemon
¼	cup grated Parmesan cheese, plus more for garnish
3	tablespoons light mayonnaise
3	tablespoons extra-virgin olive oil
2	garlic cloves, crushed with garlic press
1	teaspoon salt
1	teaspoon freshly ground black pepper
1	pint multicolored grape tomatoes, cut in half
1	medium zucchini, grated
1	cup frozen peas, thawed
¼	cup packed fresh basil leaves, finely chopped, plus leaves for garnish

1. Heat large covered saucepot of *salted water* to boiling on high heat. Cook pasta as label directs.

2. Meanwhile, from lemon, grate 1 teaspoon peel and squeeze ¼ cup juice into large bowl. Whisk in Parmesan, mayonnaise, oil, garlic, salt, and pepper. Add tomatoes, zucchini, peas, basil, and cooked pasta; toss well. Serve warm or chilled. (Can be refrigerated, covered, up to 1 day.) Garnish with additional Parmesan and basil.

EACH SERVING: About 415 calories, 14g protein, 64g carbohydrate, 12g total fat (2g saturated), 5g fiber, 6mg cholesterol, 605mg sodium ☺

TIP: *Want to cut your cook time by 5 minutes? Trade our homemade dressing for ¾ cup bottled Caesar dressing.*

9

Breakfast for Dinner

Who doesn't love eating breakfast food for supper? An omelet with a zesty filling or a stack of pancakes topped with maple syrup and fresh fruit feels indulgent (and even a bit naughty). But tucking into breakfast for dinner can also be a health-conscious strategy. After all, when you think of breakfast, the first thing that comes to mind is eggs, one of nature's most nutrient-rich and versatile foods. Not only are they an inexpensive source of protein, eggs provide a tasty base for using up leftover meat, veggies, cheese, and herbs. What's not to like about that?

In this chapter, you'll find eggs baked in frittatas with artichokes or spicy potatoes, scrambled with lox, and wrapped in tortillas with mixed veggies or black beans. Or, for something different, try bacon and poached eggs over roasted asparagus. All of these are hearty meals that will be a welcome change of pace any night of the week. We also include a recipe for a basic omelet three ways. It's another quick and affordable way to get a healthy, protein-filled supper on the table. Add a side of buttered toast, and your work is done.

For a Southern-style supper, serve up our Shrimp and Fresh Corn Grits. For more crowd-pleasing comfort food, make Potato Pancakes with Carrot Salad, and finish with a dollop of applesauce or sour cream. A side of bacon or sausage turns this into a hearty, country-style meal.

Tostada Stacks (recipe page 234)

California Breakfast Wrap

Filling and filled with good-for-you-ingredients, this wrap is the perfect way to start — or end — your day. It's packed with protein from eggs and cheese, and healthy fats from avocado.

TOTAL TIME: 25 minutes
MAKES: 4 main-dish servings

4	large eggs
2	large egg whites (see box, opposite)
⅜	teaspoon salt
⅛	teaspoon freshly ground black pepper
4	(8-inch) whole-wheat tortillas
4	tablespoons goat cheese
3½	ounces baby spinach (7 cups)
1	teaspoon canola oil
1	medium tomato, seeded and finely chopped (1 cup)
1	Hass avocado, sliced (see Tip, page 196)
1	tablespoon chopped fresh dill leaves

1. In medium bowl, beat eggs, egg whites, and ⅛ teaspoon each salt and pepper.

2. On microwave-safe plate, cover tortillas with damp paper towel. Microwave on High 30 seconds or until tortillas are just warm and pliable.

3. Spread 1 tablespoon goat cheese on each tortilla; top with spinach.

4. In nonstick 12-inch skillet, heat oil over medium heat 1 minute. Add egg mixture. Cook, stirring gently, 2 minutes or until almost set. Remove from heat; fold in tomato, avocado, and remaining ¼ teaspoon salt.

5. Divide hot egg mixture among tortillas. Top with dill; fold in half.

EACH SERVING: About 330 calories, 16g protein, 29g carbohydrate, 16g total fat (4g saturated), 6g fiber, 191mg cholesterol, 565mg sodium ☺

Egg and Black Bean Burritos

If you like your Tex-Mex fare extra spicy, use jalapeño Jack cheese. Pinto beans make a good swap for the black beans.

TOTAL TIME: 15 minutes
MAKES: 4 main-dish servings

1	can (15 to 19 ounces) black beans, rinsed and drained
1	jar (11 ounces) medium-hot salsa (1¼ cups)
6	large eggs
¼	teaspoon salt
⅛	teaspoon coarsely ground black pepper
4	ounces shredded Monterey Jack cheese (1 cup)
4	burrito-size (10-inch) flour tortillas

1. In small microwave-safe bowl, mix black beans with salsa. In medium bowl, with wire whisk or fork, beat eggs, salt, and pepper until blended.

2. Heat nonstick 10-inch skillet over medium heat. Add egg mixture to skillet. As egg mixture begins to set around edge, stir lightly with wooden spoon or heat-safe rubber spatula, tilting pan to allow uncooked egg mixture to flow toward side of pan. Continue cooking until edges are set to desired doneness, 4 to 6 minutes. Remove skillet from heat; sprinkle cheese evenly over eggs.

3. Meanwhile, in microwave, heat black-bean mixture on High, stirring once, until heated through, 1 to 2 minutes. Cover and keep warm. Stack tortillas and place between two damp paper towels. Heat tortillas in microwave on High until warm, about 1 minute.

4. To assemble burritos, place one-fourth of scrambled eggs down center of each tortilla; top with about one-fourth of black-bean mixture. Fold two opposite sides of tortillas over filling, then fold over other sides to form package.

EACH SERVING: About 575 calories, 28g protein, 71g carbohydrate, 21g total fat (9g saturated), 344mg cholesterol, 1,550mg sodium

QUICK TECHNIQUE: SEPARATING EGGS

To separate an egg, sharply tap the eggshell along its middle to make a crosswise crack. With your thumbs, gently pull open the shell along the crack, letting some of the white run into a bowl. Slowly transfer the yolk back and forth from one half-shell to the other, being careful not to break the yolk on any sharp shell edge, until all the white has run into the bowl. If any yolk does get into the whites, it can sometimes be removed with a small spoon or the edge of an eggshell.

The Perfect Omelet

Omelets are the ultimate raid-the-fridge dinner — swap in cheeses and veggies you have on hand. For lighter omelets, substitute four large eggs and eight large egg whites.

ACTIVE TIME: 2½ minutes per omelet
TOTAL TIME: 18 minutes
MAKES: 4 main-dish servings

8	large eggs
½	cup water
½	teaspoon salt
½	teaspoon ground black pepper
2	tablespoons butter or margarine
4	ounces Cheddar, Gruyère, or Fontina cheese, shredded (1 cup)

Chopped green onions for garnish
Toasted country-style bread (optional)

1. Preheat oven to 200°F. Warm four plates in oven. In medium bowl, beat eggs, water, salt, and pepper with fork, 25 to 30 quick strokes just to blend. (Overbeating toughens proteins in whites.)

2. In nonstick 8-inch skillet, melt 1½ teaspoons butter over medium heat. When butter stops sizzling, ladle ½ cup egg mixture into skillet.

3. After egg mixture begins to set around edges, 25 to 30 seconds, with heat-safe spatula, carefully push cooked egg from side of skillet toward center, so uncooked egg can reach bottom of hot skillet. Repeat eight to ten times around skillet, tilting as necessary, 1 to 1½ minutes.

4. Cook until omelet is almost set but still creamy and moist on top. Sprinkle ¼ cup cheese on half of omelet. With spatula, fold unfilled half over filling.

5. Shake pan gently to loosen any egg or filling from edge, then slide omelet to edge of skillet and tip skillet so omelet slides onto plate. Keep warm in oven. Repeat with remaining butter, egg mixture, and cheese to make 4 omelets in all. Sprinkle with green onions and serve with toast, if you like.

EACH SERVING: About 315 calories, 20g protein, 2g carbohydrate, 25g total fat (10g saturated), 0g fiber, 455mg cholesterol, 670mg sodium ☺

ASPARAGUS AND GRUYÈRE OMELET: In 2-quart saucepan, heat *1½ teaspoons olive oil* over medium heat. Add *8 ounces asparagus*, trimmed and cut diagonally into 1-inch pieces, and *2 tablespoons water*. Cook 5 minutes or until tender-crisp. Prepare each omelet as directed, but in step 4, use one-fourth of asparagus and Gruyère on each omelet. Serve with *tomato wedges*, if you like.

EACH SERVING: About 340 calories, 22g protein, 2g carbohydrate, 27g total fat (10g saturated), 1g fiber, 456mg cholesterol, 590mg sodium ☺

SPINACH, FETA, AND TOMATO OMELET: Omit cheese from omelet recipe above. Chop *2 ripe plum tomatoes*. Crumble *2 ounces feta cheese (½ cup)*. Thinly slice *2 cups loosely packed baby spinach leaves*. Prepare each omelet as directed above, but in step 4, layer one-fourth of crumbled feta, spinach leaves, and chopped tomatoes over half of each omelet. Serve with a mixed-greens salad with balsamic vinaigrette, if you like.

EACH SERVING: About 250 calories, 15g protein, 4g carbohydrate, 19g total fat (6g saturated), 2g fiber, 438mg cholesterol, 670mg sodium ☺

Tostada Stacks

Try this new spin on tostadas served with a tomato-zucchini salsa and fried eggs on top. It's a hit at brunches or a welcome weeknight dinner. For photo, see page 228.

ACTIVE TIME: 25 minutes
TOTAL TIME: 30 minutes
MAKES: 4 main-dish servings

4	(6-inch) corn tortillas
4	teaspoons vegetable oil
1	medium white onion, finely chopped
3	garlic cloves, chopped
¾	teaspoon salt
¼	teaspoon ground black pepper
1	can (15 to 19 ounces) reduced-sodium black beans, rinsed and drained
1	medium zucchini (8 ounces), finely chopped
1	medium orange pepper, finely chopped
2	cups fresh corn kernels
2	ripe plum tomatoes, finely chopped
1	teaspoon chipotle hot sauce
2	tablespoons fresh lime juice
2	tablespoons chopped fresh cilantro leaves
4	large eggs

1. Place tortillas between two paper towels on large plate. Microwave on High 3 minutes or until crisp.

2. In nonstick 12-inch skillet, heat 1 tablespoon oil over medium heat. Add onion, garlic, and ⅛ teaspoon each salt and black pepper. Cook, stirring, 8 minutes or until golden.

3. Meanwhile, place beans and ¼ teaspoon salt in medium bowl. In large bowl, combine zucchini, orange pepper, corn, tomatoes, hot sauce, lime juice, 1 tablespoon cilantro, and ¼ teaspoon salt. Add half of onion mixture to beans; add remaining half to vegetables. Mash bean mixture until almost smooth; stir zucchini mixture well.

4. Wipe pan. Heat remaining 1 teaspoon oil over medium heat. Fry eggs 6 minutes or until whites are set. Sprinkle with remaining ⅛ teaspoon each salt and black pepper.

5. While eggs cook, spread bean mixture on tortillas. Top each with 1 fried egg; serve with zucchini mixture. Sprinkle with remaining 1 tablespoon cilantro.

EACH SERVING: About 375 calories, 19g protein, 53g carbohydrate, 11g total fat (2g saturated), 10g fiber, 186mg cholesterol, 605mg sodium ☺

QUICK TECHNIQUE: REMOVING CORN KERNELS FROM THE COB

Although frozen corn is a convenient substitute, removing the kernels from a cob is easy if you follow these steps. Shuck the corn and remove the silk, then trim the tip of the cob so you can stand the ear on end. With a sharp knife, slice down to remove the kernels, cutting close to the cob. (Be sure to include the corn's sweet juices when you add the kernels to the pan.)

Artichoke Frittata

Dinner can be on the table fast when eggs are the entrée. Try this tasty open-faced omelet, packed with tangy feta and a quartet of vegetables.

TOTAL TIME: 30 minutes
MAKES: 4 main-dish servings

1   pound small red potatoes, cut into quarters
1   tablespoon plus 1 teaspoon olive oil
3/8   teaspoon salt
3/8   teaspoon ground black pepper
2   green onions, sliced
1   orange pepper (8 ounces), chopped
1   pint grape tomatoes
1   can (13 to 14 ounces) artichoke hearts, rinsed and chopped
4   large eggs plus 4 large egg whites
2   ounces feta cheese, crumbled (1/2 cup)

1. Arrange oven rack 6 inches from broiler heat source. Preheat broiler.

2. To medium microwave-safe bowl, add potatoes and *1/4 cup water*; cover with vented plastic wrap. Microwave on High 8 minutes or until tender. Drain. On jelly-roll pan, toss potatoes with 1 teaspoon oil and 1/8 teaspoon each salt and black pepper. Broil 6 minutes or until browned.

3. Meanwhile, in nonstick 10-inch skillet, heat 1 tablespoon oil over medium heat 1 minute. Add green onions and orange pepper; cook, stirring occasionally, 5 minutes or until golden. Add tomatoes and artichoke hearts; cook, stirring occasionally, 2 to 5 minutes or until tomatoes start to burst.

4. While vegetables cook, in medium bowl, beat eggs and egg whites with remaining 1/4 teaspoon each salt and black pepper and half of feta. Pour over vegetables and tilt skillet to distribute. Top with remaining feta. Cover; cook 5 to 6 minutes or until set. Serve with potatoes.

EACH SERVING: About 325 calories, 18g protein, 32g carbohydrate, 14g total fat (5g saturated), 3g fiber, 205mg cholesterol, 515mg sodium ☺

EXPRESS-LANE INGREDIENT: ARTICHOKE HEARTS

There's nothing like the tender texture and buttery flavor of artichoke hearts, but it's a lot of work to extract them from the prickly leaves and choke. Luckily, the hearts are available canned or frozen so you can enjoy them with ease, even when fresh artichokes aren't available. If you're using canned artichokes rather than frozen ones, rinse and drain them well, then position them leaves side down before chopping them.

Lox Scrambled Eggs

For this fast feed-a-crowd dish, just soft-scramble a dozen eggs with savory bagel-shop staples. Sprinkle with onions and capers and serve family-style with sliced tomatoes.

ACTIVE TIME: 20 minutes
TOTAL TIME: 25 minutes
MAKES: 6 main-dish servings

12 large eggs
2 tablespoons heavy cream
¼ teaspoon salt
1½ tablespoons butter or margarine
3 tablespoons cream cheese, cut up
4 ounces sliced smoked salmon, flaked into small pieces
2 tablespoons finely chopped red onion
1 tablespoon chopped rinsed capers
1 tablespoon chopped fresh dill leaves
2 pounds assorted ripe tomatoes, sliced
6 mini bagels, split and toasted

1. In large bowl, with fork, beat eggs, cream, and salt until well blended.

2. In nonstick 12-inch skillet, melt butter over medium heat. Add egg mixture to skillet and cook, stirring with spatula until eggs are almost done, 6 to 8 minutes. Fold in cream cheese and salmon. Cook, stirring, 1 minute longer or until egg mixture is set but still moist.

3. Place eggs on serving platter. Sprinkle onion, capers, and dill over eggs. Garnish with tomatoes and serve with mini bagels.

EACH SERVING: About 310 calories, 20g protein, 17g carbohydrate, 18g total fat (7g saturated), 1g fiber, 391mg cholesterol, 600mg sodium ☺

EXPRESS-LANE INGREDIENT: LOX

A favorite in Jewish-American cuisine, lox is a brine-cured, cold-smoked salmon. It's typically saltier than other smoked salmon, although sometimes sugar is added to the brine to create a less salty product. Lox is pricey, but you only need a little to deliver loads of luscious flavor. It's often enjoyed on a chewy bagel with a schmear of cream cheese). For a deluxe sandwich, top the lox with sliced ripe tomatoes and a sprinkling of minced red onion and fresh dill. Or flake the smoked salmon and serve it in scrambled eggs, as in the recipe above. Because lox is often sold vacuum-packed, it's easy to keep a supply on hand. Once opened, tightly wrap it in plastic then place in a resealable plastic bag; it will keep in the refrigerator for up to 1 week or in the freezer for 2 to 3 months.

Potato Pancakes with Carrot Salad

The carrot-and-parsley salad adds crunch and color to these crispy pancakes. Unsweetened applesauce and reduced-fat sour cream are yummy guilt-free toppers.

TOTAL TIME: 25 minutes
MAKES: 4 main-dish servings

CARROT SALAD

1   package (10 ounces) shredded carrots
1   cup packed fresh parsley leaves
1   tablespoon fresh lemon juice
1   tablespoon extra-virgin olive oil
¼   teaspoon salt

POTATO PANCAKES

½   cup vegetable oil
1   teaspoon salt
⅛   teaspoon ground black pepper
2   large eggs
1   bag (20 ounces) refrigerated shredded hash brown potatoes (4 cups); see Tip
2   green onions, thinly sliced
Applesauce or reduced-fat sour cream for serving (optional)

1. Preheat oven to 200°F. Line cookie sheet with paper towels.

2. Meanwhile, prepare salad: In bowl, toss carrots, parsley, lemon juice, olive oil, and salt.

3. Prepare pancakes: In 12-inch skillet, heat vegetable oil over medium-high heat until very hot. In bowl, mix salt, pepper, and eggs. Add potatoes and green onions; stir until well mixed.

4. Drop mixture by scant ½ cups into hot oil to make 4 pancakes; flatten each into 4-inch oval.

Cook until golden on both sides, 5 to 7 minutes. With slotted spatula, transfer pancakes to cookie sheet; keep warm in oven. Repeat with remaining mixture to make 8 pancakes.

5. Serve pancakes with carrot salad and top with applesauce or sour cream, if you like.

EACH SERVING: About 315 calories, 8g protein, 38g carbohydrate, 15g total fat (2g saturated), 5g fiber, 93mg cholesterol, 912mg sodium ☺

TIP: Substitute 1 cup shredded zucchini, peel left on, for an equal amount of hash brown potatoes. (Scrub well and pat dry before shredding.)

EXPRESS-LANE INGREDIENT: SHREDDED CARROTS

Grating carrots can be time-consuming work. Spare yourself time—and potentially grated knuckles!—and go for prepackaged shredded carrots instead. They're available in the produce section of most large supermarkets, often alongside grated cabbage. Tip: If you can't find pre-shredded carrots or don't have any on hand, you can grate them quickly in a food processor. Choose the grating attachment and expect to have to chop up a few large chunks that just won't grate in the machine.

Bacon and Eggs Over Asparagus

Here's a bistro-style take on bacon and eggs served over thyme-scented asparagus.

ACTIVE TIME: 8 minutes
TOTAL TIME: 30 minutes
MAKES: 4 main-dish servings

8	slices bacon
1	pound asparagus spears, trimmed
½	teaspoon fresh thyme leaves, chopped
⅜	teaspoon ground black pepper
8	large eggs
⅛	teaspoon salt
3	tablespoons packed fresh flat-leaf parsley leaves, chopped
1	tablespoon fresh dill, chopped

1. Preheat oven to 475°F. In 18" by 12" jelly-roll pan, arrange bacon slices in single layer, spacing slices ¼ inch apart. Roast 8 to 9 minutes or until browned and crisp. Transfer to plate lined with paper towel; set aside. Drain and discard excess bacon fat in pan, leaving thin film of fat.

2. Add asparagus to pan in single layer. Roll in fat until evenly coated. Arrange in tight single layer, with bottoms of spears touching one long side of pan. Sprinkle thyme and ¼ teaspoon pepper on asparagus. Roast 8 to 10 minutes or until asparagus spears are tender and browned.

3. Carefully crack eggs, without breaking yolks, directly onto asparagus spears, staggering if necessary and spacing eggs at least ¼ inch apart. Carefully return pan to oven. Roast 5 to 6 minutes or until whites are just set and yolks are still runny. Sprinkle ⅛ teaspoon each salt and pepper on eggs. Return bacon to pan; sprinkle eggs and asparagus with parsley and dill. Use wide spatula to transfer to serving plates.

EACH SERVING: About 235 calories, 18g protein, 4g carbohydrate, 16g total fat (5g saturated), 1g fiber, 435mg cholesterol, 405mg sodium ☺

TIP: *If you're worried about breaking the egg yolks, crack each egg, one at a time, into a small cup or bowl before pouring onto the asparagus.*

Shrimp and Fresh Corn Grits

Perfect for a weeknight meal, or dressed up for a dinner party.

ACTIVE TIME: 20 minutes
TOTAL TIME: 25 minutes
MAKES: 4 main-dish servings

1	cup low-fat (1%) milk
1⅓	cups water
⅛	teaspoon plus pinch salt
½	cup quick-cooking grits
1	teaspoon vegetable oil
1	link (3 ounces) fully cooked andouille sausage, cut into ¼-inch pieces
1	large onion (10 to 12 ounces), finely chopped
1	large red pepper (10 ounces), finely chopped
1	pound peeled and deveined large shrimp
1	teaspoon salt-free Cajun seasoning
4	cups fresh or frozen (thawed) corn kernels

1. In 4-quart saucepan, heat milk, 1 cup water, and pinch salt to boiling. Whisk in grits, cover, and reduce heat to medium-low. Simmer, whisking occasionally, 10 minutes or until tender.

2. Meanwhile, in 12-inch skillet, heat oil over medium-high heat. Add sausage and cook, stirring occasionally, 2 minutes or until browned. Add onion, red pepper, and remaining ⅛ teaspoon salt. Cook, stirring, 5 minutes or until vgetables are just tender and browned.

3. Stir in shrimp and Cajun seasoning. Cook, stirring, 1 minute. Add remaining ⅓ cup water; cook, stirring, 2 minutes or until shrimp just turn opaque.

4. Stir corn into grits; cook 1 minute. Serve topped with shrimp mixture.

EACH SERVING: About 395 calories, 29g protein, 57g carbohydrate, 8g total fat (2g saturated), 6g fiber, 158mg cholesterol, 960mg sodium ☺

EXPRESS-LANE INGREDIENT: QUICK-COOKING GRITS

Sometimes called hominy grits, this tasty porridge made from coarsely ground cornmeal is similar to polenta. Classic grits can take up to 45 minutes to cook. For weeknight easy, quick-cooking grits are a cinch to make: Just bring water or milk to a boil with some salt and pepper, remove from heat, and whisk in the cornmeal. Top with a pat of butter, if you like, and let the grits stand for five minutes—then eat up! This Southern side is not only delicious for breakfast; serve it for dinner with grilled meat, sausages, or seafood and a side of cooked greens.

Metric Equivalents

The recipes in this book use the standard United States method for measuring liquid and dry or solid ingredients (teaspoons, tablespoons, and cups). The information in these charts is provided to help cooks outside the U.S. successfully use these recipes. All equivalents are approximate.

METRIC EQUIVALENTS FOR DIFFERENT TYPES OF INGREDIENTS

A standard cup measure of a dry or solid ingredient will vary in weight depending on the type of ingredient. A standard cup of liquid is the same volume for any type of liquid. Use the following chart when converting standard cup measures to grams (weight) or milliliters (volume).

Standard Cup	Fine Powder (e.g., flour)	Grain (e.g., rice)	Granular (e.g., sugar)	Liquid Solids (e.g., butter)	Liquid (e.g., milk)
1	140 g	150 g	190 g	200 g	240 ml
3/4	105 g	113 g	143 g	150 g	180 ml
2/3	93 g	100 g	125 g	133 g	160 ml
1/2	70 g	75 g	95 g	100 g	120 ml
1/3	47 g	50 g	63 g	67 g	80 ml
1/4	35 g	38 g	48 g	50 g	60 ml
1/8	18 g	19 g	24 g	25 g	30 ml

USEFUL EQUIVALENTS FOR COOKING / OVEN TEMPERATURES

	Fahrenheit	Celsius	Gas Mark
Freeze water	32° F	0° C	
Room temperature	68° F	20° C	
Boil water	212° F	100° C	
Bake	325° F	160° C	3
	350° F	180° C	4
	375° F	190° C	5
	400° F	200° C	6
	425° F	220° C	7
	450° F	230° C	8
Broil			Grill

USEFUL EQUIVALENTS FOR LIQUID INGREDIENTS BY VOLUME

1/4 tsp	=			1 ml
1/2 tsp	=			2 ml
1 tsp	=			5 ml
3 tsp	= 1 tblsp	= 1/2 fl oz	=	15 ml
2 tblsp	= 1/8 cup	= 1 fl oz	=	30 ml
4 tblsp	= 1/4 cup	= 2 fl oz	=	60 ml
5 1/3 tblsp	= 1/3 cup	= 3 fl oz	=	80 ml
8 tblsp	= 1/2 cup	= 4 fl oz	=	120 ml
10 2/3 tblsp	= 2/3 cup	= 5 fl oz	=	160 ml
12 tblsp	= 3/4 cup	= 6 fl oz	=	180 ml
16 tblsp	= 1 cup	= 8 fl oz	=	240 ml
1 pt	= 2 cups	= 16 fl oz	=	480 ml
1 qt	= 4 cups	= 32 fl oz	=	960 ml
		33 fl oz	=	1000 ml

USEFUL EQUIVALENTS FOR DRY INGREDIENTS BY WEIGHT

(To convert ounces to grams, multiply the number of ounces by 30.)

1 oz	=	1/16 lb	=	30 g
4 oz	=	1/4 lb	=	120 g
8 oz	=	1/2 lb	=	240 g
12 oz	=	3/4 lb	=	360 g
16 oz	=	1 lb	=	480 g

USEFUL EQUIVALENTS FOR LENGTH

(To convert inches to centimeters, multiply the number of inches by 2.5.)

1 in	=			2.5 cm	
6 in	= 1/2 ft	=		15 cm	
12 in	= 1 ft	=		30 cm	
36 in	= 3 ft	= 1 yd	=	90 cm	
40 in	=			100 cm	= 1 m

Photography Credits

Front cover: Con Poulos

Spine: Maxg71/iStockPhoto

Back cover: (top left), Con Poulos, (top right), Anna Williams, (bottom left), Yunhee Kim, (bottom right), Kate Sears

Antonis Achilleos: 39, 82, 96

James Baigrie: 5, 36, 44, 54, 65, 91, 94, 151, 175

Mary Ellen Bartley: 199

Monica Buck: 83

Tara Donne: 66, 71, 113, 135, 179

Getty Images: Kelly Cline, 202; Image Source, 208; Michael Rosenfeld, 77

Brian Hagiwara: 117, 169, 181, 218

Lisa Hubbard: 232

iStock Photo: 203; Le Do, 112; E_Y_E, 216; Eyewave, 196; Floortje, 42, 184, 190, 235; Julichka, 121; Kondor83, 34; Maxg71, 144; Mark Swallow, 11; Alasdair James, 27; Mashuk, 87; Daniya Melnikova, 238; Julia Nichols, 137; Olgna, 166; Merih Unal Ozmen, 78 (bottom); Julija Sapic, 231; Laura Stanley, 219; Syolacan, 88; Alasdair Thomson, 21; Tomboy2290, 170

Frances Janisch: 195

Yunhee Kim: 56

Rita Maas: 141, 148, 234

Kate Mathis: 26, 46, 48, 68, 76, 78 (top), 80, 84, 85, 93, 105, 110, 114, 119, 123, 124, 126, 129, 131, 132, 139, 152, 158, 163, 172, 173, 176, 182, 185, 204, 207, 215, 217, 221, 224, 230, 241

Ngoc Mihn Ngo: 31

Con Poulos: 2, 6, 18, 25, 38, 59, 72, 86, 89, 101, 103, 106, 187, 188, 191, 197, 198, 210, 213, 239

David Prince: 29, 53, 164

Alan Richardson: 41, 63, 201

Kate Sears: 13, 17, 22, 32, 50, 61, 74, 98, 99, 108, 161, 189

Shutterstock: Bienchen's, 167; Norman Chan, 64; Dionisvera, 211; Milos Luzanin, 116; Rido, 226; Saiko3p, 28; Tkemot, 223

Stockfood: Eising Food Photography, 15; Cultura–SFUK, 145

Studio D: Philip Friedman, 140

Anna Williams: 142, 147, 154, 156, 194, 227, 228, 237

Index

Note: Page numbers in *italics* indicate photos of recipes located separately from respective recipes.

Index of Recipes by Icon

This index makes it easy to search for recipes by category: heart healthy, low calorie, and make ahead.

Note: Page numbers in *italics* indicate photos of recipes located separately from respective recipes.

♥ HEART HEALTHY

Each main dish contains no more than 5 grams of saturated fat, 150 milligrams of cholesterol, and 480 milligrams of sodium. Each side dish contains no more than 2 grams of saturated fat, 50 milligrams of cholesterol, and 360 milligrams of sodium.

☺ LOW CALORIE

These main-dish meals are limited to 450 calories. The sides and sauces are 150 calories or less.

⬛ MAKE AHEAD

You can make all (or a
portion) of these recipes
ahead of time.

The Good Housekeeping Triple-Test Promise

At *Good Housekeeping*, we want to make sure that every recipe we print works in any oven, with any brand of ingredient, no matter what. That's why, in our test kitchens at the **Good Housekeeping Research Institute**, we go all out: We test each recipe at least three times—and, often, several more times after that.

When a recipe is first developed, one member of our team prepares the dish and we judge it on these criteria: It must be **delicious, family-friendly, healthy,** and **easy to make.**

---

1 The recipe is then tested several more times to fine-tune the flavor and ease of preparation, always by the same team member, using the same equipment.

---

2 Next, another team member follows the recipe as written, **varying the brands of ingredients** and **kinds of equipment**. Even the types of stoves we use are changed.

---

3 A third team member repeats the whole process **using yet another set of equipment** and **alternative ingredients**. By the time the recipes appear on these pages, they are guaranteed to work in any kitchen, including yours. **We promise.**
